Praise for *Heali...*

"How do I become the best leader I can be? How do I grow and develop critical skills to lead, engage, and influence my teams more effectively? Dr. Baro provides unique tools and insights to answer these questions and more in *Healing Leadership*."
— **Sarah Natchez, Chief Operating Officer**

"Meeting the challenges of our time requires a significant reframe of what leadership means today. The old way is obsolete. *Healing Leadership* is the playbook for these new times, offering a wealth of inspiration and immediately implementable ideas."
— **Fabienne Fredrickson, Boldheart.com**

"Ginny Baro's powerful new book will inspire and motivate you to lead with intention, integrity, compassion, and mutual respect. *Healing Leadership* is what the world needs most right now."
— **Sandra Stosz, Trustee for the US Coast Guard Academy Loy Institute for Leadership, author of *Breaking Ice and Breaking Glass: Leading in Uncharted Waters***

"With everything that has happened over the last year, each of us will have to develop more human-centered leadership skills to facilitate healing in our personal and professional lives. Dr. Ginny Baro walks us through a process of self-discovery to help us develop a new approach to leadership that puts people first. She shares without judgment and guides with compassion. This book is a must read for anyone seeking to lead with authenticity and higher purpose."
— **Jill Johnson, CEO at Institute for Entrepreneurial Leadership**

"This book will help you tap into your personal power, strengths, and value to affect a prosperous legacy for the diverse leaders that will follow and generations to come."
— **Nate Meagher, People Operations Consultant**

"Ginny Baro teaches us that leading by example, with pleasure, ease, flow, and compassion for ourselves and others, will prepare us to lead more effectively and to manage change in these turbulent times."
— **Marina Shakour Haber, Personal Growth Coach, Speaker, Author of** *Dream a Bigger Dream: Change Your Mind to Save the World*

"The world has changed, and leadership needs to change with it. In this inspiring book, you'll discover the 21 critical leadership qualities you'll need to build your self-leadership skills, create meaningful connections, cultivate a growth mindset and become a fearless leader and role model, like Dr. Ginny Baro."
— **Chris Tomolonis, Financial Advisor, Woodstock Wealth Management**

"What do healing leaders do? They open doors and create opportunities for others to thrive. Ginny Baro reminds us that leaders have the opportunity and obligation to enable all our talent to reach their full potential, creating a culture where people feel valued for their differences, unique needs, and perspectives."
— **Dr. Karen Hare, Principal, KHare IT Consulting**

"My sense is that Ginny has an advantage over others in the leadership industry due to her dedication to her own learning process. I can attest to this fact as her somatic practitioner and coach over the past years. You can expect a deeper level of human connection through her work and leadership style."
— **Anne-Marie Duchêne CHP, CMT-P, Founder Art of Alignment Academy**

"How refreshing to read a business book which focuses on bringing our whole selves to work and the importance of leading with love and empathy."
— **Terry L. Keebaugh, Head of Strategic Sales, Southeast**

"As a cinematographer, technology and creativity are easy. Leadership is the one key component to making a production run. Inclusivity, compassion, and resilience are three of the 21 critical leadership skills Ginny Baro and her team of experts reveal in her inspirational new book, *Healing Leadership*. I will draw

on her body of work to better perfect my craft, as it is not only mind-blowing, it is essential to all paths of success."
— **Hollis Meminger, cinematographer, CEO, founder at Bridgebuilder Cinematic Arts**

"Ginny Baro's powerful insights and interviews with 41 inspiring leaders are honest, emotional and impactful. *Healing Leadership* is a must read for all leaders looking to grow to their next level in times of uncertainty."
— **Sally P. Kady, Senior Client Partner**

"*Healing Leadership* offers compelling stories and a proven framework to overcome challenge after challenge and become an inclusive leader who thrives regardless of an uncertain environment. Ginny Baro inspires each of us to become part of the healing leadership around the globe."
— **Cathy Maloney, Vice President, Mortgage Loan Officer, Guaranteed Rate**

"Do you want to know the secrets to leading, engaging, and influencing others more profoundly? You'll find them and much more in *Healing Leadership*."
— **Elaine Davidson, Founder, CEO at Beacon Lane Consulting, Beacon Lane Career Lounge**

Healing Leadership

How to Lead, Love, and Thrive in Business and Life

Dr. Ginny A. Baro

Dear Anne-Marie,

Thank you for being my journey partner. Here's to healing leadership one leader at a time.

♥ Ginny

bp

BAVARO PRESS

Bavaro Press
www.bavaropress.com

Edited by Madalyn Stone Abrams
Book design by Constellation Book Services, www.constellationbookservices.com

ISBN (paperback): 978-0-9990500-2-6
ISBN (ebook): 978-0-9990500-3-3

Printed in the United States of America

Publisher's Cataloging-in-Publication data
Names: Baro, Ginny A., author.
Title: Healing leadership : how to lead, love, and thrive in business and in life / Dr. Ginny A. Baro.
Description: Includes bibliographical references. | Branchville, NJ: Bavaro Press, 2021.
Identifiers: ISBN: 978-0-9990500-2-6 (paperback) | 978-0-9990500-3-3 (ebook)
Subjects: LCSH Leadership. | Mentoring in business. | Mentoring in the professions. | Executive ability. | Success in business. | Self-actualization (Psychology). | BISAC BUSINESS & ECONOMICS / Business Ethics | BUSINESS & ECONOMICS / Mentoring & Coaching| BUSINESS & ECONOMICS / Training
Classification: LCC HD57.7 .B37 2021 | DDC 658.4--dc23

To my son, Kyle.
The future looks brighter because of you. You are my best teacher and journey partner. Your sense of humor and sensibility fills my heart. I love you beyond words.

To my mother, Teresa Baro,
for being my role model and relentless champion. Your love fuels and inspires me daily to be my best self.

To my partner in crime, Dave.
Your perspective keeps me grounded. Life is more fun and pleasurable because of you.

To inclusive leaders who are here to thrive by serving all our talent and promoting all people of all races and genders with elegance and dignity.

Contents

Foreword

There is no question that each of us has the potential to have a positive impact on the world, but to do so requires leadership. Unfortunately, we have all seen countless examples of what *not* to do, such as leaders who find ways to undercut their teams and employees or create fear in everyone around them.

Most of the leaders I know have had to learn leadership skills on the job and adapt their style based on the circumstances. There's little room for error in an environment that's not forgiving. Rather than leaving leaders to sink or swim on their own, it makes so much sense to be intentional about developing our leaders, since these are the people who shape the minds and guide our employees and talent to achieve the objectives of the organization.

How can you develop the leadership skills to create the future you desire? You'll learn the answer to this urgent question and discover the twenty-one leadership skills and qualities that are most needed today when you read *Healing Leadership*.

Dr. Ginny Baro was inspired to write this groundbreaking guide to creating a nurturing and effective leadership style designed to meet the urgent challenges of our time. She shares her personal journey and the insights she has learned in her coaching and leadership practice. Dr. Baro also interviewed forty-one influential leaders whose leadership advice and experiences are featured in the *Leader Showcase* (the entire interviews can be heard on her *Visionary Leaders Circle* podcast). The real-world guidance and wisdom shared in these interviews are priceless.

You'll find relatable stories, practical techniques for overcoming common obstacles, and a wealth of actionable advice so you can explore what's best for you and forge your own path as a leader. The *Empowering Questions for Reflection* at the end of each chapter provide additional opportunities to think deeply about the topics discussed and apply them to your life, career, and team.

In my work at the Anita Borg Institute, I've listened to thousands of young and midcareer women who are eager to make a major contribution in their chosen field. This book provides a road map for everyone who wants to understand and implement powerful healing leadership traits and strategies. This book is pragmatic, inspiring, and empowers you to take control of what's important in your life—while taking care of your well-being and galvanizing your strengths every step of the way.

Dr. Telle Whitney
Cofounder of Grace Hopper Celebration, former CEO of
Anita Borg Institute, and CEO of Telle Whitney Consulting

Acknowledgments

I would also like to acknowledge:

My late father, Joseph Baro, and family of origin, including my dear, protective, and generous brothers, Guaro and Sandy, my sisters-in-law, nieces, nephew, aunts, and cousins for their relentless love and support.

My field study guests, interviewees, and friends—the magnificent fearless leaders who chose to share their knowledge and insights to serve the readers of this text.

My inspiring support network of journey partners, clients, friends, teachers, coaches, mentors, and role models for making introductions and everything we do and learn more enjoyable. Our love and mutual trust help us rise higher to become fuller expressions of ourselves.

My Rockstar ExecutiveBound® support team and book production team, Michelle Logan and Katie Eaker; editor, Madalyn Stone Abrams; book designer, Christy Collins; and book consultant, Martha Bullen, for making this passion project a reality. I'm grateful for your commitment and care.

My guides, protectors, and the spirits of ancestors and loved ones whose values, influence, and purpose remain alive in all of us.

THE FIVE REIKI PRINCIPLES

Reiki comes from the Japanese words "rei" (universal)
and "ki" (life energy).

Just for today, I will **not worry**.

Just for today, I will **not be angry**.

Just for today, I will **be grateful** for my blessings.

Just for today, I will **work** with **honesty** and **integrity**.

Just for today, I will **be kind** to myself,
others, and every living thing.

Introduction

There's No Time like the Present

We are calling all healing leaders! We are entering an era unlike any other we've ever experienced in modern society. Each of us is being called upon to become part of the healing leadership around the globe, to facilitate the type of leadership that honors independence, freedom, love, and trust; to create the kind of leadership that relies on the liberty, integrity, and dignity of every human being. Are you that kind of leader? Are you a healing leader?

The world is currently grappling with a global pandemic. I extend heart-felt condolences to those of you who lost a loved one or suffered due to the COVID-19 virus. For almost twelve months, many of us have lived in quarantine, worked from home, got furloughed, or lost our jobs while health-care, fire, police, and other essential workers who provided vital services for people in their communities haven't seen much relief on the front lines.

In the United States, our beautiful country clearly stands divided. Extremists exist on both ends of the political spectrum; social unrest and criminal acts sweep across the landscape of major cities over racial tension, injustice, and disagreement over how our country, borders, states, and economy should be run. There seems to be little to no appetite for finding a reasonable middle ground that accounts for the best interest of the country and its people.

Healing the politics and our economy are beyond the focus of this book. However, our political leaders could most certainly benefit from heeding the advice and applying the concepts that we sincerely put forth for healing how they lead themselves and others across our nation's highest offices.

While some people are still suffering from the aftershocks and surges of the 2020 pandemic—the loss of life, jobs, financial independence, and well-being—amid the shock, despair, and fear, many have also experienced a natural pull to slow down. Months barricaded in our homes have forced us to reevaluate and sift through what's genuinely significant and meaningful in life and deepened our appreciation for the grace and blessings we do enjoy despite the high level of ambiguity. Our individual healing is underway.

"*Healing* is the process of restoring health from an unbalanced, diseased, damaged or unvitalized organism." "*Healing* involves the repair of living tissues, organs, and the biological system as a whole and resumption of normal functioning" (Wikipedia, 2020). From where we stand today, healing leadership will require us to establish a new level of balance, looking at ourselves first. Then, we can shift our focus toward our organizations and leadership teams holistically, eradicating systemic biases and prejudice and injecting into our organizations' cultures the values, vision, purpose, and daily practices that support connection, empathy, care, and the healthy functioning, development, and ascension of its people and business ideals.

This "next normal," as McKinsey & Company refers to it, and current circumstances make us question our leadership roles and stretch us out of our comfort zones. We're transcending into new territory that requires virtuous, courageous, and virtual leadership—where not only are we still required to lead our people, deliver results, and provide solutions but also to do so in a hybrid environment. Employees may be working in the office, face-to-face, and remotely, many in fear or isolation, juggling these work responsibilities with simultaneously caring for school-age children or aging parents. In addition to ensuring our talents' safety, as leaders we also continue to face the typical challenges associated with any organization's leadership—leading, attracting, developing, promoting, and retaining qualified and diverse talent. As leaders and visionaries, it's our responsibility to help the current and new wave of talent reskill to meet the demands of an ever-changing technological landscape. Eradicating workplace inequities, the gender pay gap, sexual misconduct, ageism, and long-standing prejudices are constant battles many of us are fighting and striving to win daily. And we have a long road ahead of us. However, we're not alone.

This moment in time is an ideal opportunity to reassess, expand our way of thinking, and clarify what we can do and how to effect change, individually and collectively; to heal and improve our work environments, communities, and elevate and serve all our talent. Future generations will both benefit and feast from the fruit of the seeds we plant today or suffer from scarcity and the consequences of our neglect and short-sightedness in cultivating the land and the minds of our talent, blowing this chance to exert a significant impact on our legacy.

These difficult times are complicated but not unprecedented—people continue to be resilient. We all have been through our own version of a crisis, and it's recalling those experiences that will help us get through this and other demanding periods on the horizon to land on our feet again, as we always do. We all have our unique stories. Stories heal us, and I use mine to fuel me with compassion, love, and courage to not only survive but also thrive during this tumultuous period in our history. Sharing with each other the stories that make us who we are today is part of the healing process. By witnessing each other through these stories, we help each other heal. We realize we are not alone on our journey. Allow me to share part of my story with you.

I grew up in the Caribbean in a small village bordering Haiti in the Dominican Republic, and even as a little girl, I had a deep desire for freedom and independence that came from seeing the women in my village and their children suffer by the hands of abusive partners. For me, this became very personal when it hit my own home. When I was five years old, I vividly recall one night that my parents were arguing violently, and then my mom running, grabbing me, and locking us in her bedroom. I hid under the bed, frightened that something was going to happen to my mom while my dad kept yelling on the other side of the door. At that moment, hiding under the bed sobbing, I quietly told myself, this is not going to be me. Witnessing those early childhood scenes of emotional and physical abuse stayed with me throughout my adolescence. They gave me the determination never to be trapped by fear, to be independent, and to fend for myself.

My parents divorced shortly after that incident, and my mom eventually immigrated to New York City looking to provide a better future for my two older brothers and me. Right around my fourteenth birthday during the summer of 1983, I received my own visa to enter the United States. I started high school in a new country, a new culture, and with a new language. My dream then was to break the cycle of poverty, graduate from high school, and attend college to become an independent woman who could stand on her own. I did all I could through those four years to learn English, including attending summer school each year, joining academic enrichment programs, and sacrificing the enjoyment of extracurricular activities to complete my homework assignments. When I passed my college entrance exams. I was on my way to achieving my dream!

Once I got into college, there were multiple instances when I thought I was going to flunk—and my dad (that's what I called my stepdad), often walked me off the proverbial ledge when I would call home from the computer lab, balling my eyes out because I couldn't get a program to work. Miraculously, I graduated from Rutgers College with a major in computer science and a minor in economics. On graduation day, a sunny afternoon in June of 1991, my mother, dad, and I felt a great sense of pride, unity, and strength. I was the first in my family to attend and graduate from college.

From my first full-time job as a programmer at Prudential, I set my sites on contributing from the leadership ranks of the organization. Over the course of the next twenty-six years, I steadily climbed the corporate ladder in my field of technology in the financial services industry. I made it to the director level at the asset management firm where I worked by age thirty-seven. I went on to earn multiple director roles across the organization and held leadership roles for over twenty years of my thirty-year professional career.

During all those years, while working full-time, I also continued striving on the academic front and attended graduate schools in the evenings to earn a master's in business administration (MBA), a master's in computer science, and a PhD in information systems. I also got married and gave birth to my one and only son, Kyle, in 2007.

The scared little girl hiding under the bed had made it, or so it seemed from the outside looking in. During my experience as a leader in corporate, I was so intent on "making it" that I began to unconsciously mimic the leadership style of my peers, thinking that this was a sure path to success. Every single day, I put on my "armor." I was commuting for almost four hours a day; I was caring for my son; and I was the primary breadwinner. I felt the weight of the world on my shoulders; I endeavored to give my work and my family 100 percent. In return, I was burning the candle on both ends, and there didn't seem to be an end in sight. I knew something had to give. What nobody knew, what nobody saw, was that my world was beginning to implode, bit by bit, day by day. I realized that I was simply surviving, I wasn't thriving. I began to feel the toll and misalignment between who I was and how I was showing up as a leader. What I desired most in life—having choices and living life on my terms—was a stark contrast to the reality of the life I was actually living. After my own journey of self-discovery, I realized that success starts from within.

During this time of healing, I also noticed that I was preventing myself from expressing many natural attributes I possess as a leader. It was through a process I created called *C.A.R.E.S. Leadership Success System*™ that I connected with my own definition of success, got in touch with my life's purpose, and reignited my passion as a leader. I revealed these five transformative life strategies in my first number-one bestselling book, *Fearless Women at Work, Five Powerful Strategies to Thrive in Your Career and Life!* I began to show up more authentically in my roles and interactions, connecting with people on a deeper level, following my intuition more, listening and following my inner knowing, acknowledging my strengths as well as areas for growth, expressing my unique opinions, focusing on people, and focusing on short-term and long-term goals. Colleagues began to show up at my office door seeking connection, support, and guidance. I continued mentoring, coaching, and guiding my team, colleagues, and leaders across the organization. I noticed that people were thirsty to be seen and heard, to feel safe and supported without judgment.

While on my healing journey at the end of 2015, one of my mentors suggested I read the book *Untethered Soul* by Michael Singer (Singer, 2007), which was transformative. This book evoked a yearning to connect even more with my spirituality, that peaceful and blissful place I had been seeking since the start of a tumultuous divorce that began in 2009 and lasted until 2014. The book helped me see how I could lead a life free of drama and self-sabotage while not exerting so much effort on all fronts. I became keenly aware of how much was under my control once I focused on my inner game. I read the book whenever I could and committed to expanding my walls and stepping out into the world in a way I've never done before, coming from a place of love, openness, acceptance, and appreciation for what is, as it is. Similarly, I hope that as you read this book, in addition to others on your bookshelf, you connect with that aspect of yourself that has been dormant and wants to awaken to a new level of abundance—physically, emotionally, and spiritually.

Almost a year later after reading *Untethered Soul* on January 1, 2017, I founded a new coaching and consulting business, Fearless Women @ Work, to help individual women and leaders break through self-imposed limitations, connect with their "unique value proposition," and confidently navigate the world of biases and challenges to reach their full potential. A year later, I launched the ExecutiveBound® brand to help strategic partners and organizations to develop leadership dream teams at all levels, holistically and sustainably, with the right support structure and a human-centric approach. Making this significant transition in my life was the result of healing my "Self-leadership"—which encompasses the topics we will be engaging in together in the three sections of this book: Section 1, "The Secrets to Healing Leadership"; Section 2, "Lead, Engage, and Influence Others"; and Section 3, "Strategies for Personal Development."

My highest intention is to inspire you along your leadership journey, wherever you may be, and pay it forward on behalf of my current and past teachers, mentors, coaches, and leaders. Today, I've redesigned my life and my career and my purpose is to populate the world with inclusive leaders, live to my full potential, help my son Kyle fulfill his, and help my clients and strategic corporate partners achieve theirs. I believe that healing leaders is the solution to transforming our workplace and leadership teams to be more inclusive and diverse so that all of us benefit from opportunities to thrive based on our unique desires, capacities, and efforts.

I believe the answer lies in each one of us acknowledging and taking personal accountability and embodying our personal power, the strengths that we authentically bring to the table as leaders, and the value we bring to those we serve around us. "Healing our leaders" also means embracing and engaging with one another on a deeper level with genuine caring and compassion. It aims to elevate each of us to our highest potential, creating sustainable systems for working and living, and leveraging untapped resources—all our wisdom, intellectual and intuitive. From a place of wholeness, resourcefulness, and self-leadership, our families, communities, businesses, and the economy will thrive.

I look back at that scared five-year-old girl cowering under the bed and am grateful to have been able to overcome so many obstacles. I feel connected, aligned, empowered, energized, and guided. As you read this book, my mission is to help you remove the obstacles that are preventing you from feeling how you want to feel. Everything I share in this book I express with extraordinary love in my heart—for myself, for my family and friends, for you, and for all of us collectively. We are part of each other. We all influence each other's energetic vibration and that of our environment. Together, we impact all that we do and feel. Whenever we have the opportunity, let us listen with patience and empathy and rejoice in the moments and connections we have with one another.

There's no time like the present. Let us *be* together with curiosity about each other's similarities and differences, with compassion and harmony. *Healing Leadership*, our self-leadership, and how we lead others with a sense of contribution is one of the gateways to lead, love, and thrive in business and life, especially in this challenging period with a health crisis and social upheaval. I urge you to rise above pettiness and finger-pointing and instead invest your energy on meaningful matters that will sustain and support the freedoms we cherish right now. Let's honor our ancestors—their struggles, determination, and hard labor—and strive for breakthroughs that will affect a prosperous legacy for the diverse leaders that will follow and generations to come.

Regardless of political ideals and affiliations, a new chapter of American history lies before us. It is time to remember to live our values and the shared vision to further the well-being of Americans and the people of the world. As we move through the next era, we realize it's going to take time to heal. To the best of our abilities, let's advance as a nation by pulling our weight, individually and collectively. Each of us is called upon to use skills and talents, be productive citizens, residents, and neighbors, and contribute to economic growth and well-being. All contributions are needed in the cocreative effort to build the fabric of our country and global economy.

During times like these, I reminisce about sitting down at the kitchen table with my father discussing the ambivalent future. My late father, Joseph Baro, who is always in my heart, was born in 1945 and grew up in Havana, Cuba. He loved the United States and cherished the freedoms we sometimes take for granted—he did not. As a young man attending university to become an architect, he fought against the destruction of a Cuban economy and people under the crippling grip of a Socialist regime. He stood up for his freedoms and against a deceitful new government and as a result spent eleven years imprisoned under the Fidel Castro regime. He found refuge in the United States. Only a couple of years after immigrating, he met my mother while attending Hudson County Community College where they were both enrolled in night classes to learn English. They were married while I still lived in the Dominican Republic, waiting for my US visa to arrive.

Both my mother and father worked tirelessly to earn a living and believed that no job was beneath you as long as it was honest work. They taught my brothers and me to do the same, that nothing is free. We must work for it, pay our dues, do good, follow the law, and be kind to one another. They also taught us to think for ourselves, question everything, the status quo, analyze the issues, make up our minds, and to be diligent about retooling, learning, and remembering history to avoid repeating the mistakes of the global economy. That's what I believe today and teach my thirteen-year-old son, Kyle. Whatever situation you find yourself in today, or any posttraumatic stress you may be experiencing from decades of tug-a-wars, remember that this, too shall pass. Hold your loved ones tight, do your best, lead your team with love and empathy, and know that the sun will come out tomorrow as it always does.

"Leaders Are Born to Be Made"

What is a *leader*? There are many definitions out there! In my description, **leaders are inclusive visionaries, inspiring trust and collaboration and communicating a shared mission to achieving outcomes for the highest good of all people and organizations.** *Healing leaders* value, uplift, and mentor others; lead, engage, and influence them toward constructive action with empathy, respect, and conviction. People follow leaders they believe in and who they feel safe with. Even when people do not hear what they want to hear from their leaders, or the decisions leaders make affect them negatively, people inherently follow and work hard for leaders who have their backs. The foundation of this relationship is trust. High performance, engagement, innovation, and customer success are all the result of a leader's effectiveness or a lack thereof.

Simon Sinek (Sinek, 2019) describes some leadership qualities: Leadership is a practice, and leaders are insatiably curious, regardless of their outstanding accomplishments. They always know that there's more to know, and they learn as they go. In a TEDx Talk titled, "Leaders Are Born to Be Made," Bryan Deptula (Deptula, 2018) describes how important it is to spend time, effort, and resources developing our talent to identify leaders. According to Deptula, leadership traits alone do not dictate leadership abilities. He believes that a person must first see him- or herself as a leader, and that leaders think critically, creatively, and strategically. They coordinate and collaborate with others to create value. I've heard one of my mentors, Tony Robbins, say, "Leaders lead powerfully, intelligently, and with integrity." I agree with all these interpretations and distinctions of what it means to be a leader, as well as many others you find inside exceptional textbooks.

A criteria for powerfully leading others is learning how to lead yourself first. It all begins with you. And you can only direct yourself if you know who you are, what you are capable of, and what you desire. Self-leadership relies on your self-awareness and self-management to guide your beliefs, emotions, and behaviors in the pursuit of your worthy ideals.

As you engage with the concepts in this text, you will hear me reference

"Parts Work," which is a more common term for describing the Internal Family System (IFS). IFS is a model by Richard Schwartz (Richard C. Schwartz, 2019), a psychologist who has been expanding the IFS work for over three decades. In a nutshell, Parts Work's key concept is that everyone encompasses numerous "parts," or aspects of the psyche. In this framework, instead of seeing people as lacking resources, we as coaches assume what constrains people from using their innate strengths are polarized relationships both within (their parts) and with the people around them. Thus, Parts Work is designed to help us release our constraints and thus also release our resources to achieve our full potential and the inner state we desire—more peace, a sense of fulfillment, etc. With a capital "S," *Self* is one of those crucial parts within our internal family system, our inner community, as is our Analyst part, our Dreamer part, our Foodie part, and so on. Self-leadership hinges on our understanding and self-awareness of our Self as the "Orchestra Director" of our internal orchestra and its instruments, that is, our various parts. When healthy and accessible to us, our highest Self directs the other parts within us to rise and serve us, or to pipe down as the case may be, and to support us in pursuing our desires and goals.

Engaging in postcoaching certification work with Guthrie Sayen, a respected teacher and coach who studied directly with Schwartz and is intimately knowledgeable about the Internal Family System, I learned that "Self" is our core essence. According to Guthrie's teaching, the Self is whole, wise, loving, and kind. It is calm, clear, compassionate, curious, confident, courageous, connected, and creative. Connecting to this Self—the highest aspect of our parts—is a life's work. As a champion, student, and fan of the IFS model, I've witnessed its benefits personally and in my clients. As you connect to your Self and develop Self-leadership, you transform and enhance your outcomes and relationships in positive and prolific ways.

In this book, I'll share what I've learned to build Self-leadership as I have infused it in my proprietary coaching model and way of life. It supports us to evolve as leaders and increase our impact on our well-being and environment. As you read (or listen to) *Healing Leadership*, I intend to create a soft landing and safe harbor that will help you explore how you can powerfully lead yourself; how to lead, engage, and influence others; and how to continue to tap into your full expression as a leader, sometimes in business but always in your personal life.

The Most Critical Leadership Skills

The purpose of *Healing Leadership* is to not only present my point of view but also incorporate and feature the ideas of distinguished top industry experts and leaders. To that end, I conducted a field study that culminated in interviewing forty-one diverse and insightful leaders—thirty-four women and seven men—from emerging leaders to established senior executives to C-level leaders across the spectrum of fields, industries, profit and nonprofit sectors, company sizes, and backgrounds.

While the specifics of their lives and experiences vary, each leader shares the goal of making a difference in the wider world. Their years of work experience range from four to forty-four with a median of twenty-five years of industry experience. Their combined expertise represents over *995 years of industry know-how and best practices!* The field study occurred during the throes of the 2020 pandemic, from May 2020 to October 2020, and included a series of individual fifteen-minute interviews on average recorded over Zoom. During the interviews, each leader answered these three leading questions and any specific follow-up questions driven by their initial answers:

1. What leadership skills are most critical in this challenging environment?
2. How should companies approach developing their leaders and talent during this time?
3. What advice would you give leaders who are looking to develop a unique edge?

Throughout *Healing Leadership*, the "Leader Showcase" features are abbreviated versions of each interview highlighting its findings and usually demonstrating the power and value of diversity and inclusion. Their collective expertise presents a rich set of critical leadership skills and qualities, recommendations for growing and developing leadership teams, and best practices for leaders seeking to create a unique and competitive edge, especially during this period of high uncertainty.

This unique and comprehensive perspective on *healing leadership* would be unattainable with only my viewpoint. Although their interviews are shorter in this book, you can enjoy listening to the full versions and every bit of advice and insight directly from our new leadership podcast, the *Visionary Leaders Circle*. You can access the podcast directly from Apple Podcasts, Spotify, or wherever you listen to podcasts, or by visiting www.executivebound.com/podcast.

Finally, here's our big reveal! The forty-one interviews with industry experts uncovered twenty-one distinct critical leadership skills and qualities leaders require during this challenging environment:

1. Communicates effectively, including listening
2. Empathic and emotionally intelligent
3. Values and empowers the team
4. Sets the vision
5. Flexibility
6. Transparency
7. Manages change and transformation
8. Builds trust
9. Authenticity
10. Values diversity and inclusion
11. Positivity
12. Resiliency
13. Builds relationships
14. Creative/resourceful
15. Provides feedback
16. Practices self-care

17. Vulnerability
18. Takes risks
19. Proactive
20. Clear values
21. Commitment

We will discuss these attributes in this book. I will delve into each of these skills throughout this text with vivid examples and anecdotes from the leaders and me. I am forever grateful for each leader's generosity and feel honored to cocreate with them, to share their voices, knowledge, and stories throughout the chapters in this book.

Les Brown said, "You have greatness within you. If just one of you captures the essence of what that means that you have greatness within you and a responsibility to manifest that greatness, you can touch millions of people's lives, and the world would never be the same again because you came this way." I wholeheartedly believe this to be true. Whatever your dream, it's never too late to give it some wings.

Apply what Serves You

How many of us at this moment feel that we have a compelling message to share? What may be stopping you from moving forward and pursuing it could be that inner voice whispering (or sometimes screaming) something like, "What do I know about writing a book? No one wants to read what I have to say. I'm not an author! I know people who have done it, but who am I to write a book?" These are what I call "limiting thoughts."

Before I started writing my first number one bestselling book in 2017, *Fearless Women at Work,* I also experienced similar self-doubts. I compared myself to my role models, Sheryl Sandberg and Tony Robbins, the authors of *Lean In* (Sandberg, 2013) and *Unshakable* (Robbins, 2017), and I critically and negatively judged my level of resources to write my book compared to theirs. To move forward, I devoted precious time with my coach, shifting out of this and other disempowering beliefs and into more empowering thoughts that accepted my condition and anchored me in doing the best job that was possible for *me,* given *my* resources and circumstances.

While writing this book, I searched Google for "leadership authors," and out of the top fifty most popular authors, 90 percent were men, including John C. Maxwell, Peter Drucker, Dale Carnegie, Stephen Covey, Simon Sinek, and forty others. Only five authors were women, including Annie McKee, Brené Brown, Sheryl Sandberg, Liz Wiseman, and Susan Cain, and they were it! These results suggest that as female leaders, we either need to improve our SEO (search engine optimization) efforts or stop playing small and start stepping up as thought leaders and get our message out more prolifically. (I am inclined to believe the problem is not a technology algorithm or an SEO issue.)

Getting our message and perspective out there loudly and as clearly as possible is a privilege that we get to exercise as leaders. The world needs to hear from people with different voices and perspectives—including yours. With this book, I also intend to support you in shifting out of a fixed mindset and into a growth mindset in all the areas of your life that you want to make progress in. It will also help you align your strengths and resources to skyrocket and experience significant results in your business and personal lives. As a catalyst, I intend to help you connect to your compelling message and gain the courage to share it unapologetically. Here's how we'll accomplish this mission together.

In *Section 1: "The Secrets to Healing Leadership,"* chapters 1 through 11 are all about you—eleven intro chapters exploring your self-awareness, what it means to work and live purposefully, recommending best practices and high-performance habits to improve your Self-leadership and ability to manage your emotions, raise your energy, and boost your creativity and productivity. I also devote valuable time to discussing and assessing what it means to embrace a growth mindset, being resilient, developing healthy relationships, and tapping into all your resources, internal and external. I also discuss how to advance in your roles and enjoy a more peaceful and fulfilling existence in the various aspects of your life—career, health, spirituality, and so on. This section helps you build a robust foundation *internally* from which to launch and thrive in your role as a leader *externally*.

Section 2: "Lead, Engage, and Influence Others," focuses on your role and qualities as a leader. I dissect the leadership competencies that distinguish extraordinary, inclusive leaders from those who rule through fear, intimidation, scarcity, and a fixed mindset. By the time you finish this section, including chapters 12 through 24, you will have in your back pocket a road map for leveraging your strengths and identifying how to improve in areas that you deem critical to your leadership success. As you raise your self-awareness, specifically around your leadership abilities, one of the by-products is an enhanced ability to assess how others around you lead as well as gaining the tools to mentor and coach them to strengthen their leadership skills—it will be the gift that keeps on giving!

In *Section 3: "Strategies for Personal Development,"* you will learn how to adjust, fine-tune, and expand your self-development and evolve your personal and professional growth. This structure will help you create an attractive opportunity set for enjoying your life and career while benefiting financially, emotionally, and spiritually from your dedicated effort. This holistic benefit positively affects all areas of life. You are here for a reason, and your natural state is to experience joy and peace. Anything preventing you from experiencing these positive states is smoke and mirrors, and we're here together to blow away the smoke so that you can feel and experience life when your highest Self is in the driver's seat. Buckle up!

These topics appear in this order for a reason, focusing first on your Self-leadership, then on your leading others, and finally on a call to action to develop yourself in ways that delight your soul and bring you the most reward—according to your definition. As a certified professional coach, I'll be asking you throughout *Healing Leadership* a range of empowering questions for reflection. You will benefit from answering these questions; they will expand your emotional quotient (EQ), or emotional intelligence, above and beyond where it is now, reinforcing your intellect and IQ. Under any circumstances, your EQ will help you pursue the livelihood that's within your reach and transcend from surviving to thriving. However, it is incredibly valuable during high-demand periods such as we are in now to include caring for our talent and managing high levels of change and uncertainty.

This book, which combines my message, insights, and the diverse voices of the extraordinary leaders who participated in our field study, is my contribution to you; I offer it humbly with appreciation and gratitude. No one is perfect—I'm certainly not. Apply what serves you and leave the rest behind. Return to review the material every so often for a quick refresher. I welcome and invite you to jump into this fulfilling journey of *Healing Leadership* with joyfulness, lightheartedness, and a "beginner's mind." Experiment reframing familiar concepts, seeing them with fresh eyes from where you stand today in your growth, and get unrelentingly curious about new topics. When you encounter an unfamiliar subject, ask yourself what you could glean from it and what it could potentially activate in your life. Experiment and integrate these insights with other teachings and frameworks you've learned. Take your time. Be open to explore what emerges and how it may benefit you. To play along, I recommend that you keep a journal as you immerse yourself in this book and answer the questions. Let's engage with passion and excitement and enjoy ourselves as much as possible—otherwise, what's the point? Journey well!

"This above all: To thine own self be true."

—William Shakespeare

SECTION 1
The Secrets to Healing Leadership

1

The Self-Aware Leader

Be Self-Aware

You've probably heard the expression, "The first step to solving a problem is recognizing it." Self-awareness is being aware of your emotions, monitoring your needs, understanding your values, managing your energy and strengths, leveraging these strengths in your roles, and monitoring and acknowledging them in others. This chapter is the longest in the book because it is about learning how to build a robust foundation for becoming a self-aware leader. You are in for a treat!

Being a self-aware leader implies that we are cognizant of how our behaviors, words, and attitudes impact those around us. *Self-awareness* is one of the four components of *emotional intelligence* (Bradberry & Greaves, 2009). The other three components are *self-management*, *social awareness*, and *relationship management*. According to Dr. Bradberry, *emotional intelligence* is the "something" in each of us that is a bit intangible. He explains that it affects how we manage behavior, navigate social complexities, and make personal decisions that achieve positive results. Unlike intelligence or IQ (intelligence quotient), which is the same at age fifteen as it is at age fifty, *emotional intelligence* or *emotional quotient* (EQ) is a flexible set of skills that can be acquired and improved with practice. Dr. Bradberry affirms that although some people are naturally more emotionally intelligent than others, you can develop high emotional intelligence even if you aren't born with it. During my motivational talks and leadership training and coaching programs, I design my presentations to enhance the audience's emotional intelligence, including their self-awareness.

Part of self-awareness is sensing, pinpointing, and understanding the emotions you are feeling. This is important because once you notice your emotions, you can then guide how you respond to them—easier said than done you say? One model I've found useful in understanding the range of human emotions is the *Emotional Guidance Scale* by Abraham and Esther Hicks. In the *Emotional Guidance Scale*, they identify a range of twenty-two commonly felt emotions, including seven groups of positive emotions in the upward spiral and fifteen groups of negative emotions in the downward spiral. (Please Google the *Emotional Guidance Scale* to view the diagram.)

Self-management is another component of emotional intelligence. The key is acquiring the ability to locate your leading emotions and using emotional fitness tools to help you move up the scale to feel a more positive state to operate from. The benefit is that you will be more *response-able* and constructive in how you interact, instead of blowing up and lashing out at the people around you or making poor, critical decisions when you are in a negative emotional state. In the *Emotional Guidance Scale*, the #1 positive emotions group includes joy, knowledge, empowerment, freedom, love, and appreciation. The lowest negative emotions group, #22, encompasses fear, grief, depression, powerlessness, and victimhood. The common emotions you and others variously feel lean toward the middle and lower end of the negative emotion spectrum: #11 overwhelm, #12 disappointment, #13 doubt, #14 worry, #15 blame, #16 discouragement, #17 anger, and #18 revenge. To move up from #18 revenge to a more positive emotion—even within the negative emotions group, for example, to #13 doubt—requires *self-management*.

One way to make the shift to a more positive emotion, no matter where you are on the scale, is to intentionally shift your focus toward *gratitude*— what you are thankful and appreciative for in this moment despite what is happening. Gratitude is a tool that immediately transforms your energetic state; it helps you zoom out from navel gazing and gain a new perspective. Suddenly, when you focus on gratitude, the emotional charge that took you down the rabbit hole of negative feeling loosens its grip. Another technique to make this shift is to notice and change your physiology—move your body. Dance, jump, sit up straight with your shoulders back, chin up. Focusing on your posture and moving your muscles help you gain back your remote control and tune into a more positive and empowering mental channel. I recommend watching the TEDGlobal talk by Amy Cuddy titled "Your Body Language May Shape Who You Are." Try it. These tools work.

The most significant takeaway from this discussion is how important it is to understand and tap into your emotions, whatever they might be. After you get a hold of where you are emotionally, the next step is to self-manage those emotions. What I've described is one way to accomplish precisely that.

The last two components of emotional intelligence are *social aware-ness* and *relationship management*—noticing emotions in other people and using your self-awareness, self-management, and social awareness to build healthy, collaborative relationships. As a socially aware leader in a business setting, you can sense the vibe or energy in the room—when the team is excited, concerned, or a team member seems sad or upset. Leveraging your social awareness, you're able to observe people's emotions based on their behaviors, physical demeanor, body language, expressions, and tones of voice, to name a few. If they're yelling, they may be angry. If they are crying, they're obviously upset, sad, or grieving. At that point, validate what you notice, show empathy, and listen to their concerns in a way that cultivates relationships and addresses the issues at hand.

Why are we bringing up emotions and being self-aware? If we don't acknowledge when we feel a certain way, it will be challenging to recognize when other people are in distress and to support them. And if we tend to shove our emotions down to our feet, then we'll be likely to misjudge others who are more attuned and open to expressing their feelings, even in the workplace. Typically, our work environment isn't welcoming of employees displaying emotions. But these emotions have a source; there are bona fide reasons why people cry or display anger at the office. As an emotionally intelligent—self-aware—leader, you must be well equipped to manage and inspire different types of people; you must create an environment at the workplace that doesn't judge people for showing emotions at work. To show up fully, healing leadership requires us to embrace the full spectrum of emotions in ourselves and others, self-manage our emotions, and help our teams self-manage their emotions without losing control of ourselves and becoming disempowered by the feelings. As you notice emotions in others through your social awareness, you will become a more empathetic and influential leader; you will get to the source of the issue and strive to heal it versus ignoring the issue and letting a bad situation fester.

Another aspect of being a self-aware leader is recognizing and monitoring your *needs*. According to Tony Robbins, there are six universal human needs, which I covered in *Fearless Women at Work* and teach to my clients. I believe it's worth reiterating them here in the context of this conversation. Before I highlight them, know that we all have these needs—every one of us; the difference is in the intensity and level that we experience them.

The first need is the need for *certainty*, which includes the need for safety, having a roof over your head, a steady floor under your feet, food to eat, a job, and so on. While certainty is essential for many of us to function productively, we also require *uncertainty*, which refers to variety, diversity, adventure, breaking the routine, spicing things up. We also need *significance*, to feel that we are important and matter to someone or something. As gregarious beings, we also need *love/connection*, a sense of belonging, and if we can't have love, we will settle for connection. The last two needs are *growth* and *contribution*—the need to learn, expand, make progress, be of service, help others outside of yourself, or a social cause.

Typically, two of the six universal human needs are your *primary needs— these are your main drivers and an invisible force directing your behavior.* Before I launched my business, I assessed my human needs through this lens and discovered that my primary human needs at the time were certainty and growth. However, these needs seem to be at odds with each other. On the one hand, the potential for personal and professional development in a business of my own seemed extremely exciting and exhilarating. There was also some level of uncertainty in that, which I enjoyed. On the other hand, an intense need for certainty, a steady paycheck, and financial well-being paralyzed me when I thought about trading the relatively stable corporate track I had known as an adult in a professional career to venturing out on my own to run a business from scratch. While reconciling the levels of these conflicting needs (high certainty versus high growth), I realized that I had no chance to pursue my dreams and experience the growth and impact that I craved during this stage in my life unless I lowered my need for certainty.

These insights led me to prepare financially and transition out of the corporate world in a way that supported my need for certainty. Subsequently, I focused on saving even more, consolidating and eliminating expenses, and redesigning my lifestyle to align with my new goals. Being a self-aware leader enables you to understand your needs in different situations. Our needs may vary depending on what we're facing personally and professionally at a given time. And if we're able to notice our needs, we can articulate them and influence our outcomes.

In parallel, like a compass, our *values* guide what we believe, think, say, or do. Another quality of self-awareness is understanding what you value, what matters to you as a leader in your life. Personal freedom, family, gratitude, faith, kindness, communication, integrity, loyalty, contributing, wellness, love of career, and fun are at the top of my list.

Similar to honing in on your emotions, strengthening your understanding of the six human needs and getting clear on your values can result in advancing your relationships by monitoring the needs and values of your team, colleagues, partners, clients, and stakeholders across the organization and externally but within your sphere of influence, including your household and loved ones. It has been beneficial for my clients and my personal life to integrate the human needs and values perspectives into my leadership roles, especially when handling interpersonal conflicts. During discord, we often fail to reflect on what others also need and value. And sometimes, we obsess on satiating our individual needs and values, discounting or neglecting the needs and values of the other party. Our behaviors speak for themselves. The self-aware leader can leverage this empowering tool, seek to name and validate the needs and values of those involved, and then respond with kindness to resolve or alleviate the conflict and move forward positively.

And finally, I would like to address another feature of your self-awareness, your *energy*. When I was getting divorced back in 2009, seeking answers, healing physically and emotionally, I began to dabble into the field of energy healing and energy medicine. Learning from mentors—including Donna Eden, Barbara Brennan, Tony Robbins, and Sensei Victoria Whitfield—and as a student of energy, I am now more self-aware about how I can positively impact my energetic state. And I'm aware of the power that we each possess to direct our thoughts and energy flow to generate the emotions we desire daily. I learned that unless I first understood how my own energy worked, I couldn't grasp what would cause me to feel excited and joyful one day and unmotivated and low energy the next. What I continue to learn and fine-tune through daily practice is to put myself in the energetic state that supports my activities throughout the day. One strategy is to focus my thoughts on what I desire, not what I fear, and call out the emotions that naturally help me achieve my goals. What were foreign concepts to me growing up are now a source for managing my mental and physical wellness on a daily basis. Members of the www.ExecutiveBound.com community and visitors can download a daily practice tool and ten empowering emotions directly from our home page. This tool guides you through creating the emotional state that will automatically drive the behaviors you determine will support your success and well-being. This tool is powerful.

As a leader, having self-awareness about your energy level is a tool in your tool belt. Use it to heal how you're showing up in your roles. Get clear on what raises your energy, what lowers it, and how to shift from a low-energetic vibration to a higher one. Engage in gratitude and activities that you enjoy and find delightful. We emanate energy and resonate or clash with it within our environments.

On a business retreat with Sensei Victoria in September of 2020, I learned that "energy work is a source of personal independence." The more you know about regulating your energy, the more influential you become for yourself and others. The level of energy you bring into a space influences that space. You can become a part of the flow versus operating apart from the natural flow of the room. Once we awaken to the fact that we influence others using our energy, we'll be ready to claim it. With our energy, we positively influence the physical or virtual spaces we enter, and therein lies our power to contribute, influence, and impact the places we frequent.

And so, this is how energy works: Whatever state you are in, you put yourself there. What does this mean to you? Notice your patterns—the emotional state you most frequently experience on an average day. Suppose you've gotten accustomed to showing up with low energy and a feeling of overwhelm or worry. In this case, you can begin to shift into a more empowering, energetic state by using the tactics laid out in this chapter. Practice will help you alter this old pattern if it no longer serves you. You possess the ability to create your emotional state. To make any upgrades or shifts from old habits requires boosting your self-awareness first.

You see, we're on to something. I encourage you to begin practicing these concepts while reading this book. Notice your emotions as you read through the chapters. What needs are you looking to meet? What values support your efforts? What is your energetic state or level? Thank you for allocating this time for your self-development. Please be patient with yourself as you digest and assimilate these constructs. You're not too young, too old, or too late—you are right where you need to be. And I'm right there with you.

Your Superpowers

How do you build your self-confidence? Get crystal clear on your areas of strength and leverage them every day as much as you can. Another characteristic of being a self-aware leader is knowing your areas of strength, or *superpowers*, that is, understanding the qualities and capabilities you possess that you can offer to serve the people around you. Your strengths are the skills you are great at, the abilities you can naturally use or have learned to use over the years. Self-awareness itself is an area of strength, for example, knowing when you have reached the end of your skill set so that you can ask for support or learn something new.

We have a wide range of strengths in our area of expertise, whether finance, operations, compliance, legal, technology, education, and the sciences. Your areas of strength are at the core of your personal brand. In a nutshell, your *personal brand* is what people say about you when you leave the room or how people who know you describe you to their colleagues and friends. If you were to ask someone, "Who could I talk to about marketing for my small business?" And the person says, "You should talk to Ginny about that," that is part of your personal brand—people relate to you as an expert in a particular area. Unfortunately, if you have a reputation of *not being* self-aware or clueless, that's also part of your brand. When you know your areas of strength and you're able to articulate them as well as own them and live them consciously, others around you can count on that and recommend you to others who may need your expertise in that area.

As you may have heard, when you overuse your strengths, they can become a weakness. Therefore, being aware of where and when you are overexerting your strengths and the need to pull back are also essential. For example, as a coach, I've trained extensively to help my clients embrace their *limiting beliefs*, or "shadows," as we call them in the profession. These "limitations" are self-imposed hurdles or challenges that seem real to us until we dismantle them. While coaching, if I overuse this pathway, I may be missing out on using other techniques to help my clients move forward, for example, expanding their perspective, experiencing the moment, envisioning the future, and so on.

Another strength is listening to my clients and hearing what they're *not* saying by reading between the lines. I also listen by sensing their energy as they speak, whether they talk fast and passionately or slow and in a low tone. Yet another strength is my ability to recall information, digest it, and integrate new knowledge. I can easily connect the dots between frameworks I've learned to generate an entirely new idea. I love doing that, and it's something that my brain does naturally. Balancing out your strengths is vital in understanding the range of your strengths. There's always room for improvement and a new level of expertise.

What about you? What are some of your top strengths and areas of expertise? Become self-aware about those because knowing them will allow you to bring them forward whenever you need to. Raise your hand and engage when the opportunity to use your strengths presents itself. Just as valuable for you and your organization is also knowing when to keep your hand down. If you realize that your expertise is not aligned with a new initiative or opportunity or that you get drained by the core work required, that is an excellent time to bow out. Keeping your hand down will keep you focused and create an opportunity for someone else more fitting to raise his or her hand.

However, this approach is not an excuse to sit back and not pursue prospective growth opportunities even when they do not align with your strengths. As long as you enjoy the subject matter, are curious about it, and can add value, raising your hand in this case can offer you an opening to learn. Explore how to continue to develop and fine-tune your strengths. Complacency is the root of stagnation. Relish and celebrate what you know and stay curious and receptive to adjusting any areas within your strengths you may want to improve—technology skills, soft skills, and so on. Be honest. This text will provide ample space for self-discoveries and set you up to identify which areas you want to develop further.

As we discussed, noticing your emotions, managing them, being *response-able* by responding constructively; and acknowledging your needs, values, energy, strengths, and opportunities to contribute or grow will enhance how you monitor them in other people more effectively. These tools will help you make better decisions on your behalf and on the behalf of the people who rely on your leadership. As you hone your self-awareness, self-management, social awareness, and relationship management skills and apply them to your work teams and use them to enhance all your relationships, you can support yourself and others at a whole new level.

Empowering Questions for Reflection

1. Whatever state you are in, you put yourself there. What does this mean to you?
2. What needs are you looking to meet?
3. What values support your efforts?
4. What is your energetic state or level on a typical day?
5. How do you build your self-confidence?
6. What are some of your top strengths and areas of expertise?

LEADER SHOWCASE: BLAINE BARTLETT

"The only thing I can ever control are my thoughts, attitudes, beliefs, and behaviors. Everything else is out of my control."

Blaine Bartlett has been the president and CEO of Avatar Resources, Inc., for over thirty-three years, providing consulting, executive coaching, and leadership development training to clients from around the globe. He has spent more than forty years in leadership development. Blaine is an international bestselling author, adjunct professor, serves on many boards, and hosts a podcast, *Soul of Business with Blaine Bartlett*. He attended Nyenrode Business University and the University of Oregon.

Blaine, please introduce yourself.

I'm an author, lecturer, executive and leadership coach, and I do keynotes all over the world. I've been called a leadership development expert and have worked with some of the largest organizations on the planet. I've written five books, have personally worked with about three-hundred-thousand people, and have impacted about a million within that context.

From your perspective, what are the critical skills leaders need during this challenging time?

First, part of the answer is predicated on how we define *leadership*. I've defined it and worked with it as being the activity of cocreating coordinated movement. There are two pieces to this definition: *cocreation*, which is ownership transference; it moves us from *my* idea to *our* idea, how do I do that; and then, *coordinated movement*, getting everybody on the same page, which is a very challenging task. To your question, I think the first skill involves developing the leader's mindset. Far too often, I find that leaders believe they're in charge. They may have the idea, the directional focus. But the mindset of top-down, autocratic control, or anything associated with what we would traditionally think of as applying to leaders, doesn't work in today's environment. That mindset needs to shift to where it's far more inclusive. Within that framework, we start looking at what skill sets are present that makes cocreating coordinated movement possible. And part of that answer begins with awareness. The value of awareness can't be underestimated. Awareness increases choices. The more awareness I have, the more options I see available to me. And that's important from a skill-set perspective because, by definition, leaders are causing change. And when they're causing change, the system is pushing back. I don't care how beneficial the change is; people like comfort. They like the status quo. As a leader, I need to have more choices available to me than the system has for pushing back and resisting the change.

And then, we look at the skill of developing meaning. All behavior is associated with meaning. How do I make sure the appropriate meaning is present around what we're trying to do so that the resulting behavior is moving us closer to what we want? And part of that involves communication mastery. People will never give you what you ask for. They give you what they perceive you're willing to settle for. How are you communicating, not just with your words, but with your energetic body? We need to be aware and cognizant of how we are communicating. We need to master that process, not be accidental about it.

To connect with Blaine, please visit www.blainebartlett.com or LinkedIn.

2

Live with Purpose

Align Your Life with Your Purpose

While goals provide the destination, purpose generates the fuel to get you there. When you're self-aware about what drives, motivates, and inspires you daily and engage in activities that support your dreams and ambitions, you become more congruent in your life. Being deliberate about your goals, taking action, finding a higher purpose (the reason your goals matter), and connecting to how you would feel when you accomplish them will energize you to reach your goals. Set goals that have meaning and "move the needle"—that is, take actions that have the greatest impact toward realizing them and creating a life you love. Otherwise, you will waste valuable time and energy spinning your wheels, working very hard, but not getting any traction or seeing results that improve your quality of life.

I don't know any working professional who claims to have ample free time. These days, most professionals like you and me have a packed schedule filled with personal and professional responsibilities. Living life with purpose at any stage of your life, including retirement, involves becoming intentional about how you are spending your time and making sure that you connect with the activities you choose to engage in, professionally or personally, on multiple levels. It means you must stop chasing the wrong things to attract what you truly desire.

A global study (Malnight, Buche, & Dhanaraj, 2019) published in the Harvard Business Review, "Put Purpose at the Core of Your Business Strategy," indicates that scores of C-level leaders across twenty-eight high-growth companies in the Unites States, Europe, and India benefitted by putting purpose at the core of their business strategy. The purpose of Mars Petcare, for instance—a better world for pets—guided its expansion from pet food into the larger ecosystem of pet health. The purpose of Securitas—contributing to a safer society—led the firm to redesign its offering to include not just physical guards but also electronic services and predictive solutions. These leaders generated sustained profitable growth, stayed relevant in a rapidly changing world, had a broader impact, and more motivated stakeholders.

Individually, how could pursuing goals with purpose help you fulfill your potential and leave your mark? For example, if you decide that you want to feel more invigorated and become more physically fit, create a new regiment for your daily activity. Perhaps your daily goal would be to walk, train at the gym, hike, play tennis, or anything to get your body moving and feeling more energized. In this area, you would be aligning your life with your stated purpose.

Assess how purpose can guide your business and personal strategy and be willing to adjust as conditions change. On the business front, align your life with those goals and initiatives that propel the business forward from a people, culture, processes, systems, and regulatory perspectives. Evaluate your purpose regularly. Stay nimble as it might change monthly, quarterly, yearly, or even more frequently, depending on your environment. When we get clear on our purpose, we then arrange our goals and milestones around it. We can also discern between busy work and substantive work, allowing us to deprioritize those activities that won't make a significant difference for us and focus on the ones that will. One of the questions to ask yourself to find out whether you're dealing with a significant goal in your life is, why is this goal important to me? You will know when the answer is significant. For example, it might be, I will be able to spend more time with my son, or, I will get to be more creative in this role, or, I will have a more significant impact on my organization's growth, or, I will be able to share my experiences, enjoy myself, and help others overcome obstacles to enjoy their life more.

On the other hand, if you ask yourself why this goal is important to you and discover that the answer eludes you or does not elicit a worthy reason, I recommend you rethink it. When I enrolled to become a certified professional coach (CPC), I signed up for a nine-month time commitment and a substantial financial investment. When I asked myself, why is this goal important to me? I realized that to pursue a new career as a leadership coach, it meant I had to acquire the capabilities to become an effective and responsible coach. I also wanted to ensure that I experienced the same process that my clients would be experiencing when they coached with me—in essence, putting myself in their shoes. On the other hand, I could have pursued one of the hundreds if not thousands of three- to four-day or weekend certifications available on the market. Honoring my value of integrity was also important to me. Getting my certification from an accredited organization working with the International Coach Federation (ICF) and following professional standards within the coaching profession worldwide were goals for me. Dedicating time and money to visit a masseuse every other weekend during my divorce was also a need. It helped release my body aches and emotional stress and improved my mental and physical health during a period of high duress.

If you were to ask yourself, what goals need to be aligned with my purpose at this point in time? What do those goals look like? the answers will direct you to create the transformations that you desire most.

Living beyond Yourself

Living with purpose also entails looking at the big picture and expanding beyond your personal sphere to explore innovative and meaningful solutions to solve problems. How do we do that? One technique I use and teach my clients is to "zoom out," then look at yourself and the situation as if you're an outsider watching what is going on. In this way, you gain a fresh perspective and objectivity about the circumstances. This approach is called *expanding the view* in the coaching world. Ask this question repeatedly, what's another perspective to view this issue/situation? With patience, you will begin to expand your viewpoint and discover different angles to examine the problem from and develop creative solutions. You will learn there is never only one way to perceive a problem. All you have to do is look for other perspectives to discover them.

You can also involve others by validating how they perceive a situation by saying, "That's one way to look at it. What's another way?" This approach provides you an incredible range of resources and options. Helping others realize that different angles exist and seeing them yourself enables you to live with more purpose where the world doesn't revolve around you. Even though you're always at the center of your life, others are also playing a meaningful role (and are at the center of theirs). When you objectively experience the world from other people's perspectives, you naturally begin to lead with more empathy.

Zooming outside of yourself to see the "big picture" is a worthwhile exercise. Our perspective is the lens through which we view ourselves. The world opens up when you can perceive yourself in the context of a bigger picture. By asking these questions, what's important here? What is my role within the collective? reveals there is so much you can influence. Too often we quickly lose sight of what's most important. Get clear on what is meaningful to you, your team, your organization, and share it, proactively, with your team and loved ones.

To live with purpose and grasp a broader perspective, look at your stories, the people who made a difference in your life. When I recall the moments of epiphany and turning points in my life, those who shaped me into the leader I am today and the leader that I want to be, I think of immigrating to the United States, giving birth to my son, and starting my business. Those experiences helped me harness my purpose of caring for people profoundly, for my family and loved ones, and of course, for all of us as part of humanity. I know that if we can help each other the way that people have helped me and my family, everybody benefits—men, women, and children. And so, I care about you; I care about your success and about the impact that you have and that we can have together.

I often think of Nuni, our landlord in the Dominican Republic, and my Aunt Norma. They both took care of me for a couple of years from the time I was twelve to thirteen years old when my mom immigrated on her own to this country. Aunt Norma, Nuni and her family, Veronica and Quity, were my role models for showing what it's like to care and serve someone for the higher good even when they are not family. All of these little stories and events changed my life's trajectory, shaped me into a caring and compassionate leader, and renewed my sense of purpose.

Use your purpose as the backdrop for all that you invest in—physically, financially, and emotionally—throughout the various areas of your life. Look at your purpose from both an achievement as well as a fulfillment perspective—what brings you joy? Use this practice of asking yourself, what is the endgame here? When you meet with your team, a client, or any stakeholder in your business or in your personal life, keep this question in the forefront of your consciousness, and I promise you it will be a game changer in your level of satisfaction, effectiveness, and in your ability to influence positive results.

LEADER SHOWCASE: RACHELLE FENDER

"We need to give each other more graciousness right now."

Rachelle Fender is the Senior Manager of Strategic Partnerships with the Unstoppable Foundation, a California-based 501(c)(3) non-profit organization. She is passionate about inspiring individuals and businesses to create social impact through the power of giving. Rachelle has over twenty years of business experience.

Rachelle, please share with our leaders what you do.

I take the time to speak with individuals, families, leaders, and business owners to determine their social purpose; what really enlivens them, what they care about, and then connect them with our programming to fulfill their philanthropic goals. In 2008, I found myself laid off. And after feeling sorry for myself for a couple of weeks, I decided I needed to develop a bigger mission for my life. And I created a mantra, "I only want to work with individuals or organizations that provide products or services that help humanity, the planet, or both, and that operate in complete integrity and transparency, with no small print." Twelve years ago, I joined the Unstoppable Foundation, doing this meaningful work.

What advice would you give to the leaders looking to develop a unique edge during this time?

Add a social impact to your purpose. No matter what business you have, you can add more inspiration, retain talent longer, and attract more customers and clients if you're willing to use your voice, platform, products, and services to contribute to a social purpose in the world. You do not have to choose between domestic or international involvement; consider both. We are a global economy, we are interconnected, and if we're going to sit back and wait for government leaders to change access to education and basic needs in the world, we're going to be waiting lifetimes.

We all have the power to make a difference through our professions, companies, products, and services. By doing so, not only will it motivate you to be a part of an inspiring social purpose, but it will also inspire your customers and clients to see you differently. If they see that who you are and what you offer has a positive impact in the world, it will inspire your existing or prospective clients and customers to want to support you.

According to *The Consumer Global Good Purpose Survey*, 82 percent of customers—if they are looking at your product, brand, or service and comparing it in the marketplace to others and deem it to be about equal value—will go with whatever company is making a social impact. Choosing to make a difference does affect your bottom line. It isn't the only reason that you should be a part of a social purpose, but it's a benefit that gives you a competitive edge by adding an even greater purpose to what you're doing.

What message would you like to give our unstoppable leaders?

Remember to be gracious with yourself and with others right now. A lot of people around the world are in a tender space. We need to give each other more graciousness right now.

You can reach Rachelle at Rachelle@unstoppablefoundation. org or on LinkedIn.

Create Alignment

In the throes of surviving, we can lose sight of what's meaningful, what matters most. When we don't align what we want, what we believe, what we think, what we say, and what we do, we experience scores of negative emotions. We experience frustration, impatience, sometimes anger, and perhaps question why what we want isn't happening fast enough. Another sign or symptom of core misalignment is that we feel stuck and don't know what to do next. If you are doing work that depletes you because you don't enjoy it, there is a misalignment between what you want and what you're doing, and it's going to most likely manifest in emotional and physical ways. You may get headaches and body aches, which are physical projections of the emotional discontentment and dissonance you're feeling inside.

Part and parcel of living with purpose is creating alignment in your life, which will result in an easier and complementary relationship between living and working. And how do we do that? Answer the question, what delights you? This question helps you connect with what you want and desire. It allows you to bring awareness to what you want and align it with where you are today. It can provide you direction, which you may be asking for in your leadership career or personal life. What delights me is resting and enjoying a good book, spending time with my son, family, and friends, training and delivering motivational talks and keynotes, coaching clients, spending time outdoors, traveling whenever possible, and writing books!

We also increase our alignment by questioning what we focus on in our thinking, what we believe, and what we actually do about what we want. I can provide a relevant example. In January of 2018, I attended a Business Mastery seminar with Tony Robbins. One of the goals I identified was that I wanted to grow and scale my business. My purposes were to serve more people, earn as much as possible to sustain myself and my son, enjoy the fruits of my labor and the pleasures life has to offer, self-care, travel, and support the social causes I believe in. I started to ask myself what my *beliefs* were around achieving this goal. I noticed a stark misalignment between wanting to grow and scale my business and thinking that corporations only want to do business with established, mature organizations that conduct leadership development. At this point, my business was neither. That core (mis)belief was driving my thinking and words. Consequently, I wasn't proactive in creating a robust offering and getting the word out that I had something valuable to offer these corporations to help them grow their leadership dream teams. Working through this block, I shifted and began to crank out the materials that I knew would significantly impact leadership training for my strategic partners. Since then, Fortune 500 companies have continued to hire me to speak and deliver my coaching and leadership development programs. I've also since realized that large organizations support minority-owned businesses as part of their initiatives to diversify their supply chain. I'm on my way to growing my business exponentially and creating the impact I know I'm capable of making in healing leadership.

When there is alignment, your day-to-day activities begin to align with your daily purpose, bringing a high-level resonance to your days, weeks, and months. When your daily activities are aligned with your daily purpose, it saves you energy and creates inner harmony and satisfaction and even happiness. Sustaining alignment between what you desire and "*what is*" requires self-discipline, rituals, and *practice*—often asking yourself what delights you is a question that helps you connect with what's meaningful to you. It allows you to address and align what you want and where you are today. It can provide you a direction that you may be craving in your career or life.

What delights you? Check out your beliefs, thoughts, words, and actions. Are these four components in alignment with what delights you and your goals? If they are, terrific! Bringing this level of awareness to your life is where the healing starts. In chapter 11, we'll tackle each of these four components.

Empowering Questions for Reflection

1. How could pursuing goals with purpose help you fulfill your potential and leave your mark?

2. Why are your current goals important to you?

3. What goals need to be aligned with your purpose at this point in time? What do those goals look like?

4. How do you "zoom out" to look at the big picture and solve problems?

5. What's another perspective to view a current issue/situation? What's important here?

6. What is your role within the collective? What is the end-game here?

7. What delights you?

8. Are your beliefs, thoughts, words, and actions in alignment with what delights you and your goals?

LEADER SHOWCASE: DEB FRAZIER

"Remember, all these things we do are connected; our spiritual being, emotional being, physical being, and our psychological being."

Deborah J. Frazier, MBA, RICP is a Wealth Management Advisor for Hightower Advisors. She has over thirty-five years of financial services experience and earned an executive MBA from Columbia Business School.

Please share your background as you tell us what leadership skills are most critical in this challenging environment.

I've been in wealth management for over thirty years and a financial advisor for twenty years. I did an assignment as an international team coach in Europe, the Middle East, and Africa for three years, then came back and went into wealth management again. I've done many things as a financial advisor, in a team, and as a sole proprietor.

First, the most critical skill is emotional intelligence—having the ability to connect with others, having empathy, tuning in, and knowing when things are going on that are often unsaid. The second is communication in times of crisis. One thing I've learned as a financial advisor is that when things are really going bad, it's so hard to pick up that phone and call people. But leaders lead, and leaders pick up the phone when it's the heaviest thing to pick up. Reaching out, communicating with your clients, friends, and family, whoever, especially in crisis times—people remember and appreciate that. Third, be honest, develop trust, and show them that you care.

Recently, I called a client; I said, "I know we don't have a scheduled call today, but I've been thinking about you. The last time we spoke, I felt you were a little distracted. Even today, you sound a little bit down," and I listened for ten minutes. He shared what was going on with him, how it's making him feel, and how it's impacting him. And when he finished, he thanked me for being perceptive, for being able to tune in that something was wrong, for caring enough to pick up the phone and call him.

What advice would you give to leaders who are looking to create a unique edge?

A leader should always work to build partnership relationships. You can't do everything yourself. You have to step out of your comfort zone, create a team, and have people around you who are willing to help and be willing to share power and learn from others. Read books on leadership, for example, *Fearless Women at Work* by Dr. Ginny Baro. Leaders should get a coach. I always have one, two, or three coaches in the background. It's one of the most valuable assets I always have in my toolbox.

I want everyone to remember, all these things we do are connected—our spiritual being, emotional being, physical being, and our psychological being. We can't separate them. We have to make sure that we give each part of our being what it needs. We need to fuel those different parts of us. And when we don't, it's disconnected; we aren't as effective as leaders or as human beings.

You can connect with Deb at DFrazier@hightoweradvisors.com or LinkedIn.

3

Practice Mindfulness

Be Here Now

This moment is the *only* reality. The research by Ellen Langer (*Harvard Business Review Press,* 2017) spanning nearly four decades has influenced thinking across various fields from behavioral economics to positive psychology. Her work reveals that instead of operating on autopilot but by paying attention to what is happening around us, we can reduce stress, increase our creativity, and boost performance.

During Langer's interview with *Harvard Business Review's* senior editor Alison Beard, Langer explains the basics. From her perspective, *mindfulness* is the process of actively noticing new things. When you do that, it puts you in the present. It makes you more sensitive to context and perspective; it is the essence of engagement; it energizes not drains you. Langer emphasizes that most people mistakenly assume practicing mindfulness is stressful and exhausting—all this thinking! But what is really stressful is all our mindless negative evaluations and our worrying that we will unearth problems we won't be able to solve.

As leaders, *being here now,* being fully present to the moment, allows us to access all our resources, intellectual and otherwise. You notice where your thoughts go and can bring them to this moment through your breathing until it becomes your new state. What if we viewed today as an opportunity to experience ourselves in a new way? Be present as soon as you set down your keys or your phone and whenever you're speaking with anyone.

Practicing mindfulness became very important to me when I was going through my four-year divorce that was a period of high stress, worry, and uncertainty. That's when I began to practice mindfulness meditation, which focuses on breathing. On occasion, at the end of a hectic and long day after I put my son to sleep, I would sit on my bed, close my eyes, and focus on inhaling and exhaling. And as I did, my mind began to calm down as the craziness of the day melted away, and I found myself in complete stillness enjoying a much richer peaceful state. While I wasn't successful at clearing my mind of thoughts—which is not the goal by the way—I noticed the thoughts that came automatically and was able to let them go without attaching and dwelling on them. A few years later, in 2015, I committed to developing a regular mindfulness practice and learned Transcendental Meditation (TM). As a student, on most days, I spend twenty minutes in the morning and twenty minutes at night calming my mind and connecting within myself. My record of uninterrupted days meditating is 219. In 2020, I expanded my meditation practice to include vision journeying.

Like meditation, *vision journeying* is another tool for spiritual growth, a modality for practicing mindfulness that engages the imagination and helps you communicate on a spiritual level. I also call vision journeying an "active" form of meditation. It involves sitting down comfortably for ten to twenty minutes, listening to Shamanic drums in the background, and setting your intention on a particular question you want to explore and answer.

For example, during my vision journey, I would inquire, "Show me what my next level in business is." It is incredible what happens during a vision journey, moments of mindfulness and connection, and how much guidance I can receive as I let my vivid imagination wander. And when I am done, I journal what my vision journey uncovered. The direction I receive is aligned with my compelling vision and results in concrete, actionable steps I can implement in my business and personal life. I'll share more about it when we discuss "Tapping into Hidden Resources" in chapter 10.

"Being here now" is the greatest gift that I have given myself. It keeps me grounded where I am enjoying and experiencing the fullness of the moment. I rarely forget where I left my keys—my focus is sharper, right on the activity of the now. Practicing mindfulness as I engage in conversations, sit down to write, perform chores around the house, and focus on the activity at hand makes them more enjoyable. If I'm watching a movie or engaging in a recreational activity, then that's what I'm focused on at that moment. If it is doing paperwork, so be it. And if it is engaging with a client during a coaching call, that's what I'm present for. I prefer practicing mindfulness to my old pattern where I would get busy, ping-pong from one activity to the next, and then wonder what happened to the time.

Executive presence, and presence in general, is impossible without mindfulness. Multitasking is the killer of mindfulness. Talking to a friend on the phone while writing an e-mail at the same time robs you of listening fully to the conversation. So, one way to practice *being here now* is to focus on whatever you're doing at the moment. Do notice what else pops into your head. If you need to write yourself a reminder note to return to and deal with this thought later, do that, and then go back to what you were doing.

What is your mindfulness practice? How do you bring yourself to being here now? Consider the benefits of mindfulness meditation and commit to regularly integrating it into your leadership and personal life. The benefits will astound you.

LEADER SHOWCASE: MISHA BARTLETT

"You need to understand the individuals' needs on your team to know how to make them feel valued."

Misha Bartlett is the founder, Sales Consultant, and Sales Coach at Misha Tamiko, LLC, with over thirteen years of sales management experience. She received her bachelor's degree in biology from Rowan University.

I'd love for you to share what your background is.

I've been in sales for the past thirteen years going on fourteen years. Being a minority woman in a predominantly white male-dominated space, the thing that helped me the most was being focused on what worked for me. I learned to identify my unique skill set, how I could be most successful and contribute to the team in the biggest way. Many managers, unfortunately, aren't taught anything about being a manager. I started mentoring individuals and realized the reason why some of them, especially people who were the "other"—who may not have been as well understood or able to work exactly like another person—were getting pushed out of their roles. I started a company called Misha Tamiko dedicated to helping those professionals recognize their value and strengths, gain confidence in themselves, and then leverage that to be successful in sales.

What are the leadership skills we need most during these challenging times?

One of the things that is really important, as leaders, is the duality of **being a leader** and **doing leadership**. They're two different worlds. How you show up, your intention, your presence as a leader is something much different and often harder to work on because we're not used to thinking of it that way.

When I talk about being a leader, I'm talking about showing up and being present in your conversations, being with the other person, being nonjudgmental, curious, and trustworthy, bringing the skills that make people feel comfortable knowing that you are there to help them grow, value them, and empower them. That's one of the biggest pieces that often gets missed in leaders' toolboxes. And uncovering those skills and working on them are the connection pieces that we need as humans to feel like we are appreciated and valued within our organizations.

How should companies develop their leaders and give them the tools they need?

There was an interesting article that **Harvard Business Review** published a couple of years ago about the value of inclusive leaders. In this study, inclusive leaders' teams performed 17 percent higher than leaders who were not focusing on their teams' inclusivity. What does that mean, to be an **inclusive leader**? What I hear most from the black, Latinx, and Asian women I work with from startups to Fortune 500 companies is that if they don't feel valued, they don't show up 100 percent at work. Those feelings of not being good enough, not feeling valued will drive down performance more than not having the right skills or knowledge. You need to understand the individuals' needs on your team to know how to make them feel valued. There are many different ways that you can do this, but it's learning about the person, connecting that person to the opportunities, and making sure every individual feels valued outside of your interactions.

You can reach Misha at www.mishatamiko.com or on LinkedIn.

Forget to Worry

"Do not worry. You will receive abundance beyond your wildest dreams to focus on your real purpose—awakening the souls you are here for, serving them in the way that only you can, and teaching others this message. They will relate to you and follow you."
#The Universe

–Dr. Ginny Baro

Let's figure out your supposed "Worry Score": On a scale of 1-5, 1 being "not at all likely" and 5 being "extremely likely," how likely are you to feel worried on a typical day? Make a note of your score.

I heard once that worry is a form of prayer—however, I'm sure that is not the intention. For those who believe in prayer, we tend to use it to express gratitude, focus on requesting grace and protection over our loved ones, gaining a favorable outcome over a challenging situation, or for strength, love, and peace, to name a few examples. A prayer is a form of focusing on what we want. When worry becomes the focus of our thoughts, some suggest that we begin to manifest what we worry about because that is where our focus and energy go. According to Tony Robbins, "Where focus goes, energy flows."

Worry is a by-product of a lack of mindfulness. When we worry about things that happened in the past or something in the future, it means we are not here now. Unfortunately, both the past and future are fictitious as you can't go back or forward in time; not yet, anyway. From experience, we can agree that worrying never solves any problems and tends to create chaos for our emotional well-being. Misguided thoughts and actions directed toward the past or future are pathways to feeling guilty, angry, or disappointed without any ability for a reasonable recourse. In other words, they lead to feelings of powerlessness.

To flip this around today, find your focus and bring yourself to the here and now. Most likely, the *now* doesn't have the problems you're thinking about so intently. There's nothing we can do about the past other than maybe apologize, forgive ourselves and others, and take corrective actions so we won't repeat the mistakes we made in the past in the future. And there's nothing we can do about the unknown future. If the future you anticipate worries you, ask yourself, what worries me about the future? Use the answer to prepare and plan what you want to do from now on. The current activity could be "planning for the future," which happens to be an activity of the here and now.

Melt away your worry by becoming aware of what is worrying you, prepare for it as best you can, and then let it go. Explore whether the source of the worry is fictitious. For example, if you're worried that investors won't be happy with the stock performance, provide them with performance attribution reports that indicate the factors that detracted from the stock performance, which most likely were out of your control, and how you plan to mitigate future risks. In another scenario, if you are afraid that someone in your resource chain will delay your project and your manager will get upset, be proactive. Get commitment and progress reports from the resource personnel, communicate clearly so that all project members understand their responsibilities and potential risks to the project time line, and keep your manager in the loop. Turn your worry into actionable steps that will help you feel empowered as you focus on what's important and matters. Commit to letting worrisome thoughts melt away and replacing them with gratitude about what is working well at the moment.

It was meaningful to me to introduce you to the five Reiki principles early on. These principles epitomize the beauty of mindfulness, being here now, and directing our focus toward gratitude, fruitful outcomes, and kindness to ourselves, others, and our environment. As I mentioned—it's worth repeating—Reiki emanates from the Japanese words "rei," which means universal, and "ki," which means life energy. Reiki is an energy healing modality, and the five Reiki principles take you to the here, now:

1. Just for today, I will not worry. (focusing on being here now)
2. Just for today, I will not be angry. (choosing to shift to a more positive emotion)

3. Just for today, I will be grateful. (being thankful for your circumstances)
4. Just for today, I will work honestly. (honoring your elders in how you work, fruitfully)
5. Just for today, I will be kind to myself, others, and every living thing. (being self-aware, kind)

Forgetting to worry and taking yourself to the *here, now* will bring you more joy and remove unnecessary anxiety and stress, which you may be feeling because you are focusing on that worry. It will also allow you to reclaim and repurpose that extra mental bandwidth that worries inhabit and dedicate it toward more productive and rewarding activities. Using these techniques will flush worry from your mind and help you commit to improving your Worry Score to be as close to 1 as possible.

If nothing else, "just for today," how willing are you to commit to experimenting with these principles and see how they serve you?

Find Your Focus

All worry has a central focus. Rather than worry, what if you shift your focus to answer these two questions: What's important? What can I control? Pay attention to the intersection of these two answers to stay on point and feel empowered to do your best based on what you are *certain* about at this moment. What can you do about whatever is meaningful to you right now and under your sphere of influence? Let your answers become your new focus.

A recent example of mine is the presidential elections. I chose to shut out the vicious news cycle. Instead, I focused on having conversations with my son about the values that I want to instill in him, making sure that I voted, and staying calm among the uncertainty and controversy surrounding mail-in ballots and the indecision about who had won the presidency for the next four years. Speculation was running rampant about what would happen to the stock market based on who got elected, and many people were concerned. I chose to stay the course, focus on my work, self-care, and wait to see what happened. Ultimately, the stock market responded positively, and all the hoopla dissipated.

Finding my focus helps me stay grounded and connected to what is essential, the people I love, and those I serve. Be aware that sometimes, subconsciously, we may choose to obsess on matters that we can't control to avoid what we must do or deflect our responsibilities and instead blame others for our circumstances or feelings. The deceit is thinking that it's easier to pretend to address someone else's problems—even though we're power-less to change *anything*—instead of looking in the mirror and handling our own business. Unfortunately, that doesn't bode well for us, personally or professionally, because we cannot "fix" others' issues. If we feel upset about them, there is nothing we can do to change them. When we, instead, "own it,"—that is, take responsibility for our own issues—and direct our attention to what we can control, we become 100 percent empowered. Let's keep our house in order first, and then we can support others to do the same.

Remember those "needle movers" we spoke about—activities that generate the most impact? When you notice that others in your sphere are unfocused on what is important to them, you can ask them empowering questions to help them focus on those things that they can control and are important. With all that we must tend to daily, developing the skill of know-ing which tasks to eliminate, delegate, or tackle, and helping our teams do the same, will help all of us recoup multiple hours daily. For example, when managing a remote workforce, it is essential to stay focused on goals. Don't worry about how it's getting done or the specific activities involved. Instead, focus on the end result and accomplishments. If your team is meeting their goals, then great. Otherwise, look into the situation further. Help them stay focused on what's important, what matters, and what they can control.

How does the topic of staying focused land for you? Moving forward, what, if anything, can you begin to implement to positively impact your business, relationships, finances, health, or any other area that's important to you?

Empowering Questions for Reflection

1. What is possible if you viewed today as an opportunity to experience yourself in a new way?
2. What is your mindfulness practice?
3. How do you bring yourself to being here now?
4. On a scale of 1-5, 1 being "not at all likely" and 5 being "extremely likely," how likely are you to feel worried on a typical day?
5. If the future you anticipate worries you, what worries you about that future?
6. How willing are you to commit to experimenting with these principles and see how they serve you?
7. What's important? What can you control? And what can you do about whatever is meaningful to you right now and under your sphere of influence?
8. What are the "needle movers" in your life—activities that generate the most impact?
9. How does the topic of staying focused land for you?
10. Moving forward, what can you begin to implement to positively impact your business, relationships, finances, health, or any other area that's important to you?

4

Overcome Negative Self-Talk

Do Not Negotiate with Terrorists—Your Mind

Using mindfulness and self-awareness to notice what's happening in your thoughts will put you in the driver's seat of your life and business. We already addressed one of the gremlins in your head when we talked about *worry*. Let's call her Wendy. Now, let's chat about Wendy's cousin, *negative self-talk*, and we'll call her Nelly.

How often do you experience negative self-talk on most days? The average person has over six thousand thoughts a day, and many of those are directed toward yourself. If they are not positive ones, you are experiencing negative self-talk. Nelly can be quite insulting, calling herself names such as, "I'm an idiot" and "How could I be so stupid?" or "I can't believe how much I suck!" It can get pretty brutal up there. Nelly may also say, "Nobody wants to hear what I have to say. Keep your mouth shut. You're out of your league." Nelly can unleash any of these thoughts and put you down in ways that most people wouldn't. For most of us, this inner dialogue would, in no way, shape, or form, ever see the light of day; we would never voice these thoughts to someone else we care about. And therein lies the danger. Because Nelly is invisible, it's easy to let her carry on without doing anything about it. And yet, surprisingly, we never feel great after Nelly takes over and puts us down—that's *the* sign that something must change. That's why I want to talk about Nelly.

Becoming aware of Nelly, with her deprecating negative chatter, and befriending Nelly, the inner critic, is another way to heal as a leader and as a human. (We'll discuss further *how to do this* next when we address "Flip the Script.") In many instances, underneath the negative self-talk are judgments and unrealistic and unmet expectations, which Nelly is more than happy to point out.

Here's an example. If I'm having a conversation with a client, I may begin to feel judgmental about how I'm handling the call. As a coach, I'm trained to self-manage and notice when I'm critical, even with myself. The second I catch negative Nelly self-talk, I can stop that train of thought and refocus on my client. When speaking virtually to a group of women or a leadership team, I notice that as I share a story or listen to a question, I may judge myself harshly about how I sound. The second I catch myself, I let it go to refocus on the conversation. Stopping Nelly in her tracks gives me so many more resources to listen above and beyond the apparent words I hear. It enables me to sense where the person I am talking to is coming from and use all that intel to answer the participant's question. Negative self-talk Nelly can consume so much bandwidth in our minds and quickly sabotage us, preventing us from doing what we say we want to do.

For example, when referring to self-sabotage pertaining to your health and wellness, how often does Nelly express some version of these thoughts, "You don't want to go the gym! What difference is it going to make?" Using mindfulness, daily rituals, and practicing elevating my emotional state, I no longer negotiate with terrorists—that is, my mind, aka Nelly. Every other regular weekday, I arise at 6 a.m., sit on my bed to meditate, put on gym clothes I laid out the night before, and drive out around 6:30 a.m. to train for one hour at my local cross-fit gym for women. When I return, while getting ready to work from home in the morning, I play my favorite music through my Bluetooth speaker and dance to my favorite tunes. Then, I dress and prepare breakfast for my son—on my parenting days—and myself. After breakfast, I shoot a quick video with a microlesson to post on my LinkedIn page and my social media channels, and off I go to embrace the business day.

I no longer entertain mind battles between Nelly and me about whether I am going to the gym when I awake. I created a ritual, a structure, that supports me to stay consistent and aligned with my desires to be healthy and feel energized throughout the day. The night before, I check-in using the gym app to commit to attending a 7 a.m. class. I also leave out the gym clothes next to my bed so that after I meditate, I can jump out of bed, brush my teeth, pull my hair back, put on my workout clothes, and leave the house on time. I remove any wiggle room for Nelly to say, "I don't want to go to the gym today. I'm tired. It's too cold outside."

However, there is a difference between not listening to Nelly and listening to my body. If I intend to go to the gym, but I feel physically exhausted, I will give myself a break, cut myself some slack, and choose to rest the muscles for the day, knowing that I will go back the next day. But letting Nelly run my schedule or tell me what to do is not acceptable anymore. She and I have a clear understanding of who's calling the shots—and guess who that is? Yes, my highest Self.

Having the mindfulness to understand what is happening with Nelly and my thoughts and questioning whether that is legit for me puts me in the driver's seat. It allows me to harness my highest Self because I behave like the orchestra director that I am. As the director, I tell my *parts*, including Nelly, what to do and what the drill is instead of my *parts* piping in whenever they want and driving my actions while I obliviously pretend to drive my car on cruise control. Not negotiating with your mind also translates into generating the state that you want to experience each day. For example, I use music to put me in a cheerful, high-energetic state. I could tell myself, "Today, I am excited about meeting with my Mastermind group at noon," or "Today, I am curious about what the day will bring." That is something that I purposefully and intentionally practice and know how to do and has been an ongoing practice for over a decade.

Most nights, I sit and meditate, reflect on the day, ask for guidance on questions of the day, vision journey, and journal. These practices lay the foundation for starting and ending my days mindfully, feeling nourished, connected, and supported by myself and my creator in a highly energetic state. They help me remember that every person is experiencing a unique path and that we are human, imperfect, and prone to err. Today, my purpose is to help others connect within and accept the full range of their divinity and humanity. It is my honor to get to do this sacred work.

Don't let your head take over your state, how you feel today; you are in charge, not your brain, not Nelly. Our modern forty-thousand-year-old mind is there to keep us safe and help us "survive." It's not inherently there to help us *thrive*. Although there is no Saber-toothed tiger chasing us anymore, the mind tries to conjure up fake problems to keep us in survival mode. Our self-awareness, living with purpose, and mindfulness practices are kryptonite to Nelly and our defense against the gremlins in our mind. Over time, your brain's plasticity will enable you to create new grooves, or neural pathways, that align with your new way of thinking and feeling—thank goodness!

One at a time, as you notice and conquer the gremlins in your head, you become encouraged and increase your certainty and belief in yourself. As you do, you'll keep tapping into more of your potential and get out of your own way. You are in good company. Keep going.

LEADER SHOWCASE: ANTHONY ARIZMENDI

"Face fears, and then, as we do as business people every day, come up with the solutions for those fears to see another day of success."

Anthony Arizmendi, MBA A.AIA, is currently the Program Manager of Capital Programs at New Jersey Transit. He has over twenty-five years of experience and earned a Bachelor of Architecture and an executive MBA from the New Jersey Institute of Technology.

Let's start by sharing your background.

I manage large portfolios of projects from the financial side to the delivery side. It's my responsibility, along with my teams, to manage capital improvement projects and investments for both road and rail at many facilities and sites across the state. Career-wise, my leadership role increased, working in both public and private entities. Eventually, I realized that I would benefit from having better core knowledge of how businesses are run, so I went for my MBA. The MBA framed the knowledge that I had been gaining through experience.

What are the most critical leadership skills leaders should possess?

Change leadership is essential. You need leaders who are comfortable with change and risk. I always frame it this way, in terms of business and what we do daily: You have to make choices; either you're surfing or sailing.

When you're *sailing*, typically, you're in a vessel, and you're harnessing the resources that are around you, through extensions of yourself. I have a sail, a rudder, and the vessel itself. And by harnessing these resources, I can get from point A to point B. And typically, that's what we do every day in our careers. We manage those resources—human, financial, tangible—toward intentional goals.

But surfing is a little different. When you're **surfing**, you have to make decisions second by second. Your resources are much more limited; you have to pivot and not be afraid of risk, so a wave doesn't knock you off your surfboard and drag you back to shore. Surfers think very quickly and are very good at paring decisions down to the essentials. And they have the deep belief that their high-risk approach also has its high reward.

The people who are going to survive these "wipe-out" times are the ones who have those unique skill sets; they're okay with putting aside the search for any variables that are typically used to sustain an effort, a corporation, to identify what is available right now. In these times, the goal is to reach the other side of our pandemic and all the impact it is having on culture, politics, and the economy. Ultimately to decide on approach, you have to have your own internal compass. That has to be very clear so you can then decide which approach you're going to choose. On either framework, know how best to proceed and use the resources at hand to get to your goal.

What is your final message for our leaders?

You have to understand yourself and know that fear is your body, your mind, providing you information. Face fears, and then, as we do as business people every day, come up with the solutions for those fears to see another day of success.

You may connect with Anthony on LinkedIn.

Flip the Script

The antidote to the inner critic and negative self-talk Nelly is self-love, compassion, and becoming your own cheerleader. Isn't it wonderful to have somebody in your life who can be encouraging, carry on about how great you're doing, how kind and generous you are, and how much you are appreciated? Doesn't that feel nice? How many people do you know experience this regularly? Everybody's busy with their own lives, and most of us forget to acknowledge one another or stop and give thanks or express appreciation—it's not our automatic behavior.

How do we flip the script and put a kibosh on Nelly, the critic, and the negative self-talk to become our own biggest champion and advocate? We begin by flexing the muscle of giving ourselves more love and compassion. It starts slowly, and it could be as simple as this: Whenever you notice negative Nelly, acknowledge her: "I hear you, and you know...that was the best I could do at the moment." People are typically judgmental about themselves, and when they are, they also dish it out to others. I'm speaking from experience. When you start to give yourself more love and compassion, you will begin to extend it to the people in your life, your family, and your team.

In addition to showing yourself more understanding and kindness, one of the practices that helped me flip the script and pacify negative Nelly is *bragging,* combined with expressing gratitude and a desire. Dubbed a "trilogy," I learned about this tool while attending the School of Womanly Arts with Regina Thomashauer. It's unusual for many of us, especially women, to tout our accomplishments—you've heard or been told it's not "modest" or "becoming," right? Precisely for that reason, we use this tool to break that old pattern and elevate ourselves with truths that we wouldn't usually share, and we do it with people we love and trust.

The trilogy starts with a brag, then gratitude, and we end it with a desire. For example, "I brag that I'm publishing my second book, and I learned a valuable method to do it within three months. I'm grateful for all the support I've received from exceptional leaders, my team and family, and the time I can devote to writing. I desire to continue to empower women and leaders through my speaking, coaching, books, and leadership training pro- grams and create memorable experiences with family and friends." All the statements are factual, and the brags, in particular, help you self-acknowl- edge your hard work, all the magic you're creating using your unique value proposition, love, and passion. You can also brag how you're showing up, for example, "I brag I didn't lose my temper when my son was disrespectful."

Give it a try. Share a brag, something you're grateful for, and a desire in the following sentences (fill in the blanks): "I brag that _____." "I'm grateful _____." "I desire _____." You can use this tool by your- self or with friends. You can even use it with your team. How cool is that! And if you do this regularly, you will notice how you begin to flip the script on your negative self-talk and sabotaging tendencies.

This is a practice I continue to hone on my journey of healing and expand- ing into mindfulness, self-love, and compassion. When I noticed how I was treating myself and became more conscious about it, I could catch negative Nelly and her sabotaging behaviors. Daily, I'm growing closer to a new level of self-awareness, self-love, and self-compassion, which feels delightful.

Heal the Wounded Parts

There is work to be done. It's nearly impossible to make progress and thrive when on some level we feel fragmented and misaligned and when there's a significant aspect or parts of us that feel burdened, forgotten, or ignored. And we all possess parts that may feel hurt, neglected, or exiled from our internal community—your psyche, as we discussed in the Internal Family System model by Richard Schwartz. Perhaps it's because it is too painful or even scary to remember those times in our past. Identifying and integrating these wounded parts into our inner community (our internal family system—IFS) will help us heal them, and in turn, support healing in our leadership roles, al- lowing us to embrace others with compassion and curiosity. These burdened parts carry with them a set of *limiting beliefs*—negative self-assumptions that hold you back from showing up or executing what you want. The best way to explain this concept of *wounded parts* is by giving you a personal example.

As recently as 2018, four years after my official divorce, I struggled in my romantic relationships, a meaningful area in my life. I desired to meet a partner and lover to enjoy and share experiences, the abundance of love I felt in my heart, and the journey we call life. I knew what to do cognitively, yet I found myself closed off, distrusting, and apprehensive while dating men. Quite frankly, I can write a book on my dating escapades, and it would be a full-out comedy. I found the level of dishonesty and neglect for human values to be astounding and comical. But besides this, I was most concerned with how I was showing up to these interactions. I felt that something wasn't quite right with me. And that's when I became more inquisitive—I wanted to urgently explore what was holding me back. Through engaging in "Parts Work" with Guthrie Sayen and my coaching partner, Maria, I found the answer I desperately needed. I discovered the significant source of my dating struggles, and that's what I want to share with you in *healing the wounded parts*—the work is worth it, and the reward is sweet.

As I mentioned during the introduction, I worked with and have tremendous respect for Guthrie Sayen. He taught me about the Internal Family Systems (IFS), which is a powerfully transformative, evidence-based model of psychotherapy. The model operates under the belief that the mind is naturally "multiple," and that is a good thing. Our inner parts contain valuable qualities, and our core Self knows to heal, allowing us to become integrated and whole. In IFS, all parts are welcomed—the good, the bad, and the ugly.

Over a series of Guthrie's advanced coaching courses that focused on "Parts Work," I tapped into multiple parts of myself that felt wounded. The most pivotal wounded part that specifically affected my romantic relationships was my five-year-old *Nani* (that's what my brothers called me growing up). I told you a little bit about her already during the introduction. She was the little one hiding under the bed when my parents were violently arguing.

As I was coached through these classes with my coaching partner, Maria, focusing on my romantic relationships, I began to understand how I had forgotten about Nani. My parents' separation was such a painful and confusing time that I had suppressed a great deal about it as a young girl. For me, it had been water under the bridge—but was it? Can you relate? Many of us have suffered upsets, sadness, and hurt that we hardly want to speak about and prefer to avoid altogether. And that's the best we could do with the resources we had and our capabilities at that age. However, today, as *conscious, fearless* adults (those who act despite the fear), we're better equipped emotionally, physically, and spiritually to peel back the layers and get to the bottom of an unfavorable situation. And that's what I did.

Losing my biological family—my father and my two brothers—because of divorce was a big deal. I had to grow up fast! It wasn't merely "water under the bridge." During my coaching sessions with Maria, I learned all that Nani (my five-year-old part) wanted to say that no one had asked her before—and it was a mouthful. Nani was an adorable little girl with a tremendous capacity for giving and loving. When my parents divorced, my mother and I moved to the city of Santo Domingo, Dominican Republic, and my brothers stayed with our grandfather in the village near Haiti where we were born. My father also stayed behind in the same small village where they were living. Feeling hurt, Nani created a series of beliefs around her father's love and their separation. Through tears and sobs, Nani shared with Maria how hurt she felt from believing, "He threw me away," and "My love didn't mean anything to him," which led to the thought, "If that was my father, what can I expect from any other man?" And as Nani experienced the aftershocks from the divorce and the separation from loved ones, she built an invisible wall around her heart to protect it from getting hurt again. Even after spending almost four years throughout her divorce seeing a psychologist, I had never experienced such discovery about my parts, specifically Nani and her insights.

My healing journey in love included asking Nani (and other burdened parts that I had forgotten about and neglected) what she needed from me—she's still inside me (a part of my psyche and internal family system). As an adult aware of Nani within my internal community, I comforted and appreciated her, letting her know how courageous she was and how proud I was about her resourcefulness and sensibility. I also let her know that we are now grown-up, more knowledgeable and self-sufficient, and that it's okay for her to be a carefree five-year-old girl. Having felt seen, heard, and understood, my burdened and wounded parts eased up. When they feel welcomed and loved, they can help us move on to a new phase of our lives. When Maria asked Nani what quality she wanted to bring to my inner community (my inner world), Nani screamed, "Love!" Helping my inner child, Nani, heal, getting her back into the fold by integrating her with the rest of my parts, accepting her, understanding, listening to her, and reassuring her that she's safe now is what has allowed me to move forward and to open up my heart again after my divorce.

I expanded the work that I began with Maria and gifted myself the space to continue peeling back the layers in my romantic relationships by hiring my dear friend and brilliant coach Anne-Marie Duchene, founder or the Art of Alignment Academy, and working with her for a six-month period. What I uncovered was challenging and uncomfortable, fascinating, and rewarding. Resolved and willing to enjoy the rest of my life with a partner, I began to date again. Today, I am in a healthy, loving, romantic relationship and enjoying the fruits of this inner work, which brings me so much joy, fun, and peace.

How can you identify those parts of yourself that may feel wounded or burdened? What areas of your life are the most challenging right now? That's an excellent place to start. I specialize in "Parts Work" in my coaching practice because I've experienced firsthand and with my clients how powerful and valuable this work is. Leaders who struggle with showing up fully to their roles and in their lives can free themselves and unleash their full potential as they begin to heal wounded members of their psyche and integrate them to create more inner congruence, harmony, and authenticity. This alignment enables them to be the *same person* regardless of their environment, work or home. Engaging in "Parts Work" is the difference between leading from the wounded child versus *healing the child*. All of us can live, work, and thrive based on our desires and capabilities. Through healing and helping Nani feel safe, I learned how to integrate her within my inner world in an empowering and healthy way. This work also allowed me to grow in my personal life and build a harmonious coparenting relationship with my son's father to nurture and support my son, despite a long, litigious divorce. This inner work is priceless.

Empowering Questions for Reflection

1. What's on your mind?
2. What did you intend to do?
3. Why do you want to be successful? Why is that important?

When coaching your team:
4. What can you improve based on what happened?
5. How can you break that down into smaller steps?
6. What's another way to look at this?
7. If you only focused on one thing, what would it be?
8. How can I support you going forward?
9. What are your choices?
10. What do you care about in this situation?
11. What will you do after this?

LEADER SHOWCASE: KATHY MCKEON

"Anybody can achieve anything they want as long as they're willing to work hard, work on themselves, try to make this place, our world, a better place."

Kathy McKeon, RN, MPH, CSM, is a Senior Corporate Account Executive at Merck with over thirty-five years of experience. She received degrees from Cochran School of Nursing, Iona College, and her MPH at New York Medical College.

Please share with us a little bit of your interesting background.

I grew up one of the youngest of six kids in The Bronx, New York. I came from very humble beginnings. My father died suddenly when I was in high school, and within a year, my mother had a devastating diagnosis. But the silver lining to a very painful time through my teens and early twenties was the gift of resilience, grit, hard work, and leaning into education.

I graduated a little early from high school, went on to college, and I needed a job very badly. There was a significant nursing shortage in New York at the time. And I knew I could get through school and get a job immediately. I was a practicing nurse for about seven years. During that time, I went back to school at night for my business degree, and then I went to work for Merck and enrolled in grad school for my master's in public health and focused on epidemiology and health policy.

I just finished a course on epigenetics, aside from doing your extraordinary program, the ***Fearless Leadership Mastermind***, which transformed me. Around the time when I met you, I was wondering, "What's my chapter two?" And upon meeting and working with you, I had three significant events in my career that were extraordinary. And all of that came from the confidence, skills, and coaching that I received from you.

What leadership qualities leaders need the most during this difficult time?

A leader needs to be present, authentic, and have a high level of communication with their team. A leader needs a vision. Being honest, authentic, and showing, "Don't go where the puck is, go where the puck is going." For us here at Merck, our mission hasn't changed. In fact, it's probably more important than ever to get people healthy and moving forward.

It's crucial to be humble and vulnerable. I look to experts, ask people for their opinions, for their input. "Being authentic" is admitting when you're unsure and when you need help and you're being resourceful to get that help. I've learned that by being resourceful, branching out, and asking for help, people are more than happy to help.

Our fears are the biggest obstacles. It's looking at those fears, that self-sabotage, negative self-talk, and looking at beliefs that aren't true—looking at your beliefs and challenging them to expand. Once you can get past the fears, the energy can go to more forward-thinking projects, experiences, personal satisfaction, and professional success.

My mantra in life has always been, "Where there is a will, there is a way." Anybody can achieve anything they want as long as they're willing to work hard, work on themselves, try to make this place, our world, a better place.

Kathy is available to connect on LinkedIn.

5

Get Your Ego in Check

Don't Make Assumptions

On some level, it may feel comforting to believe that the world revolves around us, we are at the center of the universe, and everything exists to meet our needs. I was amused by a recent podcast claiming that most of us are on the narcissistic personality spectrum where we feel an inflated sense of self-importance. However, getting your *ego*, or sense of self-esteem and self-importance, in check will make you a better leader and person. Making what is happening around you about you hinders you significantly from zooming out and focusing on what's most meaningful in a situation. Instead, shift the focus to the people involved and support them in the best way possible. Let's explore how to be a more caring and effective leader by getting your ego in check.

In this chapter, I introduce you to the principles in *The Four Agreements: A Practical Guide to Personal Freedom*, the work by Don Miguel Ruiz (Ruiz, 2018). These four principles include: Be Impeccable with Your Word; Don't Take Anything Personally; Don't Make Assumptions; Always Do Your Best. When I first read this book and learned about them in the early years in 2000, they didn't have the same meaning I glean from them today. Over the decades and since starting my coaching practice, I've noticed how at the core of many of the struggles, suffering, and conflicts we endure professionally and personally is the unconscious tendency to violate one or more of these four principles. I call them the *being principles*. Since writing my first book, I realized that I teach these concepts to my clients and often bring them up during speaking engagements. If you already read *The Four Agreements*, consider how the *being principles* land for you now in the context of getting your ego in check and *healing leadership*. I discuss them in this chapter based on how popular they are with the clients I coach.

At the top of the list is *don't make assumptions* in personal and professional relationships. On many occasions, to expedite business decision making, as leaders we make educated assumptions about things such as supply, demand, interest rates, and so on. And while this may prove beneficial on a macro level and in the big picture of the business, making assumptions on a personal level, or the micro level, in our relationship about what others will say and do raises barriers and creates opportunities for confusion, upsets, and useless drama. We hold back from expressing what we really want, don't communicate clearly with others to avoid misunderstandings, don't show up authentically, and repress our ideas and hesitate to execute them.

The opposite of not making assumptions includes gathering the courage to express what we desire, validating our assumptions by asking empowering questions, and proceeding based on the information we uncover. Imagine you have a conflict with a colleague, friend, or family member, and you make assumptions about how this person will react when you approach him or her about the issue. Your conjectures typically don't presuppose a supportive or cordial response or positive outcome. We usually assume the worst and consequently either retreat—not allowing the situation to improve—approach the situation from the wrong angle, or go on the offensive aggressively, which puts the other person on the defensive and may escalate the issue rather than heal it.

This principle, *don't make assumptions*, goes hand-in-hand with *forgetting to worry*—many of the assumptions we make cause us to worry. And what we want is to remove the worry and replace it with facts as much as we can. Question what assumptions you may be making and how they ultimately influence your actions.

Don't Take Anything Personally

The second-most popular principle that clients run into trouble with is taking things personally. This *being principle* speaks to our predisposition to interpret others' behaviors as personal attacks and insults. Imagine this: Your manager decides to change your reporting line and informs you during a group meeting that you will be reporting to one of your peers. Not only is your peer less qualified and experienced in your subject matter, but you had absolutely no clue that this change was underway. Your current manager made this decision in a silo without even having the depth of knowledge about your skill set and level of expertise and experience.

Immediately, a standard reaction is to make it about you and believe that your supervisor does not value who you are and what you do. It becomes personal and feels like an offense and a bruise to your ego. The minute you take it personally, make it about you, and give it a meaning that you are not worth what you believe you're worth because of your manager's actions, you spend hours, days, weeks, mulling over the situation in your head, and quite frankly, suffering over a matter that, although it impacts you, isn't really about you.

When we apply the principle not to take anything personally, we realize that what others say or do are projections of their own reality. Their opinions have nothing to do with you, but rather reflect their inadequacy or lack of knowledge and insight (in this case) into their team's capabilities. When you don't take things personally, you're able to perceive the larger picture, get the facts, become more creative, and then proceed accordingly. In our example, you can move forward by setting up a meeting with your manager and discussing your perspective on the situation and the misalignment that you perceive between his decision and the reality about your abilities and realm of expertise. From that point forward, you have choices: Decide to stay the course, propose possible alternatives where your strengths and your skills can be best used, or consider looking for opportunities elsewhere. In any case, by not taking it personally, you bypass and avoid becoming a victim to your manager's actions, and in the process, preserve your confidence and self-worth.

With her permission, this is what Tara, one of the members of the *Fearless Leadership Mastermind™* training, says about the *being principles*: "I really relate to making assumptions and taking things personally. It takes up so much mental energy and time, and they are real barriers to being able to be at my best. It's a vicious loop to be aware of, because without awareness and reminding, we can slip into it so subconsciously with our lizard brains! What's present for me right now is to not beat myself up for the times when this has gotten the best of me, particularly in professional settings, but to move forward with awareness." What a candid expression of her experience with this lesson! And notice how much compassion she expresses for herself. Negative Nelly lost the battle with Tara!

How many times do we take things personally when somebody seems to be upset or in a bad mood during a meeting? Do you question, what did I do? How come this person is upset with me? Or do you take it personally when someone you e-mail, text, or call doesn't get back to you right away, or at all? What if you were to focus on the other person and get compassionately curious about what is going on with him or her? Then you could be fully present, ask what's upsetting him or her, or follow-up on the e-mail or text to get to the root cause. The reality could be that the e-mail got buried in the inbox, it's lost somewhere in cyberspace and was never received, or he or she meant to reply but got sidetracked with other priorities and later forgot. When we make it about us, we let our egos get in the way and create fictitious obstacles, objections, reactions, and situations. Continue to show up and avoid creating a wedge between you and the other person by not taking anything personally.

Be Impeccable with Your Word

A dear member of the *Fearless Leadership Mastermind™* program who lives in Argentina asked me recently what the principle "Be Impeccable with Your Word" means. The most straightforward response is to speak with integrity, that is, "Do as you say and say as you do," "Mean what you say and say what you mean." Don't promise somebody something and renege on your promise or commit to attending an event or working on a specific task and then back out without a legitimate reason. *Being impeccable with your word* is extremely important in following through on your commitments to yourself and others. Words matter. What we say creates our reality. Thus, speaking against yourself, putting yourself down, or gossiping about others engender negative emotions about yourself and others.

When you say yes to people to appease them and avoid conflict or to "get them off your back," that is not being impeccable with your word—that's a cop-out that comes back to bite you later. Aren't you more authentic if you are impeccable with your word and provided an honest answer along with the rationale for your answer? Additionally, you're not being impeccable with your word (or yourself) if you're not honoring how you genuinely feel.

For instance, a dear friend approached me recently about joining a business group for coaches with a multilevel marketing model. And as she explained how the group operated, I realized that this group does not align with my vision for scaling my business. And instead of saying, "Yes, I'll look into it," knowing full well that I would not, I indicated to her that based on what she shared about the group, I was going to pass and explained my rationale. She was very grateful, and from our discussion, she also gathered that this multilevel marketing model wouldn't make sense to pursue in her business structure either.

We have discussed *negative self-talk Nelly* and *flipping the script. Being impeccable with your word* will help you *flip the script* and speak more authentically, truthfully, and be more committed to being an advocate and champion for yourself and others. Notice if you disparage yourself and others. You heal your self-leadership by honoring your word, your commitments to yourself and those you lead, and by directing your words toward truth and love.

Do Your Best

"Doing Your Best" requires that you put forward your best effort. No one is a guru, and we all have a mission in this lifetime. No one is superior or inferior. If you believe you're superior to others—that your decisions, approach, and thought process are superior—that's ego talking. Question everything until you convince yourself of the right course for you. Be ready to speak your truth. Along the way, learn all that you can so that you have the worldly answer when questioned. As Don Miguel Ruiz says, your best will change from moment to moment, and it will be different when you are healthy and when you are sick. Sometimes your best is 50 percent or less if you're sick. That's okay, as long as it is the best that you can do. If you are facing a conflict or a difficult situation with someone, follow these four *being principles.* These are the questions and checklist I created and teach my clients to follow to identify the core of their problem and to address it. These are the questions to ask to resolve a conflict and assess if you are doing your best.

The first question to ask yourself in the situation is, am I making assumptions? If you are, what are they? You may find that, yes, you are making certain assumptions. In that case, which assumptions can you validate? Then go ahead and validate them.

The second question would be, am I taking anything personally? And if you ascertain that you are, what are you taking personally? And then ask, what would it look like if I didn't take this personally? What if I made it about them? What questions would I ask?

Next, ask yourself, am I being impeccable with my word to myself and others? Discern whether you are or not. Correct course as necessary.

Ask lastly, am I doing my best? When you are not making assumptions, not taking things personally, being impeccable with your word, and giving it your best effort, you are doing your best, and that's all that you or anybody can ask of yourself. Doing your best does not mean that you're perfect and don't make mistakes or that you won't regret saying or doing something that, in hindsight, you wish you hadn't. However, what it means is that given the circumstances, the information you have and collected, and the knowledge you have on the matter, this is the best decision you can make or course of action you can take.

This set of answers will guide you to get to the core problem and a fair resolution of any interpersonal conflict. As you acknowledge where you or the other party were making assumptions, taking things personally, not being impeccable with your word, and not doing your best, you will intellectually and intuitively gain insights to course correct and align with the *being principles*. And what a magnificent gift that is!

When we behave according to these principles, we can lay our head on the pillow and rest peacefully at night knowing that we performed, acted, and communicated in the best way possible. Again, it's not about perfection; it's about ensuring that your highest Self is in the driver's seat—not ego, negative self-talk Nelly, or worry Wendy. You may find when you ask yourself, did I do my best? that you didn't do your best. So, these four questions will help you identify the source of conflict and a direction to generate solutions to tackle the problems.

I remember when I was buying my home in 2014 in rural Sussex County, New Jersey, the house where I would live full-time with my son after my divorce. We finally found a place we liked within two miles of my son's school and central to my former marital home where my son's father lived. We learned during the inspection that the septic system was a big issue. The house was built in 1989, and the septic system's lifespan was twenty-five years! It was at the end of its life, and it was essential to replace it to enjoy functional indoor plumbing. At least that was my perspective. My lawyer and I requested to have a septic replacement clause as a contingency clause to close the deal. The estimated replacement cost would go into an escrow account to expedite the closing and relieve me of the responsibility and cost of incurring over twenty thousand dollars in repair costs within months of moving in.

This request became a sore point for the realtor, who was a dual agent for the seller and me, the buyer. She became very vocal and judgmental about my being too demanding by asking the sellers to replace the septic system. She wanted to make the sale regardless of the facts and didn't want to jeopardize losing the deal and her sales commission. Rather than make assumptions about the septic replacement cost and underestimate the repair price, I went out and requested three different quotes. While I could have become exasperated with the realtor for pushing the issue and insisting that I close on the house without a new septic system, I looked at the situation from her perspective. I reasoned with her that if I were to buy the house in the condition that it was, it would be equivalent to buying a home without viable bathrooms, which would be a problem for me and most likely for other potential buyers. She and the homeowners got the point. I was impeccable with my word with them and to myself by speaking my truth. I followed through with the purchase once they placed the septic replacement money in escrow. And at the end of the day, I did my best to be fair and defend my interests while also striving to meet the seller's and the realtor's needs.

Had I not practiced these principles, I would have raged and gotten insulted by the realtor's lack of consideration toward me and the expense that I would have had to incur after buying the home. The whole deal could have fallen through because of this conflict, and I would have had to start a new home search costing me months of additional work and effort. I appreciate that the *being principles* and my approach salvaged the deal and created a reasonable outcome. The sellers, who had the house on sale for over a year and wanted to relocate to be near their parents, finally sold their home. I needed a comfortable home to live with my son and be close to his school and my ex-husband with whom I share custody. And the realtor earned her commission on both ends. My home purchase scenario is one straightforward example of how using these principles supports life decisions, reduces chaos, and aligns solutions to truth and love.

Whether you already knew about *The Four Agreements* or are just learning about them now, I encourage you to apply them proactively—and you can completely transform your life.

Empowering Questions for Reflection

1. How many times do you take things personally when somebody seems to be upset or in a bad mood during a meeting?

2. How often do you question, what did I do? How come this person is upset with me?

3. How often do you take it personally when someone you e-mail, text, or call doesn't get back to you right away, or at all?

4. What would be different if you stopped taking things personally?

5. What if you were to focus on the other person and get compassionately curious about what is going on with him or her? What questions would you ask?

6. What assumptions are you making? How are they impacting you?

7. How can you be more authentic and impeccable with your word when people ask you to do something and you can't?

8. What does doing your best look like?

LEADER SHOWCASE: HARRY ELSINGA

"Always be authentically yourself."

Harry Elsinga, MA, is a global Chief Human Resources Officer for Fortune 150 companies. He's a coach, board, and start-up advisor with over thirty years of experience, including working at General Electric for over nineteen years. Harry attended Hogeschool Rotterdam and Erasmus University, Rotterdam and earned a master's in sociology.

Please share a little bit of your background.

I'm from the Netherlands originally. I started my career as a sociologist in human resources for a big construction company—big according to Dutch standards. And I was very fortunate to work for them in various countries. I worked in Hong Kong, came back, and then started working for GE Plastics in the Netherlands. And then, there was an opportunity to go to the United States.

As a family, we moved to beautiful Pittsfield, Massachusetts, then moved to Fairfield, Connecticut, where GE had its headquarters at the time. I worked as the manager of executive development for GE, and in 2008, I moved over to Oil and Gas, now known as Baker Hughes Oil and Gas. We did over forty billion dollars in transactions, and then in 2017, we merged and became a publicly traded company. You and I met in that period when Baker Hughes and GE came together, working on projects with the HR leadership team.

What are the most critical leadership skills leaders need in this turbulent environment?

It's important to listen to the vibe in your organization so you can try to instill a culture that's based on a particular set of values, in compliance, and with a high level of integrity. These are all great things to write in a pamphlet and publish online. But you need to be out there and see the organization, not the way you would like to see it, but the way it presents itself. And ask yourself questions such as, does this organization reflect a true representation of society? Do we have the diversity that we see in the environment that we operate in? Most likely, it's not always a perfect representation, so why is that?

What would you say to leaders who want to create a unique edge?

If you're going to pick up something or advance in a particular area, do something that you really like, not what somebody else tells you to do. You cannot train for the Tour De France if you don't like biking. It has to motivate you and excite you to get the best work out of you. If you find that area you're interested in, spend time researching it. Talk to people that have done it or are active in that field. Find a group with interests connected to this particular domain. Connect with other people because in the networking you do, the people you meet might be your next employment opportunity or engagement.

You can reach Harry via email at harry.elsinga@icloud.com or via LinkedIn.

6

Commit to Your Success and Well-Being

Define Your Success

Who succeeds? In his video, *The Strangest Secret* (Nightingale, 2019), Earl Nightingale highlights that the only person who succeeds is the person who is *progressively realizing a worthy ideal*. It is the person who says, "I am going to become this," and then begins to work toward that goal. This definition includes the teacher, salesperson, a stay-at-home mom or dad, the person running the gas station, the entrepreneur, and so on—all who are pursuing a predetermined goal because that's what he or she decided to do deliberately. As he points out, only one person out of twenty does that.

In his example, one hundred people start even at the age of twenty-five and claim to want to be successful. They are hungry, eager, and have a sparkle in their eye. But by the time they're sixty-five, only one will be rich, four will be financially independent, forty-one will still be working, and fifty-one will be broke, depending on others for life's necessities. Out of the one hundred, only five made the grade. Nightingale further concludes that the reason for so many failures is *conformity*, people acting like everyone else, or at least 95 percent of the population. And so, he asks, why do people conform? We don't know. Most people seem to believe their lives are shaped by circumstances, things that happen to them, and exterior forces. They are "outer-directed" people, or what I refer to as people with an *external locus of control*. In this book, one of my objectives is to shed light on what it means to have an *internal locus of control*—a belief that you can shape and influence your environment and that your actions determine the rewards you obtain.

If you were to subscribe to Nightingale's definition of success, those who are *progressively realizing a worthy ideal*, what is your worthy ideal? What are your important goals that you pursue deliberately with purpose while also taking care of your well-being? What is success to you? I've noticed that my definition of success evolves depending on the stages of my life and career.

When I began my career at the age of twenty-two, success was getting out of economic poverty, living on my own, paying my rent and later a mortgage. It was enjoying financial independence from my parents, doing work that I was good at and appreciated, traveling to countries I had only dreamed of, and learning as much as I could. Later, it was having my own family, getting married, giving birth to my son, and spending time with loved ones. As life went on and I attained those things, my definition of success included living peacefully, enjoying a healthy lifestyle, tapping into my creativity, dancing, spending time in nature, and developing a mindfulness and spiritual practice.

At this stage in my life, success is reaching my full potential, supporting organizations to build their leadership dream teams, helping individuals reach their potential, living in peace with my family, being in a loving relationship, and contributing to my clients, country, and the gross domestic product (GDP) the best way possible. Writing books are passion projects that allow me to collaborate with generous and talented individuals. Being able to connect with people and listen to them brings me joy, which is part of my success. Giving my son support, love, caring for him, teaching him, and helping him gain life skills and make his way in the world is also part of my success. Helping anyone that I can to rise and make progress is part of my success.

How do you define success, and what does it look like for you today? What is starkly different about your definition of success today versus what it was five, ten, or twenty years ago?

Prioritize Self-Care

Prioritize and commit proactively to your success and self-care as a way of life—that is courageous and reflects your commitment to living your best life, serving, and bringing joy to yourself and others. The alternative is burnout—physical, intellectual, and emotional. Get yourself on your priority list once and for all. What does that look like? What can you do daily to strengthen and expand your self-care?

Create a self-care ritual, rest, get moving, calm your mind, strengthen your body, have fun. Nutrition is at the core of my self-care. Growing up, I often heard my mother say, "If you have your health, you have everything." With that belief and modest financial means, my mother always cooked healthy meals by our Dominican standards: rice, beans, lots of salads, vegetables, meats, poultry, and fish. We seldom ate out, not because we didn't want to, but because we couldn't afford it. As a teenager, it was a privilege and a treat once in a blue moon when my mom and dad took us out to dinner.

Interestingly, growing up in a household where my mother cooked every night helped me develop healthy eating habits, which have supported me physically to live my best life. Even during the busiest of periods when I commuted for hours and my son was a toddler, I spent the weekends preparing the main course of our weekly meals to expedite preparing dinner when I got home. It was fun to plan the week's menu. And although it wasn't fancy, I fed my family home-cooked food. Today, as a single mom, I continue to enjoy preparing quick meals for my son, partner, and myself and teaching my son to cook simple dishes, for example, scrambled eggs, so he can learn to prepare his meals as he gets older. In addition to nutrition, I incorporate physical activity into my self-care.

Three days a week, I strive to train at my local cross-fit gym. During the lockdown of 2020, I joined my gym coaches for online training via Facebook Live and Zoom. I used gallons of water for weights and improvised with household items to perform some of the exercises. Gifting myself this time for movement and exercise during quarantine was crucial to staying healthy, physically and mentally. Activity is ingrained in my way of life and daily structure. From the time I launched into the business world after finishing college in 1991, I've done one or more of these activities at once: aerobics, running, volleyball, kickboxing, working out at my gym, yoga, and cross-fit training in the morning, lunchtime, or on the weekends. Recently, I train early in the morning and get through my day with more energy, less stress, and feeling physically strong. However, I'm not a saint. On occasion, I enjoy a piece of Dominican cake, chocolate chip cookies, Halloween candy, and recently discovered black-and-white cookies, which are so hard to resist! Like many, my metabolism has slowed down as I age, and I've noticed that I'm training a little bit harder to stay in the same shape. In my view, it's about moderation. I don't deprive myself of anything that I enjoy—I don't believe that's sustainable. Whatever your goals are for your physical fitness, it's never too late to start.

If you have a fitness regime that you follow and works for you, that is excellent. And if you don't, take a look at what's around you, maybe focus on what you like to do based on the options, and choose one. Then begin to use that option once a week, twice a week, three times a week, and see how you feel. But no matter what you do physically, if you don't watch what you eat, the portions and the quality of the food, it will sabotage any efforts you take through exercise to be physically fit. I have found that it's the combination of watching what I eat and physical activity that has kept me in the shape that I want to be and with the energy level I desire to get through my day. If you find this to be a challenging aspect of your self-care, I recommend hiring a coach who can help you develop the habits that will work for you specifically.

You may already *know* what to do for your self-care. I may be preaching to the choir. In these chapters, I am recommending that you begin to implement what you know about self-care. Having a cognitive understanding of what it means to self-care and doing it are two different things. What are you committing to doing that will motivate you in your self-care?

Another simple and accessible way that I self-care after a long, busy workday is by applying a hydrating or detoxifying Burt's Bees face mask—there are many other great ones. I apply it, lay down for twenty minutes, close my eyes, and meditate. I buy them in a pack and keep them handy. Miraculously, the stress and responsibilities that may be weighing on me melt away. I become more clear-minded, feel more centered and organized, and more easily prioritize what needs to get done next. Every two months or so, pandemic permitting, my mother and I have a ritual where I pick her up to attend our scheduled facials together, which feel exceptionally rejuvenating while spending quality time with each other. The combination of having your success goals, being directed to make progress in those goals, along with your self-care will help you attain those goals without burnout.

And let's not forget that creating downtime with friends and family and games or movie nights are also part of your self-care. There was a point in my life when sitting down to chill without being productive seemed pointless. I learned the hard way from years of hard work that it's necessary to give yourself the mental space to enjoy spending time *being*. Once I figured it out, I began to enjoy my life more, noticing all that's around that's already great. However, there's ample room for improvement for me on this front. And even though I am still ambitious to grow toward my potential, develop leadership dream teams, and focus on growing my business, I'm doing it with peace and a mindset of abundance and purpose, knowing that it is not a race but a lifestyle I deliberately choose.

Before the pandemic, one of my favorite self-care fun and recreation activities was meeting up with my friend Jannette and driving to Nyack, New York, to dance Latin music, salsa, merengue, and bachata. During our outings, not only did we have a blast, belly laughs, and enjoy connecting, we both created an opportunity to unwind from a busy work week. Afterward, around 2 a.m., we'd drive to a local diner and while waiting for our food, book our next outing. What a hoot, and as busy working women, we both looked forward to the next adventure. My takeaway for you is this: Schedule your self-care as if it were a doctor's appointment. When you need it most, in the middle of a tough week, month, or quarter, you will be so glad to see your self-care appointment on your calendar. That's how you prioritize yourself.

Finally, another way that I self-care is by dedicating time to my connection practice. I check-in with myself daily. This daily practice keeps me grounded and centered, removing any anxiety and overwhelm that I may feel. One of my coaches, Anne Marie, says that if you don't have twenty minutes to meditate, you need to set aside one hour! It's very telling if, on a typical day, you can't set aside twenty minutes for yourself. Even if only for five minutes, put it on your regular schedule to connect, meditate, and make it a priority. If you already do it, great. And if you don't know how, search YouTube for "guided meditation" to assist you. Let your soul settle and rest. Stay present. Bring your attention to your breathing. Afterward, you can write down what bubbled up for you. Notice the patterns and the quality of your thoughts. If you're trying to learn this new skill of connecting to yourself as a practice, don't leave it up to chance or a whim. Please put it on your calendar. And if your calendar changes, adjust accordingly.

Don't let random impulses dictate the routine and structure that will help you feel empowered. And while many of us may resist structure, the people I speak with—friends, clients, mentors, and teachers—have found more ease and flow in creating a support system, a routine that works for you, that invigorates you. Your self-care is one aspect of your life that you can control and that's meaningful—an ideal area of focus. Think of the movement, the foods that will nourish you, the connection practice that will help you center and rest—those we discuss here and others you may know and choose to add them to your calendar. Honor them, be impeccable with your word to yourself. And if you fall off the wagon, it's okay. Pick up where you left off and keep moving, doing your best.

LEADER SHOWCASE: DR. ALICE FONG

"You need to refuel, refresh, reinvigorate yourself, so you can keep going and support your people."

Dr. Alice Fong is a naturopathic doctor, CEO, and founder of Amour de Soi Wellness and Thriving Wellness Practice. She is known as the "Virtual Stress Doc" and helps busy professionals break free from stress, anxiety, and burnout so they can focus on what matters to them. Dr. Fong co-hosts the video podcast show *"Happy Talks with Dr. Alice and Donovon,* and she has given several talks around the country.

Please share the perspective from which you'll be answering these questions.

I am a naturopathic doctor and stress expert. I take a holistic approach to health and well-being, helping people go from surviving life to thriving in it. Stress is something that impacts everyone, especially right now, during this difficult time in the world with the pandemic.

We cannot always change the stressors in our life, but we can change how we respond to stress. *Naturopathic medicine* is about addressing the root cause and getting to the source of the problem to address it so it's no longer a problem. It's important to start with the foundation of health, such as eating clean, exercising, and getting enough sleep and water. Mindfulness practice is crucial too because it helps us become present in the moment, rather than dwell in the past or worry about the future.

What leadership skills are the most critical in this challenging world?

As a stress expert, I think leaders need compassion and understanding because when people are stressed and anxious, they are not typically performing at their best or being the best version of themselves. When we're anxious, we're more reactive and don't think things through. And biologically, what's happening when you're stressed and anxious is that blood leaves your brain and pumps into your heart so it can beat faster so you can run away because it's anticipating danger.

We as leaders need to practice being calm and not taking things personally in the face of other people's reactions. Then, that would give us the skill to be with them—however they are—and inspire them to know that they're being heard, understood, and that you get that they're anxious.

How should companies approach developing their leaders?

Companies should focus on training leaders to respond to stress in a healthy way. Training them to deal with stress and be that source of calm for others will help everyone else down the line feel more at ease. If a leader is frantic and anxious because of everything going on, that's going to trickle down, and everyone's going to be anxious.

Maybe we don't know exactly how to handle things correctly all the time because we're learning as we go along, and that's how we get better. We need to be okay with that and do the best we can. Ultimately, everyone tends to feel happier when they feel safe and comfortable in their environment.

Please connect with Dr. Alice on www.dralicefong.com or LinkedIn.

Listen to Your Body

It was Friday, December 11, 2015, one year and a few months after settling into being a single woman again. I was home sick, tired, a little hopeless, and shut down. Lyon Goldman held a teleclass where he was teaching the *body wisdom technique*, or the Somatic Wisdom Technique (SWT), a way of accessing the body's innate wisdom. By connecting and focusing on the body sensation, asking empowering questions, and listening, it's possible to gain insights and messages to improve your health, vitality, and well-being. After the class that night, I decided to give it a try. My body sensation was a sharp pain around my heart. By asking a series of questions about its shape, color, depth, and message, I intuited that my heart looked like a five feet by five feet round crater taking in what seemed to be vast amounts of water from the ocean. The edges were smooth and the depth immense. After asking for the message, I heard, "Listen to your heart. You already know the answers." And almost instantaneously, as soon as the message ended, I saw in my mind's eye the crater, the hole in my heart close, and the ocean that had been draining into the crater of my heart started to fill up again. As the ocean filled up, it nourished and filled me up, and the sharp pain in my heart subsided. Just like that. I was pleasantly surprised.

I continued to play with this concept a few more times and to journal my findings. The following Saturday, I felt an ache on my side as I lay on a massage table while getting a facial. I began to ask questions. What does it look like? It appeared as a long tear with jagged edges from the side of my back to the left of my spine. I asked what message it had for me and heard the response, "You are healing from the inside out." And then the pain went away. I tried it again one night when I felt a heavy weight on my left eye and at the back of my neck. As I sat up in bed, I closed my eyes and connected with it. I felt the sensation of a house sitting on my head. I felt its weight on my neck. As I asked what message it had for me, I heard in my mind, "What is true today will not be true tomorrow. Making these life changes will give you positive surprises you cannot imagine." This message was in reference to the court-ordered arrangement where I have a financial obligation to pay my ex-husband child support. The message continued, "The scale will be evened and all involved will contribute the same." On a different day, I felt a sharp throb around my heart again, and as I focused my attention on it but before I could ask any questions, it disappeared.

In December of 2015, Lyon taught me that paying attention to my body in a mindful way, something that I had never done or experienced before, would allow me to tap that inner wisdom that lives within. And I realized that this technique would help me release my inner healer. I was on to something and felt a tug to move toward the light while allowing the experiences and source to lead me, knowing that it's all happening as it should and that I'll always be safe, protected, taken care of, guided, and supported

For many years, I suffered from back pain especially in my lower back. I guess having a profession where I sat at my desk or in meetings most of the day didn't help. To alleviate the back pain, I would come up with excuses to get up from my desk and walk to the kitchen to make coffee or tea. Or during the nice weather in the Northeast, at lunchtime I would walk outside for ten or fifteen minutes with my friends and move my body around. Sitting in the car for long hours while commuting also contributed to the back pain—there were days the pain was so bad I thought my back would snap in two. Adding massages to my self-care practice helped tremendously with the back pain as did going to the chiropractor. And then I noticed that when I began to practice yoga, the chronic back pain improved significantly. A little stretching and strengthening of the back muscles and my abs released much of the stress that my lower back had been feeling.

As you pursue the goals that define *success* using *your* definition, and as you self-care, *listen* to your body. Notice its sensations, focus on them, get curious and ask to see their color, size, depth, texture—bring mindfulness to your body's sensations. Then ask for the message your body wants to deliver to you. The body is full of wisdom and it is always speaking to us. It lets us know when we need rest, water, fresh air, a nature walk, or movement. Our bodies are full of "transmitters." And as you get to know your body, you will notice when something's not working as it should. For example, experiencing headaches and muscle pains are indications of something not quite right happening within us.

The messages your body sends you will be meaningful and inspiring. Nothing happens by accident. As we learn to interact with our environment through our senses, our intuition, and body wisdom, we'll find meaning in everything around us—now wouldn't that heal leadership? We will lead by example with pleasure, ease, and flow. We will ask for guidance and be open to listening as we build a bridge to get from where we are to where we belong. You got this!

Empowering Questions for Reflection

1. What is your worthy ideal?
2. What are your important goals that you pursue deliberately with purpose while also taking care of your well-being?
3. How do you define success, and what does it look like for you today?
4. What is starkly different about your definition of success today versus what it was five, ten, or twenty years ago?
5. If you were to prioritize yourself once and for all, what does that look like?
6. What can you do daily to strengthen and expand your self-care?
7. What are you committing to doing that will motivate you in your self-care?
8. What messages are your body sending you? If you were to pay attention, what would you do differently?
9. What emotions will you feel when you improve your physical, emotional, or spiritual well-being?

7

Develop a Growth Mindset

Assess Your Mindset

According to the Neuro Leadership Institute, a *mindset* is a way of thinking about the goals we pursue personally and professionally. Your *mindset* determines the kind of information you focus on, how your brain handles errors and mistakes, and how you interpret successes and failures. Carol Dweck introduced the concept of a *growth mindset*.

People with a *growth mindset* believe skills and abilities can improve over time. They see potential in themselves and others, see change as a positive challenge, find new ways to take constructive action, and look for opportunities to learn. On the other end of the spectrum, people with a *fixed mindset* believe talent and intelligence can't change over time. They perceive change as a threat. Because people with a fixed mindset create negative scenarios, they experience highly negative emotions, and by exhausting their mental capacity on worries and these negative emotions, they learn at a slower rate. People with a fixed mindset also tend to critically judge and evaluate their performance to test their competence and worth.

However, it is not uncommon to have a growth mindset in one area of your life and not in another. For example, I have a growth mindset on my career—I believe I have potential, and so do my clients. However, I struggled with a fixed mindset around romantic relationships for many years as

I shared earlier. I didn't see any chance of finding a romantic partner in the rural area where I lived.

What is your mindset about your role as a leader? Knowing where you are on the spectrum of a growth versus a fixed mindset will inform your understanding about yourself and how your mindset will either support or prevent you from being the leader you want to be. To assess your current mindset on a particular area of your life, pay attention to that area and answer this set of assessment questions: Do you:

1. Believe talent and intelligence can't be changed?
2. Experience highly negative emotions regularly?
3. Judge and evaluate your performance as a test of your competence and worth?
4. See change as a threat?
5. Feel anxiety about your performance?
6. Feel concerned about how you "appear" to others?
7. Fear asking questions or admitting what you don't know?
8. Avoid challenging yourself and stick to what you already know?
9. See setbacks as a personal attack?
10. Give up quickly?
11. Hide mistakes?
12. Criticize yourself often?

As a leader, answering yes to the previous questions indicates a tendency toward a fixed mindset. How do you interpret errors and mistakes in your leadership role? Do you learn from them and try again or see them as a hit to your value and self-worth? What kind of information do you focus on? The problems or solutions? What meaning do you give to successes and failures? If you see the world from the perspective of gloom and doom, you most likely have a fixed mindset when it comes to that aspect of your life.

When you're assessing your mindset, look at your finances, career, health, personal development, physical environment, fun and recreation, and spirituality and assess your mindset in those areas, too. Suppose that you believe you can't improve in a particular area of your life such as your finances. Here is the risk. Believing that, are you more or less likely to stick to a budget where you save at least 10 percent of your income or lower your credit card purchases to reduce your discretionary spending? Your mindset determines your actions toward improving your overall personal well-being and toward your team and organization.

Cultivate a Growth Mindset

There are ample personal and professional benefits to understanding, cultivating, and investing in propagating a growth mindset culture. Research by the Neuro Leadership Institute (Weller, 2019) indicates that two years after launching its growth mindset initiative, HP Inc. saw a 22 percent increase in employee engagement. A global pharmaceutical company saw a 14 percent increase since starting its growth mindset journey. The research attributes these gains to the growth mindset culture. Teams in such a corporate culture don't think the same way as teams in other organizations do. Growth-minded teams see challenges as opportunities and leap at the chance to take on new problems. With a growth mindset culture, the goal is not to be the best—it is to make progress. And if they make mistakes, they look for the lessons to be learned and do all they can to improve next time. Here's a sample list of behaviors and attitudes that embody a growth mindset:

1. Believe skills and abilities can improve.
2. Find new ways to take constructive action.
3. Create realistic life goals grounded in a sense of purpose.
4. Take positive action toward goals daily.
5. Keep a realistic perspective (big picture).
6. See change as a positive challenge.
7. Look for opportunities to learn.
8. Nurture confidence and a complimentary view of yourself.
9. See the potential in yourself and others.

10. Cherish social support and interaction.
11. Treat problems as a learning process.
12. Avoid making a drama out of a crisis.
13. Focus on what will empower you.
14. Practice optimism.

As an individual, cultivate a growth mindset by reframing life's situations as opportunities to learn and evolve; this will make you more resilient and resourceful to recover from failures and execute your ideas. Author Byron Katie puts it this way: "Life is simple. ***Everything happens for you, not to you.*** Everything happens at exactly the right moment, neither too soon nor too late. You don't have to like it…. It's just easier if you do." When you begin to perceive and give a more empowering meaning to what is happening in your life as an opening to get to your next level of growth, you'll get patiently curious and begin to look for the lessons and the opportunities.

It takes the same mental energy to believe in the possibilities as it does to falling prey to doom-and-gloom scenarios—a balanced viewpoint helps you make informed decisions and take calculated risks. Embracing a fixed mindset keeps you relatively "safe" from taking those calculated risks and simultaneously and significantly limits you from fulfilling your full potential. You get to choose what helps you stay energized and hopeful. The alternative to developing a growth mindset is experiencing a downward spiral of negative emotions.

How do you reframe a situation to cultivate a growth mindset? Ask yourself quality questions: What is this situation helping me learn? How is this challenge helping me grow? How can I become a better version of who I was yesterday with self-compassion? Regularly, I connect with one of my dear mentors, entrepreneur, and author, Dean Graziosi, to reinforce a growth mindset and stay plugged-in with like-minded business leaders. When you cultivate a growth mindset, failures are but gifts that take you to a new level of expertise and insight.

In 2018, I launched my first online program, *Land a Job You Love*, and it turned out to be a massive flop. Only two students registered for the course.

I was disappointed in the results for sure! However, the lesson I learned from that experience was that I had to substantially improve my marketing and messaging. The modules' content was voluminous and difficult to digest in small bites. I only shot a few videos and provided too much text. From that experience, I realized that to have a successful program launch I would have to course correct. Using these insights, I started to craft my flagship program, the *Fearless Leadership Mastermind*™ (FLMM).

I enlisted Priya Kapoor, an expert in workplace learning and performance, to flesh out the course curriculum and content layout on a mobile-friendly platform. Throughout 2019, I designed the content and created training videos for each lesson, including video transcripts, audio-only files, and a downloadable Word workbook with exercises. These measures made the training student friendly, engaging, and tailored to different learning modalities. I hired a brilliant copywriter and marketing specialist, Lauren Doucher, to finalize my sales pages, created a sustainable back-office process for our members, and implemented a launch campaign that led to record sales in 2020 during the pandemic, exceeding all expectations. The FLMM members' testimonials validate the impact and value the program delivers. I couldn't be happier to host weekly Masterminds, teach, and coach on the concepts we discuss in this book to bright and growth-minded leaders on their unique leadership path. I then leveraged this approach and virtual team to successfully launch the *Personal Branding Masterclass*™, a rebirth of the original *Land a Job You Love* course. Because of this failed attempt, I'm now more aware of the importance of continuing improving marketing and operations efforts and creating a repeatable process and support team.

Another key to developing a growth mindset is not to link your self-worth and value to the outcome. If I had made any connection between the value that I provided in my program and the dismal enrollment and sales during the first failed launch, I would have not learned from the experience and been able to redo it. No one likes to feel bad at something and have that feeling reinforced! If you make that connection—that because you failed, you stink—the fear creeps in to prevent you from trying again. That is the danger. The growth mindset perspective questions, what can I learn from this? What can I do differently next time? Instead of blaming and wanting to stay stuck in a problem, you can choose what helps you stay energized and hopeful.

With this new understanding, how can you arm yourself and your team to cultivate a growth mindset culture? One of my favorite quotes about the importance of developing a growth mindset is by a fellow coach, Cynthia Occelli:

"For a seed to achieve its greatest expression, it must come completely undone. Its shell cracks, its insides come out, and everything changes. To someone who doesn't understand growth, it would feel like complete destruction."

–Cynthia Occelli

Empowering Questions for Reflection

1. What is your mindset about your role as a leader?
2. How do you interpret errors and mistakes in your leadership role?
3. How do you learn from errors?
4. What kind of information do you focus on? The problems or solutions?
5. What meaning do you give to successes and failures?
6. What is this situation helping you learn?
7. How is this challenge helping you grow?
8. How can you become a better version of who you were yesterday with self-compassion?
9. What can you do differently next time?
10. How can you arm yourself and your team to cultivate a growth mindset culture?

LEADER SHOWCASE: KIMBERLY KALOZ

"Encouraging a growth mindset is also encouraging time for professional development."

Kimberly Kaloz is a Senior Account Executive for a global biopharmaceutical giant where she has been influencing health-care market trends for over fifteen years. As a native New Yorker, Kimberly's experience spans over twenty-five years collectively in the market working with the top Fortune 100 companies. She received her bachelor's degree in marketing and advertising from Pace University.

Kim, please tell us about your background.

I started out with my current organization as a sales representative and have progressed over my career into an executive management role. Previously, I had been a self-taught web developer and a graphic designer. What I've learned most in my life and throughout twenty-five years in my career is that anything you want to transition to, you can do, as long as you believe in it and work hard.

What are the most crucial leadership skills that leaders should have today?

I'm always taken by leaders who exhibit a very calm, confident, controlled, nonreactive personality toward this challenging environment. We're not all born with these traits, but I believe that they are muscles worth exercising.

The only thing we really know right now is that change is constant and it's going to happen whether we like it or we don't. It's a matter of focusing on the opportunity in the change and adapting to it. There have been many curveballs thrown my way in my career. I have learned to befriend change and get comfortable with it instead of fearing it. Today, it fuels my confidence. Now, I know I have a strength inside me that can handle the changes as they come.

How should companies approach developing their leaders?

Organizations should be open to feedback and hearing the insights from colleagues of all skill sets and levels—because I believe that we work among some very creative and problem-solving minds. When we come together and brainstorm ideas, it can create new strategies to catapult on. Encouraging a growth mindset is also encouraging time for professional development.

I enjoy immersing myself in both personal and professional growth opportunities. It is essential for organizations to encourage their peers, colleagues, and employees to focus on that to better themselves as an organization. Find a mentor; it's very important! It has been crucial for me, especially working with you over all these years. It's been a tremendous help for me, in my career, and for my confidence as well.

What advice would you give to your younger self if you were looking to develop a unique edge?

People have said to me, "You can't do that because you need to be at a certain level." I've learned that's ONE person's opinion. Find the person who believes in you and says yes to who you are. Who knows what you're capable of, what you can become, and that you are capable of developing, growing, and learning.

Kimberly is available to connect on LinkedIn.

8

Be Resilient

Be Flexible and Adapt to Change

I hope you're starting to see a pattern. All the themes we have covered thus far inform and facilitate the next set of topics. Adapting to change is implausible without a growth mindset. Adapting to change by being flexible will help us heal, eliminate the pain associated with those changes, and experience growth from the challenges we face. From corporate reorganizations to changes in macro- and microeconomies, major life transitions, continually evolving relationships, and our rollercoaster shifts, change is inevitable. The concept of resilience and adapting to change goes hand-in-hand with mindfulness and being here now.

It is challenging to be flexible and adapt to change because we tend to project our fears and biggest worries onto the future. We assume that the current, troublesome situation will persist into the future. However, this usually proves *not* to be the case. Circumstances change rapidly. People move around and leave, companies shut down, you make a different decision today from the one you made yesterday. Bringing mindfulness to the changes and staying focused on what's here, now, while still planning as best as possible for the future will serve us immensely. I often bring up the quote by the Greek philosopher Heraclitus who said, "Change is the only constant in life."

Resilience is defined as the ability to go through periods of high demand and land on your feet. Look back at the different instances in your life when you felt you were in the middle of a storm and dealing with significant transformations. You somehow figured out how to get through that storm and get to the other side. *Flexibility* is vital in helping us navigate those stormy waters, and so is an open mind. How do we frame change as a positive challenge and adapt to it with flexibility? We harness our growth mindset and look for the lesson in the change.

Many times we think what is happening to us at a particular moment is utterly devastating. However, when we get out of our heads and look at our circumstances more objectively, we may notice the change was the catalyst to take us to our next level. Sometimes, working with an ineffective leader is a catalyst to anchor in our values, strengths, and convictions for what we want to see and create in our careers. The challenge emanating from conflict or discord or disagreement at work or home helps connect us to the next best version of ourselves. I believe that the purpose of every single change or challenge is to get through it and come out stronger and wiser until it's time to physically depart from the earth.

When my stepfather was diagnosed with lung cancer in July of 2002, I was devastated and felt the world was crumbling around me. He was a rock for our family, someone dear to me, a man who had taken me and my siblings under his wing and treated us like his own blood. I looked up to him, not only as my *father* but also as a mentor, teacher, and champion. And during that time when he was sick, I was working full-time and attending graduate school at night, but I was the family member managing and attending his doctors' appointments because I was fluent in English and was best equipped to communicate with the doctors. That was a very tough period, but it helped me see very clearly what was most important, which in this case was my stepfather and his health. At work, it pushed me to communicate and confide to my manager at the time, Rich, what I was going through, to be vulnerable, and receive the support I needed to get through that time.

It wasn't until months after my stepfather's passing, which was only three months after his diagnosis, that I was capable of expressing the grief and pain

I had suppressed during his illness. While sitting in the middle of that storm, I had held it together for my mother, brothers, and the critical work I was responsible for completing. After that experience, I was grateful for my dear colleagues, friends, and family members who supported me and my family. I also appreciated my own resilience and that I had been able to show up for my stepdad and my family and that I had done so with so much love in my heart.

I owed it all to my mom. As my role model, my mother has taught me what it means to be resilient. She has endured so much in her life with little support. She is one of those people who always looks for a positive way forward, learns from her mistakes, and never dwells on the problems but only on the solutions. Now, it's my turn to teach and model those qualities for my son and those I lead.

The pandemic of 2020 has been a real test for the world about what it means to be resilient. We've had to adjust and reinvent how we work, learn, collaborate, network, and operate practically overnight. We've leveraged technology in innovative ways to connect, mourn, and celebrate with loved ones, both healthy and suffering from illness. Months into it, what seemed foreign is now the new norm. Technology can be a valuable tool as long as we don't let *it* use *us*. Leading by example, with pleasure, ease, flow, a growth mindset, and compassion for ourselves and others will prepare us to continue adapting as changes ensue.

Because they always do.

LEADER SHOWCASE: RITA MITJANS

"Anything is possible if you want it badly enough, you put your mind to it, and you do the hard work to make it happen."

Rita Mitjans, MBA, is the founder and President of BizGuru, LLC. Rita is a strategic advisor, speaker, and coach who helps her clients elevate their performance through inclusive practices. Rita has over thirty years of corporate experience and received her BS from St. John's University with the honor of summa cum laude and an MBA from Harvard Business School.

Please tell us a little bit about yourself.

I was born in Cuba and came to the United States as a young child. I grew up in New York City. My parents valued hard work and education, so I spent a lot of time working hard in school—I have an MBA from Harvard, which I'm very proud of considering I was the first in my family to graduate from college. I cut my teeth on Wall Street then joined ADP and spent the last twenty years of my career there in various roles—everything from leading Marketing and Strategy to my favorite role, the position I retired from, leading Global Diversity and Inclusion for the company, as well as Social Responsibility.

What are the critical skills our leaders need in these times?

I think of five key things that I would say are particularly useful at this time and generally good skills to build on. The first one is **resilience**. In any environment, the ability to be resilient, overcome challenges, and come back from adversity is essential, not just a leadership skill but also a life skill.

The second one is **adaptability** and **flexibility**. I think those two go hand-in-hand, especially given the environment we're living in. There are so many unknowns. The ability to adapt to different environments and different challenges is critically important.

The third skill is the ability to **collaborate** and be **inclusive**. Inclusivity is important as a leader because you really can't do it by yourself. You need to engage others in that mission, and having the ability to connect with people who think differently from you is vital to promote innovative thinking.

The fourth skill is **courage**. Sometimes as a leader, you have to say and do unpopular things. You have to be willing to stand up when you see something isn't right, stand up for your convictions, and not compromise your values. Demonstrating that courage is crucial to being an authentic leader.

And the last thing is **self-empowerment** and the **empowerment of others**. Self-empowerment is about believing in yourself, investing in yourself, and making enough time for yourself. To carve out time to be healthy, both mentally and physically, but also to do that for your team. Especially for women, there's this balancing act that has to happen with competing demands from work and home. And the ability to empower our teams to take control of their own lives, their situations, and make decisions that can help achieve that elusive balance is incredibly important.

You can reach Rita at Rita@bizgurullc.com, www.bizgurullc.com, or on LinkedIn.

Take on Challenges

"The tragedy of life is not death but what
we let die inside of us while we live."

–Norman Cousins

Suppose that we appreciate and develop a growth mindset and accept that every challenge we face is there for a reason and is an opportunity for growth. How does a healing leader take on challenges? We think about the circumstances, the stakeholder groups involved, and strategize around the right steps to take on behalf of all the stakeholders. In a work-related example, when a project is in trouble suffering from delays, stakeholders are not accountable, the project manager has lost control of the project, and the business partners are not organized and continue to change the requirements. As difficult as this situation is, keep your cool and look at these challenges as opportunities. As a leader, my priority is always relationship building. Devising the solution includes answering the question, how can I preserve these relationships, or improve them, from the challenge(s) we are facing?

Individually, get clear on your *endgame*—what you desire to create on behalf of your team and organization. As you face challenges, question what is most important. What would be the ideal outcome? And then, what would be the next ideal outcome? And then shepherd resources and people around the problem to envision that ideal outcome or the next ideal outcome. This is the time to get resourceful and communicate powerfully and with integrity; the time to lean on others in your team to generate ideas, and ultimately being decisive moving forward. The alternative is to throw in the towel and quit. That's always an option, but before you do, make sure that you've exhausted your possibilities.

One of my biggest challenges at work was dealing with a botched vendor selection project. We were looking for a system to help us enhance the sales process and ultimately increase assets under management (AUM) by automating the management of requests for proposals (RFPs), and requests for information (RFIs). I was the project manager responsible for initiating, conducting, and implementing the vendor search and solution. The team and I had followed the best practices for vendor search and due diligence, demos, client referrals, vendor site visits, and so on. After selecting a vendor and signing the contract, we implemented the new system.

During the end-user testing, we learned that some of the features we expected based on our specifications and vendor demonstrations were not available in the product. The product was substandard, and we had to abort the implementation. We had been duped! I felt like I had been hit over the head with a two-by-four as I had never experienced anything like this throughout my professional career. Due to this breach of contract, we were able to nullify it but incurred some financial consequences. As a relatively new member to this division but a long-standing employee at the company, this was a challenge I had to face with everyone in mind—the least of which was my concern for my reputation within the team.

Taking on this challenge meant owning it. Despite our efforts to follow the due process, I had made a mistake in making this recommendation. I communicated with the stakeholders and addressed their concerns. The team regrouped to pursue a different avenue and select a new vendor. We ended up buying another system, implementing it successfully, and everything worked out okay. However, this experience taught me to dig even deeper when looking at a vendor to provide a service or technology. In this case, I could have dug in my heels and clamored that I had done everything that I was supposed to do. This approach would not have been supportive of my internal partners who desperately needed to alleviate the chokehold on the team who was processing the RFPs and RFIs manually. They needed a swift solution that would provide operational efficiencies, minimize manual errors, and lead to increasing the sales of our mutual funds. Focusing on the endgame of implementing the right product helped me to bypass and avoid wasting time on making excuses, finger-pointing, and blaming.

How we handle challenges becomes part of our personal brand and speaks directly to our character. With transparency, honesty, and a sense of urgency we can address challenges head on and do what is best for the people involved.

Think of a time when you encountered a challenge in business or personally. What would it look like to take on that challenge today with a growth mindset and resilience? What would you do differently?

Grow while Pivoting

Every challenge creates an opportunity for personal growth. The beautiful thing is that challenging scenarios help you identify yours and others' strengths and weaknesses, which are merely areas to improve. In a professional context, it could be a people, process, or system issue, and so on. In any case, performing root-cause analysis will identify whether people need to be trained. Leaders may need to become better at communicating goals, handling conflicts, or unearthing competing agendas. It could be that you ascertain the process is not efficient and needs an overhaul—which may involve enlisting cross-functional stakeholders to agree and commit resources. You may learn about system breaks where data is not flowing from one source to its destination as expected.

Growth comes from pinpointing problem areas and looking for constructive action moving ahead. And that requires us to be self-aware and examine the *being principles* for ourselves and others. Look at the *assumptions* you're making; what you may be taking *personally*. Observe how you are being *impeccable with your word*. Also, notice if you're focusing on fears versus ideas and any potential concerns with placing blame. If we do this right, the problem will help you and the entire team grow. It's sometimes hard to accept making a mistake—I know it was for me as a new member of the group—or when we're not communicating well or dropped the ball. It's crucial to have checks and balances throughout the problem resolution. The team—especially if it's a dynamic production support group, or a front-office, client-facing type of group—may continuously be pivoting around problems with clients, processes, or systems.

I used to joke around whenever we had a business problem. I used to call it "job security." If there were no problems for us to solve as professionals, what would be the point of having us around? As knowledge workers, we have a role to play that machines can never replace, and that is to look at the big picture, use our critical, analytical, and strategic thinking to connect the dots and find solutions.

On a personal level, relationships provide a rich source for growth and learning, in some instances stretching us way out of our comfort zones. And a similar strategy applies here, too: Get to the root cause, clarify what's most important in the long game, be present in the short game to bring your highest Self to the interaction, and cocreate a desirable solution.

You can do it. Try it, it works!

Empowering Questions for Reflection

1. How do you frame change as a positive challenge and adapt to it with flexibility?

2. How does a healing leader take on challenges?

3. How can you preserve relationships, or improve them, from the challenge(s) you are facing?

4. What would be the ideal outcome? And then, what would be the next ideal outcome?

5. What would it look like to take on a former challenge today with a growth mindset and resilience? What would you do differently?

LEADER SHOWCASE: MARIA SANTOS VALENTIN

"This is a time when all of humanity has to be at our most resilient because we are faced with unprecedented challenges and hardships."

Maria Santos Valentin is Secretary and General Counsel for the Rockefeller Foundation. Maria has over thirty years of international transactional work in developing markets, working for large law firms, the US federal government, and the nonprofit sector. She has a BA in economics from Fordham University and a law degree from Yale Law School.

Maria, for our leaders, what is your background?

I was born in Puerto Rico in the outskirts of the city of Ponce to a single mom. When I was about five years old, my mother brought me and my older sister to New York looking for better opportunities. She taught us that your circumstances don't define you and what you're capable of achieving.

My mother encouraged me and my sister to go to college as a way to open doors. Going to Yale Law School changed my life in terms of the opportunities that opened up for me. My time at Yale made me aware of how difficult it is for a minority and an immigrant to get to that place, and how out of place you can feel in that environment when most students come from a different and more privileged background.

After law school, I was on my way to becoming an international corporate lawyer in developing markets, eventually working for the Overseas Private Investment Corporation, the US development finance institution, and then to become an expert on charitable investments that have a social impact working for The Open Society

Foundation, and now as the second General Counsel of the Rockefeller Foundation.

What would you say are the most critical skills leaders need today?

What comes to mind is **resilience**. And there can be a positive lens to that—resilience to keep going at your vision, but also resilience if you have obstacles. You don't let those get you down. You overcome them and actually look at those obstacles as opportunities for growth. And the other is **empathy**, putting yourself in other people's shoes because as a leader, you need to motivate others. And you won't be able to motivate them to join this journey with you if you can't anticipate their needs.

What would you advise when it comes to developing a unique edge?

It's important to have different viewpoints so that you're not all patting yourselves on the back and having a herd mentality to your operations. Part of that is acknowledging, especially in this time, racial justice issues and diversity from that perspective. Knowing that there are things we don't know and being open to finding out what that is.

This is a time when all of humanity has to be at our most resilient because we are faced with unprecedented challenges and hardships. I believe that there are many opportunities for personal, professional, and communal growth coming out of this crisis if we open ourselves to them.

You can reach and connect with Maria on LinkedIn.

9

Develop Relationships

Connect with Your Centers of Influence

As leaders, developing relationships, virtually or live, is our most precious currency. In our leadership training and coaching programs, I teach our members and clients about the importance of developing healthy relationships with their centers of influence. Knowing which people are within your sphere of influence is crucial. Your *centers of influence* involve you at the very center of the diagram, and then it includes each of these groups of people who influence your role, and vice versa, in a separate bubble around you: your manager (or the board); your manager's peers; your peers within the organizational structure; your team and direct reports; internal partners; and clients, mentors, sponsors, vendors, and any other stakeholders, that is, affiliates, venture partners, industry liaisons, and so on. They each get a bubble on your centers of influence diagram. After you create your map, healing leaders are deliberate about developing these relationships and nurturing a supportive network and ecosystem of people.

What is significant about that? In the next segment, I will share the distinctions I make between being *transactional* versus *relational* in our approach. For now, building relationships with your centers of influence will expedite your achieving strategic objectives while also enjoying the process, the vision and mission, spreading trust, collaborating, and influencing a growth mindset culture that slowly immunizes people and protects them against a fixed mindset.

As I mentioned in the beginning, **as healing leaders, we value, uplift, and mentor others; lead, engage, and influence them toward constructive action with empathy, respect, and conviction.** These kinds of transformations occur when you build relationships with your centers of influence. What are some recommendations for connecting with them regularly? This point is even more critical now that many of us are working virtually or in a hybrid model, making face-to-face interactions less viable, at least until we introduce a sustainable, healthy treatment to this current virus and future ones. If you are not used to networking or new to the leadership ranks, it's worthwhile to share these best practices. If you are a seasoned master networker, I will love to hear from you about your favorite techniques for connecting with your centers of influence.

One of the simplest ways to connect with your centers of influence—once you identify them—is by setting up a fifteen-minute cyber-coffee or tea (as I call it) with them. Use either a work project, a milestone, an achievement, a post you saw on their social networks, to e-mail, call, or text message them to say something along these lines: "Hi Ginny, congratulations on getting promoted. It's been a while. Would you be open to connecting for a fifteen-minute cyber-coffee or tea to catch up?" In your message, include a couple of dates when you are available so that the person can say, "Yes, that works," or "I'm not available on those dates, but here are some dates that work on my end." And give the person some time to get back to you.

If you don't hear back after reaching out the first time, don't give up. E-mail or message the person again five days later, more or less. People are busy and their inboxes are overflowing. So far in my experience, it's been rare for someone to say they don't have fifteen minutes to connect. It is much harder to say yes to a one-hour meeting. Keep it brief. Bring any bullet points you want to address during your cyber-coffee or tea and get curious about the person—how is he or she doing during this time, professionally and personally. Keep your comments and remarks professional whether you are speaking about work or family. If you don't know the connection that well, see if anyone in your network can make an introduction. Either way, do your research beforehand, check out the LinkedIn profile, see what articles are posted or have been liked recently, and you can use that intel for conversation topics. Make sure to share what you are up to, which appeals to their interests. When the time is up, if you are still engaged in conversation, inform the person, "It has been fifteen minutes. I want to be respectful of your schedule." The individual can let you know how much free time he or she has available and your meeting can proceed accordingly.

Connecting with your centers of influence is a two-way street—a give-and-take. This includes connecting with your mentors and sponsors. Depending on your career trajectory, you might be clear about mentors' and sponsors' roles, or maybe you haven't dabbled in this area yet. Suppose you fall in the latter group of leaders or could use a refresher course on their importance. In that case, the benefits of forming relationships with mentors and sponsors are essential to develop, accelerate, and expand your influence and impact within the company and externally.

Your mentors are people you trust and can tell them just about anything and ask for their advice. They can be people in your line of work, your direct reporting structure, or anywhere within or outside your organization, in your industry, or elsewhere. I recommend that you focus on fostering internal and external mentorship relationships. One quick word of caution: Avoid approaching people and asking, would you be my mentor? I cringe when I hear that question. I am so busy that I can't even imagine committing to the typical one-hour meetings. However, if you were to approach me and say, "Ginny, I know you wrote a book; I've been thinking about writing one also. Would you be open to a fifteen-minute cyber-coffee or tea to briefly share your insights?" I would make fifteen minutes for you for sure.

On the other hand, your sponsors are people with seniority who can assign you a new role, a stretch assignment, or put you in charge of a new initiative. If you are at a senior level of management, sometimes your sponsor plays your mentor's role when there's a great deal of mutual trust. To connect with your sponsors, find common ground. Again, notice what they're talking about, what interests them, and approach them with those topics in mind.

Consider what you can contribute to the conversation that would catch their attention and bring that up when you invite them to connect, for example, "Hi Ginny. I see that the team is getting ready to launch a new product line. Would you be open to connecting for a fifteen-minute cyber-coffee or tea? I have some thoughts about how we can use this occasion to enhance client success." Sponsors are quite busy and typically rely on an assistant for scheduling meetings—so do mentors if they're in senior-level roles. Rather than providing dates, I would also ask them, "If you are agreeable to a fifteen-minute cyber-coffee, should I reach out to your assistant directly to set it up?" And wait to hear back. Remember to follow-up and be proactive in reaching out.

Your sponsors provide an opportunity to share ideas they would find exciting and better understand the vision for the organization, your field, or industry. Strive to make a contribution when you talk to your sponsor. Great sponsors value your perspective. While sharing insightful information in which you have common interests, keep the focus on your sponsor—you already know what's in your brain; you want to understand what's in theirs. Become genuinely interested in their perspective and express your appreciation for their time and ideas.

Whether referring to mentors, sponsors, or anyone else in your centers of influence, how do you proceed to deepen the relationship after you connect for cyber-coffee or tea? At the end of fifteen minutes, you can say something like this, "This was a very insightful conversation. Would you be open to briefly syncing-up in a couple of months?" Then schedule it on your calendar to reach out again in the agreed-upon time frame. If the person suggests alternatives to the cyber-coffee or tea, be open and flexible. Use your own words and expressions during your communication, of course. This is a proven and plausible approach to developing healthy, organic connections with the people in your centers of influence. It works, and it has served me tremendously over a thirty-year career.

Since graduating from college, I began to network and build my centers of influence—I didn't refer to them by this name back then. I've treasured these relationships and gained great advice and wisdom from those interactions. A few years ago, when I assembled a new company deck to introduce ExecutiveBound® to my strategic corporate partners, I connected with several industry leaders in the C-suite from my LinkedIn network. My goal was to get to know them better and ask for feedback. Rita Mitjans, Bob Selle, and Harry Elsinga among others generously provided practical feedback to enhance the presentation. It takes courage to reach out, and it requires us to stop making assumptions about how others will respond. Every leader I reached out to for our field study agreed to participate in a fifteen-minute video interview. Go ahead, validate your assumptions; send the invitation and then wait patiently for the response. The reality is that people are generous, and everyone has a need to contribute. When you ask anyone in your centers of influence for a connection, you enable them to contribute to you. And likewise, you get to contribute to them, too.

Spread synergies around the human need to contribute by staying in touch with your centers of influence. Commit to creating and nurturing your professional and personal networks of colleagues, mentors, sponsors, friends, and so on. If you were to connect with even one person a week for fifteen minutes, that translates into making fifty-two connections per year. Taking this deliberate action not only expands your exposure and visibility but you also learn what is going on around you, pick up on the latest trends, contribute your thought leadership while building your unique edge, and take care of your well-being. If you've been passive on this front, this is your cordial invitation. Let's get moving.

LEADER SHOWCASE: JENNA HENDRICKS

"Be curious, be a business partner, create great relation-ships, remember that every relationship matters."

Jenna Hendricks is the Senior Vice President of Global HR for Michael Kors/Capri Holdings. Jenna has over twenty years of human resources experience and has been with Michael Kors for over seventeen years. She graduated from the University of Pennsylvania with a degree in psychology.

Let's start by learning a little bit about you.

At the beginning of my career at Michael Kors, I started as a team of one. Now fast forward seventeen years, and there has been amazing growth. My role has been all-encompassing. I've touched on everything in the HR space including taking the company public and learning what that entails, acquiring two other brands, and subsequently becoming a holdings company. For me, the most crucial piece of my growth and development—it doesn't mean it's right for everyone—was having to figure out things on my own and learning trial-by-fire.

Early on, my boss described my experience with this quote, "We threw her into the deep end of a swimming pool without knowing how to swim, and she had to figure it out." I think people perform best when they have the autonomy and ability to be creative, to figure out their own way of doing things versus following specific direction. This leads to more dynamic perspectives because not everybody has to get to the same answer in the same way. That's the beauty of having a diverse team that comes to the table with different viewpoints.

What approach should companies use to develop their leaders?

Set a standard baseline of what it takes to be a leader. Make sure those standards are communicated and people are aware of where they fit on that spectrum; then create leadership programs around those standards, tying them to business results. Then keep those learnings alive and continue to fine-tune those skills. It can't be a one-size-fits-all answer because everyone has different strengths and developmental needs. Creating flexibility around those programs and making sure companies know it's a part of their job to help their leaders be successful must be weaved throughout your culture.

What would you say to leaders who are looking to create a unique edge?

Take advantage of any opportunity to learn. Whether it's learning from a senior-level leader in the organization or an offered program, know what your options are and take advantage of them. This is easier said than done, but it's critical to focus a bit of your time, whether it's daily, weekly, or monthly on being able to think and not just getting through the day.

In any function you do, there should always be a connection between the business and the human side. Be curious, be a business partner, create great relationships, remember that every relationship matters. It doesn't matter if you don't think it does right now. It may, at some point. Treat everyone fairly and equally. Finally, people work for people. Lead the way you would want to be led.

You can reach Jenna on LinkedIn.

Transacting vs Relationship Building

In the book, *The Seat of The Soul*, Gary Zukav (Zukav, 2014, p. 242) states, "The deeper you allow yourself to go with yourself and others, the more you will accelerate your growth and become a conscious, heart-centered contributor to your evolution and the evolution of the species."

In everyday work situations, rushed people lean on being *transactional* (fixated on the short game) versus *relational* (focused on the long game). Many feel comfortable in a demand/supply exchange: I need something, *demand;* you provide it, *supply;* or vice versa. Somebody asks you for a deliverable, you supply it, and that's the extent of it. When working with a *team*, a set of people working together to achieve a common goal, focusing on relationship development means aiming beyond the work-related item and connecting with people on a much deeper level to "see" and appreciate them. My recommendation is to make a concerted effort to shift toward a relationship-building paradigm. As healing leaders, what are the tangible benefits of deepening relationships with our team and the people in our workplace? What's the carrot we're chasing?

The answer is: *employee engagement. Engaged employees* and teams are "those who are involved in, enthusiastic about, and committed to their work and workplace" (Gallup, Gallup, 2020). It is also "the emotional commitment the employee has to the organization." When employees feel engaged, they care about the company and do their best work to achieve the company's goals (Smarp, 2020). For decades, leaders have battled the crisis around low-employee engagement. As of 2017, 85 percent of employees worldwide are *not engaged* or are *actively disengaged* in their jobs. Conversely, only 15 percent of employees *are engaged* (Gallup, *State of the Global Workplace*, 2017). And while 71 percent of executives say **employee engagement** is critical to their company's success, employers spend approximately $1.1B per year looking for replacement workers (Smarp, 2020), or roughly 20 percent of a salary to replace a lost worker (Spencer, 2019).

Employee engagement increases retention, customer success, morale, and lowers turnover costs (Spencer, 2019). During hard economic times and massive disruption, employee engagement drives *team resilience* and *company performance*, which is essential for organic customer growth, delivering on the company's brand promise, adapting to a rapidly changing marketplace, and persevering through unplanned disruption (Gallup, Gallup, 2020). From a practical firsthand, thirty-year career perspective, I'd add that I've witnessed the organic by-products of engaging with my team and colleagues—building trust, empathy, and understanding of a person's needs, values, beliefs, and stories. We help each other heal and fulfill our potential when we share our stories and listen, seeking real understanding first. In Stephen Covey's *The Seven Habits of Highly Effective People*, the fifth habit is, "Seek first to understand, then to be understood" (Covey, 2004). At one point in my corporate role, I created a poster with this quote and pinned it on my team's whiteboard.

Our work culture and business benefit when we expand work relationships and assist our teams in engagement. With this awareness, how do we, as healing leaders, become more *"involved in, enthusiastic about, and committed to"* our work and workplace? How do we increase the "emotional commitment" that we have to the organization? And how do we navigate doing so in-person or remotely these days?

Every day we have opportunities to deepen our relationships. Unfortunately, this is the part that many of us skip. When you first connect with someone, depending on your style, you may dive right into the business at hand, and that's understandable. Time is of the essence, we're all pressed for time and have deadlines to meet. However, bring a renewed mindfulness to your daily interactions—despite a virtual or face-to-face medium—be here, now, come equipped with a growth mindset, and start simple. It's most important to be true to your communication style and voice. These are straightforward examples to give you an idea of what to talk about, which depends on the work context and your familiarity with the person.

In essence, engage from a relationship-building angle, and before you go into the business at hand, make a *human connection*. Here are a few examples: Go beyond saying, "Good morning, Dave" and ask, "How are you?" "How's the family?" and then finally ask, "How are things at work?"

And here's the most significant component: Genuinely listen to their re-sponses, patiently and without interruptions. Get comfortable with silence. Pause any conversations happening in your head. Instead, take the person in. Notice the body language, demeanor, voice quality, pitch, rate, and cadence. Bring your whole Self to the conversation.

Based on what you hear or see, name what is present, what you noticed, such as, "You sound very excited about that!" Or, "I'm sorry to hear that. Please let me know if there's anything I can do to help." And ask follow-up, empowering questions if appropriate. For example, if he says that the family is going on a vacation to Costa Rica, follow-up with something relevant, "Why did you choose that destination?" You might learn that he loves scuba diving—now you know something new about Dave. (Please note that this doesn't have to be a fifteen-minute exchange. It could be as short as a couple of minutes. It all depends on the circumstances, length of the meeting, and so on.)

After you make the human connection, dive into the work. During meetings, look for authentic ways to appreciate the participants and what they are doing well. When you speak about the strengths you see in people, you call out their power by reflecting who they are. And when you finish, express appreciation for the time you spent together. You'll transform from being another person in the meeting to being an engaged, trusted advocate, and ally. That's the type of workplace and team where I want to spend my hard-earned days.

Using our previous example, under a typical scenario, Dave may ask you similar questions. When it's your turn to answer, be thoughtful and answer him authentically and professionally. Set healthy boundaries, remembering that you don't have to share as if you were shooting the breeze with your best friend. Being *professional* to me means being respectful to the person when sharing the information that's essential to get the message across without getting into deeply personal details. Nonetheless, share highlights that speak to your truth and lets the person know how you are really doing. There will be occasions when the person does not ask you any questions. I can't tell you how many times I've asked people at work or in social circles, "How are you?" and they responded and did not reciprocate. Regardless, share your perspective as well, briefly. I mention this because my concern is on how you show up to the interaction as a healing leader. Maneuvering the conversation depends on the dynamics. Use your self-awareness and social awareness to sense when you're ready to dive into the work issue(s).

Through your approach and behavior, you will be role modeling for your team and colleagues, and it will be up to them to appreciate the benefits and decide to connect on that level. Your engaging behavior will inevitably generate a ripple effect. It will take time to *heal* how we interact with each other. However, with consistency, care, and love, the relationship will expand over time.

It took me a full year of focused training and over one hundred hours of coaching practice to become a certified professional coach. I realize that it is challenging to flip a switch and begin interacting at a deeper level overnight. As a leader, the goal is not perfection; it's progress.

These simple examples describe the essence of some of the tools a great coach uses during a coaching session. Use them as a practice to self-manage, notice how you're feeling, and to listen with a heightened level of self-awareness and focus. Like driving a car, with practice, it becomes automatic.

This approach and tactics to engaging apply to your social circles as well. Connecting more profoundly, listening on all levels, and sharing authentically, with curiosity and patience, will make you a safe leader—and one who sees in the dark, tapping into your intuition to hear what's present and silent. As you continue interacting like this regularly, your *emotional commitment* to the organization and the people in your life will flourish, and collectively, you will feel more engaged. Bring on the benefits!

LEADER SHOWCASE: JOHNNA GINGERELLI

"Leaders need to value, respect, and foster their relationships across the organization and make themselves available."

Johnna Gingerelli, PMP, PMI-PBA, VLSS Black Belt, is a Program Manager at Verizon. With over twenty-five years of finance experience, Johnna graduated from Fordham University with a bachelor of science degree in business and received dual MBA degrees from Fairleigh Dickinson University and Montclair State University.

Please provide a brief description of your background.

I work at Verizon in the Financial Transformation office. I have two master's degrees, one in finance and one in accounting, as well as several project management-related certifications. My career has spanned both Fortune 100 companies and startups that cross varied industries including communication, banking, media, retail, and advertising. My career at Verizon began in IT Governance, Risk, and Compliance, then to Global Supply Chain, and now Finance. Before joining Verizon, I worked at JP Morgan in Corporate HR Finance.

What advice would you give leaders looking to develop a unique edge?

Leaders looking to develop and carry out a unique edge for themselves need to show up as leaders every day. In the here and now, this means making time for themselves and their teams to connect and examine their processes, deliverables, and time constraints. Leaders need to create a "safe space" for their team to make suggestions, freely ask questions, and feel heard and included. Leadership requires "fellowship."

Leaders also should have a long-term vision plan for themselves in writing and encourage their team to do likewise. This drives intent and culture while demonstrating foresight. The long-term vision requires planning a path that can be accomplished in short-term palatable commitments, such as taking coursework, networking with others who are in a position to provide guidance and insight, and staying on course.

What do you recommend to leaders who are coasting right now?

Coasting stagnates growth and progress for the leader, their employees, and ultimately the organization. Coasting does not drive change, creativity, or innovation. For me, **coasting** implies a lack of ambition, enthusiasm for the position, and minimal effort. The team often can sense this lack of enthusiasm, and in turn, becomes disillusioned with their position and contributions.

What last message do you want to leave for our leaders?

Leaders need to be role models and remain self-aware and vigilant about how they show up each day and how their behavior impacts those around them. They need to set a daily intent to keep their emotions in check, not be reactive, engage their teams, and have both short- and long-term goals in writing. Leaders need to value, respect, and foster their relationships across the organization and make themselves available.

Johnna is available to connect on LinkedIn.

Lead by Contributing

Some people are skeptical of others' intentions. Some aren't trusting of others for various reasons. We've grown accustomed to watching our backs, protecting our turf, sometimes because of our past experiences with colleagues, partners, or managers who have taken advantage or overstepped to advance their agenda without regard for others. We all have agendas or ulterior motives, but that doesn't necessarily mean they are malicious. To help each other heal, lead by contributing. Let others know that you intend to contribute and that you mean it.

One of the most effective ways to build relationships is to consider it from the perspective of contribution—being of service to people, helping them advance, and so on. How can you contribute to the people around you? This is the foundation for propagating goodwill and meeting your human need for contributing while also building relationships. It's a give-and- take. As you deepen your relationships, share your intention to support them in any way possible. This approach is disarming—it brings down the guards of people. It creates a sense of safety.

As you begin to notice the people at work and in your social circles who are more transactional versus relational, let them know it's okay to check-in whenever they'd like. Those are the people who come around only when they need something. Some assumptions we make can stop us from reaching out when we don't want anything other than to connect, for example, we might think, Ginny may be busy. Why would she want to hear from me?

In what ways can you contribute to the people in your sphere of influence? Your mere presence and your ability to listen is a form of contribution to someone without having to fix anybody's problem. People aren't heard enough and we desperately seek it. We tend to anxiously await our turn while the other person is speaking, listening only superficially. We're all guilty of this at some point. Listening and validating what you heard makes a person feel seen and understood. Sharing a resource, connecting an individual to someone in your network, providing a referral or recommendation are ways to contribute, and so is asking for other people's advice or opinions about a situation. How so? When you ask for advice, you enable them to contribute to you, plus you're giving them *significance*. You're making them feel important and valuable, meeting one of their human needs.

The last example I'll cover is *appreciation*. As I already mentioned, when you express your gratitude to someone and highlight their strengths, you also contribute to them.

To connect with your centers of influence, to *build* relationships versus *transacting*, all you need is to think about contributing to that person. Most likely, any hesitation, apprehension, and fears that arise when you think about connecting with people will melt away as you focus on contributing. It will make a world of difference. And ultimately, you will have more engaging and enjoyable connections and a network of people you get to influence and who influence you, which is something to respect and honor.

Empowering Questions for Reflection

1. What are some recommendations for connecting with your centers of influence regularly?
2. Who is in your sphere of influence and how are you cultivating those relationships?
3. Whether referring to mentors, sponsors, or anyone else in your centers of influence, how do you proceed to deepen the relationship after you connect for cyber-coffee or tea?
4. As a healing leader, what are the tangible benefits of deepening relationships with your team and the people in your workplace?
5. How do you, as a healing leader, become more *"involved in, enthusiastic about, and committed to"* your work and workplace?
6. How do you increase the "emotional commitment" that you have to the organization? How do you navigate doing so in-person or remotely these days?
7. How can you contribute to the people around you?
8. In what ways can you contribute to the people in your sphere of influence?

10

Tap Hidden Resources

Affirm Your Faith

We all possess a wealth of resources, including our intellect. Growing up, I was most familiar with my intelligence quotient versus my emotional quotient (EQ), or emotional intelligence. Over the years, I've been unlocking hidden resources, including my faith, intuition, and divine guidance. As a leader, understanding these resources in myself helps me acknowledge and appreciate them in others and to grasp the extent of my potential and theirs.

I'm not a religious person. However, I have a strong spiritual connection to my Creator and connect with my version of the Divine and work on my faith daily through meditation, vision journeying with my tribe of visionary entrepreneurs, and by focusing on gratitude. Practicing my faith through daily rituals replenishes my strength to continue to ride the inevitable storms that cross everyone's paths time and time again. My faith is a guide that I relish and helps me move toward my fullest expression each day. I've noticed that my faith works in mysterious ways. While connecting one evening, I received this message, which I share with you here:

Ease and flow. Let us do all the work. You only focus on pleasure so that you can be open. In fact, the feminine energy is the only way in which men [and women] receive the offerings of wisdom, grace, knowing, truth, and authenticity. Masculine energy does not allow this, only the feminine does. Both men and women integrate the two to blossom in career and life. Teach this to both genders. This is not a female conversation. This is a leader conversation. Both genders are powerful, smart, capable, resourceful, loving beings. We are not meant to be at odds. We are meant to collaborate in harmony, complementing each other.

This message was so rich—and its intention is not to exclude or dismiss those who do not identify with one gender or the other. To translate this message from my perspective, focusing on pleasure translates into engaging in activities that light me up. To clarify, we all possess masculine and feminine energy, regardless of gender orientation or identity. The *feminine energy* is intuitive, flexible, collaborative, creative, spontaneous, playful, transformative, caring, and attuned to how people feel. It also engages and arouses the senses through beauty, the physical environment, music, scents, foods, and fabrics. The *masculine energy* is focused, results oriented, assertive, dominant, commanding, inflexible. It's beautiful, too. Integrate the two, and we accomplish incredible feats, get things done, and simultaneously enjoy the beauty and people we experience. Leaning mostly on your masculine energy can lead to working yourself into burnout, breakdown, focusing only on the end goal, and forgetting to have fun on the way there. Many of us in the corporate world overuse our masculine energy—it tends to be the most "valued" and financially rewarded paradigm in modern societies since it is about progress and moving forward. Similarly, relying solely on feminine energy, we may lose sight of the end goal, the results, and the structure that would support getting things accomplished. We would struggle to be decisive and direct our people toward the desired outcome.

As a woman operating primarily from a masculine framework for decades, my fervent yearning was to synchronize the two, the *masculine* and *feminine* energies—to chill, enjoy my hard work, and smell the roses, too. Still, I didn't know *how* to let go. I felt most comfortable when I was "on" and working toward a result. That posture pretty much invalidated entertaining seemingly mundane, recreational activities that ironically, when integrated with achievement, led to enjoying the journey. Getting to this level of self-awareness and noticing the misalignment, I joined the School of Womanly Arts. I tentatively accessed my inner goddess—symbolizing the feminine within—while being surrounded by other women who role modeled for me how the feminine shows up. This search ensued from my faith and belief that more abundance and joy awaited me than I had ever known.

This hunch proved to be true. I felt a pull to rest and enjoy the fruits of my labor, which had been ongoing for decades. During the months I spent exploring my feminine layers, I discovered how closed-off I was to "flowing" with it and being flexible and playful—my modus operandi was control, which is the opposite of the feminine. Sticking with a plan was within my comfort zone, playing it by ear was not. Since this journey began in 2016, it has been a work in progress. I've been learning to "turn on" to life more each day, self-care like my life depended on it—because it does—filling my cup often. I'm asking for help when I need it and receiving it gracefully and graciously, going on business retreats with other goddesses, relishing nature, and opening up to flow daily. And to enjoy any of this, self-awareness, mindfulness, and a growth mindset are essential.

I'm inviting you to explore your faith, to entertain these concepts, and be receptive to what you discover—regardless of your gender identity. Do your *pleasure research*, find out what delights you, and pay attention to notice any differences in your being as a result. What is your source of faith—whatever faith is? And how can it support you in your leadership and propagate wellness in your world?

Lean into Your Intuition

Your intuition, your "gut," encompasses the hunches and sometimes precognitions that you receive. When you learn to listen to your intuition, you tap into resources inaccessible by the senses. Before starting my own business and when I was working full-time in my corporate role as a director in a technology division, I remember vividly how, on many occasions, my intuition guided me to work on a particular deliverable apparently out of the blue. Because there were no apparent reasons why I should do so, at first I would question, where did this idea come from? Over time, I learned to listen to my intuition and began following it—even if it didn't make sense to me *yet*. What started to happen was nothing short of mesmerizing. Shortly after following an intuitive message, my manager would ask me for that same deliverable. These repeated experiences taught me to stop questioning my intuition and start following it faithfully.

According to Gary Zukav (Zukav, 2014), *intuition* is that sensory system or sensory capability that allows you to know more than your five senses can tell you. Similarly, Sensei Victoria (Whitfield, 2016), a dear friend and mentor, describes that the first most significant step you can take on your journey to developing and mastering your natural intuition is this: Accept the fact that you are an empath. In her description, an *empath* can perceive and send sensory information, or "energetic data," in a more than five-senses fashion. She highlights that your empathic sense receives information in the form of energy distinct from that of sight, sound, taste, touch, and smell. As she states, this type of energetic data has to do with ambient feelings and emotions in people, places, and objects.

According to *Psychology Today* (Orloff M.D., 2016), empaths highly attune to other people's moods, good and bad. They feel everything, sometimes to an extreme. They take on negativity such as anger or anxiety, which can be exhausting for them. If they are around peace and love, though, their bodies also take these feelings on and flourish.

Before I knew about this "empath," concept, I couldn't understand or explain why the news stories of gloom and doom impacted me in such a negative way. Those stories and friends' or colleagues' sad stories often left me feeling deeply sad and troubled. Intuitively, I stopped watching the news and only consumed the highlights whenever I wanted them to stay informed about the world and the domestic socioeconomic outlook and the latest events. As an empath—and I attract and work with many empaths—I feel very deeply. The gift is feeling empathy and connecting to others' conditions and feeling an urge to support them as best you can. When you're not self-aware, the extreme side of being an empath is absorbing other people's emotions and confusing it with your own. If you can relate to this discussion, begin to explore it further, let's connect over a fifteen-minute cyber-coffee if you believe it would serve you. If you are not familiar with these concepts, use this information as a prompt and data point to raise your self-awareness and perhaps understand colleagues, team members, and others in your personal life who may also be highly sensitive. From this perspective alone, it's clear how we influence each other. My goal is to expose these resources to influence each other to *heal*, including healing our workplaces.

We all have an innate ability to tap into and expand our intuition. To hone my connection, on a typical day I sit to calm my mind through meditation as soon as I awake and before I go to sleep. Feeling a tug to expand my intuitive vision and evolve past my current abilities, starting in 2020 I joined a one-year spiritual business program with Sensei Victoria Whitfield. I devote two hours a week to mindful training and vision journeying with other like-minded leaders on a similar adventure in this safe space. As leaders in our lives, tapping our hidden resources begins by becoming more self-aware and conscious about our ability to connect and getting curious about it. You may then accelerate the transmissions by practicing regular rituals, such as meditation, vision journeying, and any other mindfulness habits, which generate the safe space and stillness for the connection and expansion to occur.

What do you appreciate the most about your intuition?

LEADER SHOWCASE: KRISTINA SMITH

"You need to hire good performing people and make your environment and culture better so that everybody is raised, finding people with different strengths and diversity."

Kristina Smith, MBA, is an engineer and Director of Research and Development. She has over 18 years of experience and attended Tulane University, Duke University, and received an MBA from Villanova University.

Kristy, please tell us a little bit about your background.

My academic background was biomedical and mechanical engineering at Duke. And then, grad school at Tulane in biomedical engineering. A year ago, I finished my MBA at Villanova. Career path wise, I have been in the medical device field since 2007 and held various roles in Operations and R&D. While in college, there were many more women in biomedical engineering as a pathway into medical school. But once I continued as an engineer in the real world, the numbers got smaller, so it's definitely been one dynamic in my career, especially working in manufacturing engineering and operations roles.

What leadership skills do you believe are the most essential these days?

Listening to your gut is something that has benefited me in my career as I've progressed, not to be so analytical. Listen to team members, different groups, different leaders, and trust your gut for what you think the right decision is. Many times, especially in technical paths, there are many options and analysis. It benefits leaders when they trust themselves enough to stand up and make what they believe to be the right decision. Some of my proudest moments as a leader have been when my team has echoed that doing the best right thing is always the answer.

What would you say to women and leaders who may be not trusting their gut?

It's true for many people. But especially in technical career paths, it's difficult for women because there aren't many of us. I've seen women who suit it up; act like they have to conform and display more masculine traits to feel like they fit in and are listened to. I've even been told to speak in a deeper voice while giving a presentation so that I can be taken more seriously. That eventually comes off as inauthentic. If it doesn't align with who you are, even your leaders above you will see it in the long term.

I have met some amazing women throughout my career, women who make you better, lift you up, support you. I've heard the phrase, "Surround yourself with people you want to be like." And with your community, I feel like every woman I've met on retreats, in our group calls, and Masterminds, they're positive, empowering women. When we leave those calls, I feel better about everything. And I know there are women working hard, doing the right thing, and feeling the same way that I do about our struggles.

Like yourself, like Simon Sinek, certain leaders understand the humanity of the work environment. You need to hire good performing people and make your environment and culture better so that everybody is raised, finding people with different strengths and diversity.

Connect with Kristina on LinkedIn.

Seek Divine Guidance

We are not alone. I believe that each of us is divinely guided—especially when we ask for that guidance. As a visionary, I felt a need to expand to receive intuitive and divine guidance more readily and deliberately.

Following my inner guidance and intuition as a leader, I began to develop my first, 100 percent virtual leadership development program early in 2019, *The Fearless Leadership Mastermind™*. I felt a strong pull to create this remote offering combining virtual live-group coaching and masterminding with on-demand virtual learning. In January of 2020, I launched the first cohort of leaders who enrolled in the program. A few months later, the timing made sense when our country and the world shut down because of an unprecedented pandemic and many knowledge workers decided to work from home, face-to-face events vanished, and business as usual came to a screeching halt. In the middle of chaos, my business was ready to scale and support and serve individual clients and strategic partners 100 percent remotely.

If I believe that I'm not alone, but instead that I have guides and protectors, then that means that I'm not alone when pursuing my goals, either. The concept for this book was directly the result of following my divine guidance. In May 2020, I prepared to launch the *Fearless Leaders Challenge*, a five-day training program that I run multiple times a year. Starting in 2020, it would be the first launch. While preparing for the *Challenge*, sitting at my desk one afternoon, I began to draft "Secrets to Develop Fearless Leadership." As if hooked to headphones, effortlessly, the topics and content began to pour out of me, and I faithfully banged away on the keys of my laptop to capture all of it. When I finished, glaring back at me from the glow of my screen were three sections and thirty topics. I set it aside and sat with it for a few days. What became abundantly clear as I reviewed what I had created was that what I had channeled was much more than the content for a five-day challenge. The structure and the thirty topics and concepts were the makings for my new book, *Healing Leadership*. These are the themes in the thirty chapters you are currently reading. The book structure that required

LEADER SHOWCASE: SENSEI VICTORIA WHITFIELD

"Faith is an internal guide that is strong, steady, and clear, holding you no matter what's happening outside, externally and circumstantially."

Sensei Victoria Whitfield is the owner of Victoria Whitfield, LLC, and a Certified Reiki Master. Victoria is an internationally recognized energy healer who has specialized in supporting entrepreneurs for over nine years. She is the hostess of *The Journeypreneur Podcast*. In addition to Victoria's extensive Reiki training, she attended Boldheart Academy and received her degree from Rutgers University.

Please tell our audience who you are and what you do.

I'm Sensei Victoria Whitfield. I happen to be the world's first Business Reiki Master, which means I help visionary leaders like you get and stay grounded and clear in mind, body, and business. The more we can balance our energy as leaders, the more we become safe leaders to follow.

We want to have people out there who lead our teams, our companies, our families, and our communities living authentically. And we want them to be guided from that internal compass of intuition, which never gets tired, never gets old, so that you don't have to worry about always being on top of everything—and **working so hard.** And you are getting better and better at not working hard. There's going to be a point where we don't work at all because we are **being**.

What are the most critical skills that leaders need most today?

The most critical thing that leaders need now more than ever is faith, systems of faith. Now, that is a very loaded word. People may immediately think they need God. Let's unpack that. **Faith** is the felt sensation of trust. **Faith** is an internal guide that is strong, steady, and clear, holding you no matter what's happening outside, externally and circumstantially. **Faith** is that inner clarity.

Having a system of faith, something that generates certainty for you is primary above all else. You could forget all the techniques, accolades, and all the things you studied, are working on, or trying to achieve, and so on. No matter what, things could go completely upside down. If the leader has faith that we are going to make it, transform, that we are going to go even higher because of the challenges that we've faced, what's beautiful about that is that it opens up basically like a vacuum for all of creation to answer and pour into. It also opens up a vacuum of creativity in the people that you lead. If we assume that this is happening "for us," if we have someone who can exemplify what it is to have faith if we are thinking, what are we going to do? People fall into that vacuum. That faith opens up, and they feel it with their creativity.

The number-one ability that leaders need now more than ever is to have a system that generates faith for them, which creates certainty. That's the gift from leaders to those who have the courage to follow them. It's insurance that they're headed in the right direction.

To connect with Victoria, please visit www.naturalintuition.com and LinkedIn.

11

Operate from Alignment

Notice Your Beliefs

As leaders, we will only achieve if we believe it's possible, including healing our leadership. Everything you achieve is ingrained in your belief system. Your actions follow your beliefs. If you're not acting in a way that supports your vision, begin to question the beliefs lurking in the shadows, one by one. Replacing the disempowering beliefs with empowering ones is where the magic happens. And if you don't believe in yourself, who else is going to believe in you and help you? Work through those limitations. Place all bets on you! Your life and happiness are worth it.

In this chapter, we bring it all together. All the concepts we've discussed thus far culminate in operating from *alignment*: the self-aware leader living with purpose, practicing mindfulness, overcoming negative self-talk, getting the ego in check, committing to success and well-being, developing a growth mindset, being resilient, developing relationships, and tapping hidden resources. We integrate all these concepts and harmonize your beliefs with your thoughts, words, and actions to generate momentum in your career and personal life. *Alignment* accelerates your ability to manifest and fulfill your goals and desires from a place of empowerment, self-care, and abundance, not from scarcity, fears, shame, guilt, ego, and so on.

Alignment begins with your beliefs—the thoughts that seem real. Imagine that you are building a skyscraper. The foundation of that building is your *belief system*, hiding from plain view. Your belief systems and structures can either support or sabotage what you desire as a leader. Your belief system has been with you since you gained consciousness. Events, people, culture and upbringing, environment, experiences, emotions resulting from those experiences, and the meaning you assigned to those experiences have molded your belief system. The interpretations you have given all of these events make up the fabric of your belief system. Examining your beliefs is extremely rewarding and cannot be circumvented if your goal is to heal your Self-leadership.

How do you explore your beliefs? I suggest taking a systematic approach, breaking it down by looking at the different areas of your life. Perhaps looking at it holistically first to say, overall, what are my core beliefs about life—what do I believe to be my truth and worldview? A clear set of beliefs is going to emerge. And then, break them down by the different areas in your life. Look at your career, relationships, health, finances, and other areas and the beliefs you have around each one. Specifically, delve into areas where you struggle or have neglected, perhaps because taking a look could be too painful. Those areas will probably generate the most enlightening discoveries.

When I began to seriously entertain the idea of starting my own business, I was in the car with a dear friend returning from Newport, Rhode Island, heading toward New York City. During the conversation, my friend, a coach, asked me to write down my beliefs about starting my own business. I was astonished to see in black-and-white what was at the forefront of my thoughts—a set of limiting beliefs from doubting my ability to replace my corporate income to not sustaining the business once I started it. I also discovered how attached I was to a corporate job's financial certainty despite the challenges. When I questioned my beliefs and faced them, I couldn't hide anymore, and I had the answer to why I was so indecisive. All of it stemmed from my views about not being successful in my business and its consequences. This process was the catalyst to turning around my ship and pointing it to a new destination.

By questioning the beliefs and where they came from, I realized that growing up in a third-world country, being poor—never starving, thankfully—and not having much more than the essentials had created within me a sense of scarcity. Even though I had transcended poverty beyond my wildest dreams, I still operated from a scarcity mindset. That's how beliefs work. They trick you into thinking that they are factual even when they are not. One technique to dismantle those disempowering beliefs is to dissect them. And so I did.

I started by recognizing that I was in a much better financial position to pursue my dream of starting my own business than I thought. Instead of creating obstacles, I began to leverage my resourcefulness to develop solutions and workaround strategies. Fearing that the company would not succeed, I came up with a backup plan—look for a corporate job. I also gave myself a one-year trial period. Proactively, I also began cutting back on living expenses, anticipating a lower income when the business was getting off the ground. Fortunately, I had always saved over 10 percent of my income, so I had savings to rely on but did not want to dip into them and remove that cushion. I had to dismantle my negative belief system around my value, resourcefulness, connections, and knowledge of the marketplace. Little by little, I began to replace the limiting beliefs with empowering ones and shift my actions to reflect a new set of beliefs. The alignment was on the way.

Struggle, resistance, fear, lack of flow around your most cherished goals are telltale signs that you should question your belief system in that area. By raising your self-awareness, you can heal your beliefs to support you in your endeavors at self-actualization.

Think about what Matters

In *The Greatest Secret*, Earl Nightingale (Nightingale, 2019) emphasizes that the key to success and failure is that "we become what we think about." He indicates that wise men, teachers, philosophers, and prophets have disagreed with one another throughout our history on many different things. It's only on this one point that they are in unanimous agreement.

Your beliefs support the thoughts you have about your goals. Aligning your beliefs by tearing down those that oppose your plans will lead to ideas that align with your vision and goals. This alignment becomes another pathway to healing leadership—aligning our beliefs and thoughts with the goals we're seeking to reach in our organizations and teams. Do your thoughts align with your empowering beliefs?

In Nightingale's analogy, the mind is like fertile land; however, it doesn't care if you plant success or failure. Whatever you plant, it must return to us. Along with the concepts of growth versus fixed mindset, are you focusing on fears of potential failures of the initiatives you pursue or the possibilities for success, development, and innovation? A growth mindset and your interpretation of your results will empower you to seek opportunities and reframe setbacks to maintain momentum toward your vision.

Visualization is a powerful technique for many reasons. As you picture yourself already enjoying your goals, doing what you would be doing when you reach them, it enforces your faith that the goal is possible. It *solidifies your beliefs* (what you believe to be true) and aligns your thoughts (as many of the six thousand per day as possible) with the vision. In the brain, visualization triggers the *reticular activating system* (RAS), which, simply stated, acts as the brain's filter; it allows through information related to what you're visualizing. For example, you decide you're going to buy a Toyota Highlander. Suddenly, you begin to notice all the Highlanders on the road. Let's use an analogy: The "match" is having clear and concrete goals that are significant to you. The "wood" is the set of beliefs, thoughts, words, and actions, which we'll discuss shortly. Put the match and wood together and you generate fire in your life—the good kind.

Contemplate your goals with a growth mindset, visualize yourself enjoying the achievement, and bring self-awareness to your beliefs and thoughts. With mindfulness, direct your thoughts toward the achievement of your goals. And as we practiced in dealing with negative self-talk Nelly, release negative thoughts contradicting your vision. If it's this simple, why don't more people use this knowledge? As Nightingale points out, humans typically devalue what is free and in the process stay enslaved in believing that our circumstances control our lives. Let's correct this behavior and stop the madness.

Choose Your Words Carefully

Along with our beliefs and what we think, our words *express* those beliefs and thoughts. *Words* create the commitment that we are making with ourselves and others about what we are going to do and how we're going to live our lives. If your words misalign with what you want to create and accomplish in your beliefs and your thoughts, you will experience *cognitive dissonance* (internal conflict), which causes stress, anxiety, and other negative emotions.

We typically voice what we believe to be true. I believe that we will get through this pandemic, my business will continue to grow, and we'll continue to travel worldwide as a family. But if I were to say, "There's no way I'll be able to afford a twenty-thousand-dollar trip to Australia with my family," which is contradictory to my desire to visit Australia, most likely based on this misalignment my trip to Australia won't happen. I would not start saving toward it and imagining the adventures we could enjoy.

The words we speak *matter*. Like our beliefs and thoughts, words also create our reality. Pay attention to the words you're using to describe your life and emotions. For example, we discussed being proactive and putting yourself in an emotional state to support your day. If the words you often use express that you feel anxious, sad, or alone, that seals the deal. You will continue to feel more of these emotions. It's your belief, your truth, and what you are thinking. Miraculously, the opposite works the same way. If I believe that I'm going to feel motivated today, that things will turn out alright, that I will do the best I can and speak the words that reflect my positivity and optimism, I will create my reality based on the words I use that day and every single day.

Stand guard of your mind and mouth. I remember when I decided to write my first book. I started writing the first version while still working full-time at an asset management firm. I believed that I had a book in me and a message that I wanted to share. I often thought about the stories that I wanted to share in the book. I visualized myself sitting at my dining room table at home, writing not only one book but a series of them. I thought about how exciting it would be to finish writing it and getting my message out there. I started to tell my friends that I had already written a few chapters of my book. Speaking my goals generated accountability, and it allowed me to verbalize the actions I was taking to make it happen.

As soon as I started my company in 2017, writing my book was at the top of my priority list. Within six months, I had a coach and learned how to organize my ideas, create the book structure, speak my book, edit it, give it to my official editor, work with my book cover and layout designer, and get it published on Amazon by September 2017. On October 11, 2017, we celebrated the book launch and the number-one bestseller, *Fearless Women at Work*.

What are you saying and speaking about your life, your leadership, the team, the culture, your vision? Begin to notice any misalignments and pivot. You'll see a significant improvement in how you feel as you give breath to your goals. The same applies to your relationships, especially your romantic partnership. Watch how you speak about your relationship—your words create your reality there, too.

Take Action and Build Momentum

Operating from alignment requires that you execute! As I often share with our audiences, *knowledge and execution are power*. If we have the beliefs, thoughts, and speak our intentions supporting our goals, but we don't take action, unfortunately what we want to happen will most likely not occur—there is no silver bullet.

Taking action is the embodiment of your beliefs, thoughts, and words—that what you want is attainable. What do we execute? It can feel overwhelming because there's so much for us to do. This question brings us back to living with purpose. When it comes to taking action, direct your efforts toward those things that would help you live your best life. Do you want to become a patient person? Give back to your community, learn French, become a better salesperson? Invent a new technology that will help people connect? What has purpose and meaning for you? Do you want to become healthier, study history, politics? Implement those ideas and remember your self-care and well-being.

Nightingale gave us the insights that *we are what we think about*, that *people who succeed have goals*, and *people who don't "fail."* Following his advice, it would make sense to clarify the goals you want to achieve—with purpose and adhering to *your* definition of success. Showing up aligned among your beliefs, thoughts, words, and actions generate momentum in your life and help you tap into your full potential.

Here's how momentum works from what I've learned and experienced. When you believe that you have the potential to achieve a compelling goal, you're going to think along those lines as well. You're going to imagine yourself achieving the goal and already enjoying the fruits of your labor. Your conversations communicate your intent to those around you. And these precursors fuel your actions to bring that goal into reality. As you start to implement and take action, you'll experience the results, tweaking as you go, with a growth mindset. Those results validate your belief that you are on the right track. Then you tap into more of your potential and continue to execute toward your goal, which delivers results, which validate your belief, and motivates you to go back to tapping more of your potential. The positive loop continues. And this is how you experience forward momentum.

The inverse is true as well. When you doubt that what you want is even attainable and focus on thoughts of fear and worry and verbalize your insecurities and concerns about the goal, you tap into just a little bit of your potential and sheepishly put little effort into the steps toward achieving the goal. Little action leads to dismal results. The "failure" or disappointing results, combined with a fixed mindset, validate your belief that this goal is unattainable. You then tap into even less of your potential and barely take any action, which leads to even shoddier results. Again, the poor outcomes reinforce your belief that you don't see this becoming a reality for you, and then you tap into even less of your potential. The negative loop and negative momentum continue until you finally quit.

As I stand in front of my storyboard of my book, I'm having flashbacks to 2016 when I was sitting in my dining room in my apartment in Jersey City, New Jersey. Then, I imagined myself working from home, taking care of my son, writing books, coaching, creating my schedule, serving my clients. Today, at fifty-one years old, sitting at the same table in Sussex County, New Jersey, I'm celebrating the following: Five years since building my company from scratch, living my compelling vision, and realizing what initially seemed impossible goals; finding ease and flow in everything, tapping my full potential, contributing in my unique way, and finding the love in all of it. I am living my worthy ideals. The healing principles and practices in the first eleven chapters of this book lead you through an enlightening self-study process and teach you fundamental techniques to create profound transformation with compassion and understanding. They support you to build a positive momentum loop to realize purposeful goals in your life. Bearing witness to the value in integrating this knowledge and applying it in your business and personal life, you possess the *secrets* to healing self-leadership and the keys to unlocking human potential. Continue to practice, question, celebrate, and be mindful of your mind, body, and spirit. Bask under the shade of the tree of self-awareness, feeling rejuvenated, faithful, and aligned with your purpose as a healing leader.

Empowering Questions for Reflection

1. How often do you believe in yourself?
2. If you don't believe in yourself, who else is going to believe in you and help you?
3. How do you explore your beliefs?
4. What do you believe to be your truth and worldview?
5. Do your thoughts align with your empowering beliefs?
6. Where is your focus? Are you focusing on fears of potential failures of the initiatives you pursue or the possibilities for success, development, and innovation?
7. What is your response to this statement? "Humans typically devalue what is free and in the process stay enslaved in believing that our circumstances control our lives."
8. What are you saying and speaking about your life, your leadership, the team, the culture, your vision?
9. How do you decide what you execute or do?
10. What has purpose and meaning for you?

LEADER SHOWCASE: OSATO CHITOU

"There is something to be said about leaping. We sometimes block our blessings without even knowing it."

Osato Chitou, ESQ, MPH, is the founder and Principal Consultant at Compli by Osato, LLC, specializing in health-care regulatory compliance. She is also an adjunct professor of law and public health at Rutgers, Newark, New Jersey. She has over eleven years of experience in health-care law and compliance. Osato attended Canterbury School, Boston University, Rutgers University School of Law, and received her MPH from the University of North Carolina at Greensboro.

Please share what you do and your background.

I am an attorney by training, and my background has always been in the health-care compliance space. Effectively, I build compliance programs for health insurance companies with government health-care products and health insurance providers that have to comply with government health-care requirements because they accept government health-care program dollars. The purpose of engaging in that area is to ensure that the end-users—which are me, you, your mom, my dad—that use both those health insurance companies and those health insurance providers are getting good care.

What are the most critical leadership qualities leaders need to embrace?

Individuals have to be flexible. If you are so rigid in your mindset and stuck on holding onto what you know as "normal," you hinder your ability to move forward and embrace the opportunity that sudden change may provide. Flexibility is key. The inability to be flexible will keep you behind. You can have a growth mindset, even in periods of uncertainty and discomfort.

How have you personally had to pivot during this time?

There was a spot of fear initially, given the health-care space in which I operate. There was a potential client, which ended up being a huge client. However, before landing that client, I had to go onsite to this facility—a large hospital system in New York City. We are in a global pandemic, and that area was hit very hard. I had to process this potential opportunity and step into the fear and lean into what was being provided to me. Once I took that step, a number of doors proceeded to open. There is something to be said about leaping. We sometimes block our blessings without even knowing it. We create all these stories in our minds to keep us from moving forward because we sell ourselves a story that keeps us safe. We end up blocking a great deal of abundance that would be otherwise available to us if we leaned into that fear and uncertainty. This has been a fascinating lesson for me over this last year.

Be comfortable in discomfort and embrace discomfort, which is important for your growth. When we are living life coasting in a space where we don't feel challenged, or if you   are someone that says, "I can do this job with my eyes closed," then you need a new job. We should not be afraid of uncertainty and discomfort because it is in those spaces that we grow.

Connect with Osato via osato@complibyosato.com, www.complibyosato.com, or LinkedIn.

"A leader's job is to figure out what the next right thing is and then do it."

–Brené Brown

SECTION 2
Lead, Engage, and Influence Others

12

Lead with Empathy

Connect to Others

As discussed in chapter 9, one of the biggest problems today is that as of 2017, approximately 85 percent of the global workforce is not *engaged*—not committed to or emotionally invested in their companies' success. As leaders, what is preventing us from engaging our talent? And if we don't have their attention, how can we effectively lead and influence them in positive ways toward the organization's vision and mission? I believe it must start with us, the leadership, which is why we spent a substantive effort going through "Section 1: The Secrets to Healing Leadership." As leaders, it always starts with us. Let's build on this foundation and explore how to lead, engage, and influence others powerfully and compassionately.

In Section 2: "Lead, Engage, and Influence Others," we shift our focus outward toward the teams and people whose lives we impact. Along with our "Leader Showcase" features, I personally share insights and recommendations for leading, engaging, and influencing others. My perspective is that of a leader in financial services and technology for over twenty years, as a leadership and executive coach, and draws from my experiences inside and outside the organizations I've served during a thirty-year career.

The 2020 pandemic and our new way of working and living highlight the importance of *empathetic* leadership that values and embraces a *human-centric* approach where people's well-being is at the forefront of all business imperatives and ideals. Specifically, the massive numbers of people working remotely presents an opportunity to distinguish between leaders who are ill-equipped and struggle to connect with their people and those who thrive. Forming human connections with our talent outside of work builds relationships that encourage employees to bring their whole selves to work and engage on a meaningful level with the organization's goals. It also helps employees find common ground between their purpose and the organization's objectives, values, and so on, both professionally and personally.

According to Brené Brown (Brown, 2018), "Empathy is not connecting to an experience. Empathy is connecting to the emotions that underpin an experience." Leading with empathy is by far one of the most empowering qualities for leaders at any time, especially during a health crisis when human lives are literally at stake. Our field study uncovered that leading with empathy is among the top five—the second-highest to be exact—critical skills leaders need during these uncertain and complex times. The top critical skill is communication. To lead with compassion, we must deepen our connection with our people.

It's often automatic and perhaps more comfortable to relegate human connections with work colleagues to work transactions—the project update, the sales report analysis, the client complaint, and so on. However, understanding complete human beings and what they're currently going through will help you provide the support they need to get on with the project or team goals and outcomes. Leading with empathy enables you to see the world from the other person's perspective. As you connect personally, you can hear in their voices and words their current emotional state, whether that is worry, stress, fear, excitement, or contentment.

Curiosity, acknowledging what is happening in the moment, and staying present to those emotions helps you connect on a deeper level. Letting employees know you notice their emotional state and asking simple empowering questions provides an opening for them to share their concerns. What's the benefit to the relationship? It shows them that you care and provides the vehicle to voice and release what's concerning to them—which is essential to heal and get through it. Without prying and with the spirit of contribution, as a leader you might say, "I noticed you sounded a little worried. What's going on?" or "How can I help?" You might find out the issue is work related, and as a leader you can do something to guide and coach them through the next steps to take. If it's personal, just being there as a witness and listening could be the release that the individual needs to move on with his or her day.

I remember when one of my former managers was going through a difficult situation with his mother who was elderly. During our weekly check-in, I noticed he looked a little anxious, and I asked him, "How's everything going?" And he opened up about the challenges of finding a nursing home for his mother and how time-consuming and frustrating the process was. I listened, and when he finished, I let him know that I empathized with him and asked him if it would be valuable for him to connect with someone I knew who had been through a similar process. He was extremely thankful, and once we wrapped up that topic, we were able to move on to our weekly check-in. In this example, I used my resources to assist him. However, that's not the objective. Instead, it's about providing emotional support.

Empathy is a gateway to more profound emotional connections that transform people. To empathize doesn't imply that we agree with others' perspectives; it means that we're able to, for a moment, put ourselves in their shoes and see the world through their eyes. That insight informs our approach and helps us position our message in a way that resonates with their angle and perspective. That is how we influence them positively. For example, suppose I learn that the team is concerned about the tight deadline. In that case, my message can focus on how we plan to address meeting the significant milestones, maybe with the collaboration of another group, and how we plan to mitigate the risks associated with potential delays.

A factor that usually prevents people from engaging more profoundly is *fear*, which stems from distrust or a lack of confidence that the leader is honest or can be trusted. When we connect with empathy, we increase the level of trust and safety on both sides. The other party, feeling vulnerable, may fear what the leader may do with the shared information. Fears also arise from assumptions that the leader doesn't care or does not want to hear what we have to say.

As the leader, your reputation precedes you. Without knowing where your people are coming from, the only aspect of the relationship you can control is how *you show up* from this day forward. Getting your ego in check and being mindful of each of the topics we raised in section 1 are extremely valuable and relevant. Connect authentically. Share what is on your mind and heart, professionally, and see how the other person reacts. And based on that reaction, you can make an informed decision about what you may need to do to uplift the person's trust and confidence level. As long as you are doing your best, with self-awareness, social awareness, and a growth mindset, that's what's most important.

It is those generous connections with your team, manager, and stakeholders that over time build a trusting and gratifying relationship and transform how we relate to each other from being transactional to being relational. Humans are gregarious mammals. Make it a pleasant habit to reach out to team members, colleagues, and the people in your personal circles.

LEADER SHOWCASE: PAIGE GRANGER

"We can face every challenge and come out on the other side, better because of it."

Paige Granger is the Director of Grants Management at the Rockefeller Foundation. Paige has been working in grants for over ten years and has more than seventeen years of business experience. She received her BA at Boston College and her MA in international affairs at Columbia University.

Please tell us a little bit about your background.

I became the director of Grants Management here at the Rockefeller Foundation in April [2020]. I've been in the field of philanthropy for about ten years. I started at Rockefeller about a year ago. Previously, I was camp director at a camp for children with HIV/AIDS. I developed some leadership skills there and in other nonprofits. It's a different experience but a challenge in and of itself. And so, I've taken lessons from that experience to where I am now.

What are the leadership skills that are most critical during this time?

For this time, specifically, empathy is the biggest one—to understand what people are going through, be mindful of everybody's situation. Everyone's experiencing this time in such different ways. There are people with kids, people without kids, people with aging parents, and caretakers now in full-time jobs at home.

There's so much on everybody's plate. As a leader, you have to take into account all of those situations, listen, understand, and then step in where needed to help people prioritize and even lighten their load. Sometimes they don't like to let go of their responsibilities, but you should step in and say that we need to make a change here for you for the better. Make clear it's not a referendum on anybody's job or skills but is being mindful of the situation that they're all in right now.

What advice would you give leaders to create that unique edge?

Look outside your own four walls or your own screen not only at how your organization's functioning but who else is out there. Now that we have this virtual way of living in so many ways, there's access to many more people, and connecting virtually is possible. I'm part of a grant-making association that has been beneficial for meeting other leaders, thought partners, and organizations across the country that are doing the same work differently. There's always something more to learn. It starts with listening because you can't pull it all out of thin air. You need to ground your ideas somewhere. It's always helpful to talk to others to learn more about what's in the field.

This time has shown us how flexible and adaptable we are, that everything can be overcome. We can face every challenge and come out on the other side, better because of it. And we need to hold on to that. We can rise above it all. There are lessons from this time that we need to hold onto and not let go of.

You can connect with Paige on LinkedIn.

Build an Empathetic Culture and Team

How do you build an empathetic culture and team, a team where individuals aren't only looking after themselves but also after each other's best interests? Having empathy requires us to be self-aware about our own emotions and exercise our social awareness muscle to perceive other people's feelings. An emotionally intelligent team can notice what's happening within the group. As the leader, you lead that undertaking, and we'll discuss role modeling in the next section. An empathetic culture demonstrates compassion for what other people are going through and understands the challenges others face.

One of the easiest ways to acknowledge what is happening and elevate the team's self-awareness and social awareness is to raise the topic when you notice you or someone else in the group is experiencing difficulties. In particular work situations, there is a high likelihood that if you or one of the team members is struggling, others are struggling, too. Leading with empathy and building that culture of compassion means that you articulate what you're going through and what you're feeling in a way that supports anyone else in the team who may be feeling similarly. Your actions will encourage them to feel safe and come forward and say, "yes, I'm feeling that, too," or it lets them know that if they're facing a specific problem, it's okay for them to approach you or others to discuss it. You know that you have an empathetic team and workforce when issues are brought to light because there is a sense that the team will understand what's going on, be open to listening, and then move forward together toward a resolution. If you're finding that the team is hiding issues when they arise, people are not talking with each other when there is conflict or disagreement, that's also a telltale sign that your culture lacks empathy and trust.

A proven tool or strategy for cultivating an empathetic culture and team is promoting an attitude of gratitude within your team. A team gratitude practice will enhance your level of energy and joy—based on what is working on a specific day—and also that of the group, allowing them to celebrate the wins despite the difficulties. It will also help you and the team become more resourceful in addressing the challenges that you're facing. It's undeniable that there will always be what I call a pile of "bad stuff" in front of you— issues, problems, misunderstandings, disappointments, or disagreements. And there will always be a pile of "good stuff"—the projects that you're cranking out, the clients that you acquired, the customers who wrote stellar reviews, the partnership that is helping you grow the business. Being mindful about where you focus is significant.

When you direct the team's attention primarily toward the problems and pile of *bad stuff*, they are likely to feel low energy and weighed down. It's not unusual that even when we successfully finish a project, we're already looking at the next thing without taking a moment to celebrate the accomplishment. A celebration is a ritual that helps you and your team with self-care. To create more positive emotions within the team and influence the culture, shift your focus to the pile of *good stuff* while acknowledging and working on the *bad stuff*. Allow yourself and the team to be thankful every day. Communicate to the group what you're grateful for about them and notice the difference—everyone's spirits will start to rise.

Expressing and living in an attitude of gratitude and compassion with yourself, others, and your environment does not mean ignoring everything else. It translates to filling up your cup, refueling your tank with the strength that will support you and your team as you tackle the challenges at hand. Remember to show the people in your life who support your success—your peers, managers, team, family, partner, mentors, caregivers, and support team—that you care and appreciate them. Show them that you notice and care—this will go a long way in creating and building an empathetic culture and team.

Role Modeling

As a leader, you are a role model by default. Your team, partners, and people you lead and serve look up to you. When you embrace a *role model* identity, you aspire to be your highest Self for yourself and others. If you show care and empathy in your personal interactions and business dealings, others will have a pattern, a model to emulate. Unfortunately, it works in both directions. People will emulate your behaviors and attitudes regardless—even if they produce a toxic culture that propagates fear, distrust, dishonesty, blaming, and so on. When a leader operates from this toxic position, those who are empathetic may hold back from showing it in the workplace. Only a few courageous souls will continue to be compassionate toward each other when their leader is not. These dilemmas are the fundamental reason why leaders have a tremendous responsibility to lead with a role model identity.

Where do you start? Begin by role modeling for your team the qualities that you appreciate in a leader. Getting feedback will help you identify which areas you excel in and which require improvement. (We'll address feedback in chapter 24.) You've most likely heard about the concept of role modeling for children. You can say whatever you want to kids, but nothing speaks louder than your actions—what children actually witness you doing. Similarly, to create a culture and team that's empathetic to team and organization members, show them how it looks.

If you work in a cutthroat and extremely competitive work environment, you may feel apprehensive or concerned about how others will perceive you or that they might even take advantage of your empathetic approach. You probably know someone who has taken advantage of your kindness—it happens. For example, suppose you set a policy to allow people to take time off after working long hours and using personal time to fix a production problem. An employee might try to find loopholes to take advantage of that policy. Rather than punishing everyone and getting rid of the policy, it is crucial to have an empowering conversation with the individual attempting to abuse the system. You might learn other facts about the situation when you connect with the individual through a coaching and mentoring conversation. (We'll dive into mentoring and coaching in chapter 20.) Being an empathetic leader does not make you ineffective or does not mean you don't have a backbone. Instead, you become more respected and trusted and are viewed as a fair leader when you lead powerfully, confidently, and show empathy to your talent.

When you consider what identity you want to role model, what will you continue doing and what will you stop doing to foster compassion, connection, and collaboration among teams?

Empowering Questions for Reflection

1. As a leader, what, if anything, is preventing you from engaging your talent?

2. What's the benefit to the relationships with your team members when you acknowledge their emotional states?

3. How do you build an empathetic culture and team, a team where individuals aren't only looking after themselves but also after each other's best interests?

4. How do you role model for your team the qualities that you appreciate in a leader?

5. What will you continue doing, and what will you stop doing, to foster compassion, connection, and collaboration among teams?

LEADER SHOWCASE: BOB SELLE

"Lead with L.O.V.E. Great things will follow."

Bob Selle, SPHR, SHRM, SCP, is the Chief People Officer for Ocean State Job Lot. Bob has more than fifteen years of experience in HR and received the 2019 HR ICON of the Year Award for his accomplishments. He has been in the industry for approximately thirty years and has earned various certifications, including a Senior Professional of Human Resources —Masters of HR from the HR Certification Institute.

Which leadership skills are most critical in this challenging environment?

Empathy is, hands down, one of the essential skills. The second one is trust. Now more than any other time in our history, people are vulnerable, and they are showing their vulnerability at work. As a leader, we are held to high standards with the trust that our associates and the people we work with are giving us. I have broken it down into the acronym L.O.V.E. Lead with L.O.V.E. is what I've been sharing with people. L.O.V.E. stands for Listen, Observe, Voice, and Empathy. Take the time to listen. Listening is really important now in making sure you take the time to hear what's going on in their lives, not only what's going on at work.

Here's an example. Someone called me on Saturday. Like you and me, he has children. **What's going on with school and the kids?** He has aging parents. **What's going on with them?** He is also responsible for a team and trying to be that calm leader. **What's going on with his team?** And then, **what is going on with all this political unrest in the world?** I practiced what I preached. I listened attentively, and although I couldn't see him, I was trying to **observe** how he was feeling. I followed-up with many questions to ensure that I understood exactly what was taking place. Then I used my

voice. I spoke with his leader on behalf of this person and with other leaders to make sure they understood that he was going through a vulnerable time.

I believe it is how we handle these situations that determines where we're going to be from a retention standpoint because people know that we care about them as a person ***first***. Our talent is going to put in the effort, which should drive sales. But then, it always goes back to where I started. The ***E*** stands for the most critical leadership skill—***empathy***.

I also make sure that we don't make assumptions when we're listening. We have to make sure that we heard what we thought we heard. And it takes practice. I've handed out the book ***Change Your Life, Change Your Questions*** by Marilee Adams to more people these days because it helps you ask good questions. Reinforcing what you heard before you go any further is important these days as well. If we do all of that, the trust that was initially formed with our team is heightened, and it's further enhanced because they realize that we care more about them than we care about profits. And that speaks volumes to people today.

What we have been talking about right now will be the future of leadership. It is making a human connection and understanding that everyone in the workforce is human. Lead with L.O.V.E. Great things will follow.

You can reach Bob Selle at www.bobsellethehrguy.com or on LinkedIn.

13

Build Love and Trust

Display High Integrity and Character

Displaying high integrity and character is one of the qualities of great leaders. Living in *integrity* means embodying your values, being impeccable with your word, and as we discussed, saying what you mean and meaning what you say. It is standing behind your statements and your decisions, and when you falter, which is human, acknowledging when you're wrong or made a mistake. These are a few instances of a person who honors his or her character.

In life, especially in your career, one of the worst reputations anyone can have—which sooner or later catches up with you and jeopardizes a viable career—is consistent dishonesty. Work circumstances may prevent a leader from sharing confidential information—that's not what I'm referring to here. There are a multitude of reasons why a leader's character would be in question. One is when a leader purposely disseminates inaccurate information to persuade an audience to do whatever the leader wants without regard for their well-being. Other reasons are when the leader deflects blame or responsibility, wants to get out of a situation that went awry, and so on— sometimes out of fear or assumptions about the consequences if the leader told the truth. These character flaws create a wedge between a leader and the people the leader serves, drastically reducing the leader's effectiveness and eroding the quality of the organization's values and culture. Being self-aware helps everyone evaluate if this is an area of concern, personally and within the team.

People with high integrity and character build the trust that people need to follow them and achieve business imperatives. It can happen in subtle but consequential daily gestures. Suppose that you promise a team member a promotion, already knowing certain factors could prevent you from doing so. When you don't pull it off, this will tarnish your character and trust with that individual and those who hear about it later; *what you say matters*. Be thoughtful in your comments. Instead, you could indicate that you will advocate and do your best to secure the promotion during the next budget cycle and follow through. Communicate why you can't do it if that's the case.

What determines your character is not the actual outcome—getting the promotion or not—what matters is how you handle the situation and your truthfulness and respect in communicating the results to the person. I have heard leaders in a meeting express that they had already discussed an essential issue with a critical stakeholder only to learn later that was not the case. Although subtle, these instances and similar ones plant seeds of doubt about these leaders' characters that spreads to other team members, leaving them questioning, in what other instances is this person being dishonest? If you are on board already, displaying high integrity and character, this topic may seem redundant. However, from personal experience and the recounts of clients, these behaviors are widespread in corporate cultures and work environments.

Others will discern your character and integrity when you act reasonably and recognize the team's efforts, giving credit where credit is due. And that sometimes means standing up to people who are spreading misinformation about your group or others around the organization who are absent during the conversation and cannot defend themselves. It would be easy to remain silent, specifically when it doesn't impact you directly. However, taking a stand when you know the truth and clarifying that you have a different perspective on the person or events in question will demonstrate that you are trustworthy. The workplace has bullies, too. The people in the room who hear you defend the absent person will realize that you would also stand up for them when they're not in the meeting. Trust begets more trust.

Your word is your bond—what's your word's value? How are you showing your team and others that you are trustworthy? When team decisions back-fire, how do you stand behind those decisions? Your team will respect when you back them up and take responsibility, even when you know it may be a difficult situation. Lean on your resourcefulness and creativity to role model for your team what you expect from them and what they should expect from each other. They are learning by witnessing you, and every challenge creates an ideal opportunity to demonstrate your integrity and character.

Show up Authentically

An *authentic* leader speaks what is in his or her heart and mind, knows the audience and understands its needs, and speaks truthfully. In the context of meeting their needs, express what is on your mind—your ideas, concerns, motivations, goals, and vision—and what is in your heart—your dreams, hopes, desires for the team, and so on. Expressing and sharing yourself without shame or guilt lets others know that it is acceptable to do the same.

A compelling and heartwarming vehicle to show up authentically is to share your stories. In addition to being memorable, stories help your team know you personally. People make assumptions about their leaders. They might think that our current status has been that way for our whole lives. They don't know your history—where you came from and how you grew up—or the difficulties and challenges you faced throughout adulthood. Sharing your stories will help them understand you, build trust, and cultivate appreciation and love. When people can connect on a human level, authen-tically sharing who they are, it weaves a direct cord to their heart center, a bond that goes beyond a contract or paycheck. You begin to build friendships within the team that are respected and not abused under any circumstances. Instead, these deepen your experience as an engaged team, which benefits the individuals and the organization's well-being and performance.

Showing up with authenticity begins with self-awareness. How do you express what you notice and speak your truth about it, compassionately, grounded, and empathetically? Sometimes, it's invaluable to be able to call out the elephant in the room, to say what you sense is happening that no one else is articulating; that's showing up authentically. It's also opening a little window into your heart to let others look inside. It's letting them know that you don't have all the answers, that you may also be feeling a bit afraid of what is coming, and injecting hope and ideas as to how, together, you're all moving forward.

Be Transparent

"I have no idea what's going on around here! I don't know why we decided to go this way. What was she thinking?" Fear of pushback, rejection, losing authority, and so on can lead us, as leaders, to make decisions and not articulate how we arrived at those decisions. You may have conferred with other people to come up with your decision. However, when you lack transparency and avoid letting your team and others know how you arrived at that decision, it can confuse them. And confusion does not lead to engagement, influence, love, or trust.

Whenever possible, take the time to explain the rationale behind a decision. Sometimes, it requires courage to do so. Let's not confuse being transparent with keeping *confidentiality*—information that's sensitive and you are not privy to disclose. What is the appropriate amount of information to share to be transparent? In my opinion, it all depends on your audience—*who* needs to know *what* level of information? In the case of your direct reports and other leaders, they are the conduits of your message to the rest of the organization or team. They also have the need for *certainty*. Thus, give them enough information to generate the certainty they require individually and the level of detail that will support them to generate confidence among their staffs as they communicate the message. Give your direct reports, managers, and supervisors the tools to communicate a message that is both truthful and logical behind a particular decision, why it was important to make it, and what the objectives are. And when talking to your talent, in general, provide information that helps them understand that decision as it relates to their roles.

Transparency also means treating people respectfully as you plan to move roles and responsibilities around in your organization. Give the people impacted an opportunity to chime in. I can't tell you how many times I noticed people were moved around as if they were a bag of sugar. They weren't told there were plans for them to move to a different group and often learned about it after the fact. What are the implications for the people impacted when you as the leader disregarded or didn't consider their preference? When there is a choice, you may be assuming that you know best how to direct their careers. If you are not being transparent because you are afraid people may choose not to move, you can make that clear during your conversation, for example, "We are planning to move you to this new group. Here's why I think this would be a good move for you and for the new group." Talk about their strengths, the things they do well, and the knowledge they have. Highlight what the new group needs and how they can develop from a career perspective by joining it. That's a very different conversation from the one where an employee finds out for the first time at a meeting that he or she is working for a new group.

I've experienced this scenario secondhand on multiple occasions over the last thirty years of my career, in organizations I've worked with and with my individual clients, and it is a prevalent leadership faux pas. Be thoughtful and put yourself in someone else's shoes. How would you like to receive that news for the first time at a group meeting?

When considering how to be transparent, also understand that different people possess different styles and unique needs levels—from informal to formal, low- to high-degree of details, for example. As you get to know your team because you regularly connect with them, you will know the nuances about who needs more details and who requires less. These are additional benefits to connecting with your team and the people in your organization. If you're limited by time, be transparent by providing high-level information and creating another outlet for those who need more details. Everybody is different, and if we treat everybody as if they were the same, it's going to get us in trouble as leaders. And then we won' be able to lead, engage, and influence them in a way that is beneficial for everyone.

Empowering Questions for Reflection

1. If your word is your bond, what's your word's value?
2. How are you showing your team and others that you are trustworthy?
3. When team decisions backfire, how do you stand behind those decisions?
4. How do you express what you notice and speak your truth about it, compassionately, grounded, and empathetically?
5. What is the appropriate amount of information to share to be transparent?

LEADER SHOWCASE: NICK DONOFRIO

"You have to see the horizon better than anyone, look out there, and create an aspirational view."

Nicholas Donofrio, MSC, retired as IBM's Executive Vice President of Innovation and Technology in 2008 after over forty-four years with the company. Nick is currently an IBM Fellow Emeritus and founder of NMD Consulting, LLC. He earned his BSEE from Rensselaer Polytechnic Institute and received his MSEE from Syracuse University and has since received nine honorary doctorate awards from universities around the world and one honorary associate degree as well.

Nick, let's start by sharing your background with us.

I'm a second-generation American. I was born in Beacon, New York, one of four children. In typical first-generation Italian families, my dad was a hard man, a mechanic in the army air force during World War II. There's now an acronym called ALICE, **A**sset **L**imited **I**ncome **C**onstrained and **E**mployed. That acronym didn't exist when I was growing up, but that's what we were. My dad had three jobs and my mom raised four children and worked at home. We had a strong work and family ethic. I had many jobs. My paper route paid off for me because I won the Newsboy Scholarship that allowed me to go to RPI, Rensselaer Polytechnic Institute in Troy, New York. My work ethic is truly from my parents. I'm an electrical engineer and started my IBM career in September of 1964, and I ended my IBM career in September of 2008, forty-four years later.

What are the leadership skills that are most critical during these challenging times?

Leaders have to have the courage of their convictions, see the horizon better than anyone, look out there, and create an aspirational view. Then, you have to be an inspirational leader to inspire people to follow you; it's not merely a matter of command and control. And the last element of being a good leader is perspiration—a lot of hard work. It's something you have to do every day. And the mixture is very biased toward perspiration, ninety-five percent perspiration; the other five percent is a combination of aspiration and inspiration. Also, the more authentic and closer to the ground you are, the more you understand the problems.

Make sure people know you understand the issues. Be connected with people. They need to believe that you're real—that you know what's working and what isn't.

How would you recommend that companies approach developing their leaders?

The critical element is to figure out if they're really committed. Are they authentic? You don't need to be the smartest person. It's sometimes better if you're not. I managed 240,000 IBM technical people; I was definitely not the smartest person. Look at this whole issue of the traits that I shared. Can that leader fulfill those traits? Is that leader adaptable? If you're going to be a leader, you have to change your style. If you're not a problem solver, don't be a leader because you're kidding yourself, especially if you're in a company that creates things. If you're managing something, then you'd better become a lifelong learner. You better realize that it's not all about you. If you're not an enabler, I don't think you deserve to be a leader.

You can contact Nick on LinkedIn.

14

Be an Inclusive Leader

Value Diversity, Equity, and Inclusion (DE&I)

When we value *diversity* (recognizing our differences), *equity* (focusing on our individualistic needs), and *inclusion* (valuing the quality of the human experience), we serve our talent and all our people. Being healing leaders requires that we account for and consider the range of voices, perspectives, experiences, and points of view to be heard and valued, whether in teams, organizations, or when interacting with our products or services. Carol Copeland, a global diversity, empowerment, and leadership issues expert with C Thomas & Associate, describes diversity as follows: "Diversity is understanding, appreciating, and ultimately managing differences and similarities at the same time." Equity, openness, and belonging are core components of inclusion. It is said that "diversity" is an invitation to a party, whereas "inclusion" is being asked to dance.

Diversity Wins is the third report in a McKinsey series investigating the business case for diversity (McKinsey&Company, *Featured Insights*, 2020). The report shows that the business case for diversity remains robust while the relationship between diversity in executive teams and the likelihood of outperforming financially has strengthened over time. Their latest analysis reaffirms the strong business case for gender diversity and ethnic and cultural diversity in corporate leadership—and shows that this business case continues to strengthen. The most diverse companies are now more likely than ever to outperform their less diverse peers and be more profitable.

Their analysis finds that companies in the top quartile for gender diversity on executive teams were 25 percent more likely to have above-average profitability than companies in the fourth quartile—up from 21 percent in 2017 and 15 percent in 2014. Moreover, the study shows that the greater the representation of gender diversity, the higher the likelihood of outperformance. Companies with more than 30 percent of women executives were more likely to outperform companies where this percentage ranged from 10 to 30 percent. In addition, companies with more women executives were more likely to outperform those with fewer women executives or none at all.

In the case of ethnic and cultural diversity, McKinsey & Company's business case findings are equally compelling: In 2019, top-quartile companies outperformed those in the fourth quartile by 36 percent in profitability, slightly up from 33 percent in 2017 and 35 percent in 2014. As they have previously found, the likelihood of outperformance continues to be higher for diversity in ethnicity than for gender. What's most concerning is that, overall, progress has been slow. According to the study, in the company's original 2014 data set based in the United States and the United Kingdom, female representation on executive teams rose from 15 percent in 2014 to 20 percent in 2019, a 5 percent increase across five years. They highlight that *more than 30 percent of the companies* in their data set *still have no women on their executive teams*. The study concludes that this lack of material progress for executive women is evident across all industries and in most countries. Similarly, the representation of ethnic minorities on UK and US executive teams stood at only 13 percent in 2019, 5 percent higher than it was in 2014.

The McKinsey & Company report also provides new insights into how inclusion matters. It shows that companies should pay much greater attention to inclusion even when they are relatively diverse. The findings highlight the importance of inclusion, overall, and specific aspects of inclusion. Even relatively diverse companies face significant challenges in creating work environments characterized by inclusive leadership, accountability among managers, equality and fairness of opportunity, and openness and freedom from bias and discrimination. We have our work cut out for us.

The nemeses of diversity, equity, and inclusion are *unconscious biases*. Specifically speaking about gender biases, and according to the *50 Ways to Fight Bias* cards created by LeanIn.org, we keep struggling with seven core biases in the workplace. These biases include: *(1) affinity bias, (2) likability bias, (3) performance bias, (4) attribution bias, (5) double discrimination bias, (6) motherhood bias, and (7) double discrimination and intersectionality bias*. It is worthwhile to briefly describe each of these biases to raise awareness and ultimately address their sources; this knowledge will support you to heal these biases in your culture.

Affinity bias indicates that we gravitate toward people like ourselves in appearance, beliefs, and background and we may avoid or even dislike people who are different from us. *Likability bias* is rooted in antiquated expectations, such as men being assertive, so it feels natural when they lead. However, we expect women to be kind and communal, so we like them less when they assert themselves. *Performance bias* is based on entrenched and incorrect assumptions about women's and men's abilities. We tend to underestimate women's performances and overestimate men's. *Attribution bias* is closely linked to performance bias: it is the false perception that women are less competent than men. Thus, we tend to give them less credit for accomplishments and blame them more for mistakes.

LeanIn.org also indicates that women can experience biases because of their race, sexuality, age, religion, disability, and other aspects of their identities. When these biases are compounded, the discrimination people experience is even worse. This is called *double discrimination and intersectionality bias*, and it applies to men, too. For example, women of color often face double discrimination: biases for being women and biases for being women of color. Imagine the compounded effect of being Black, Muslim, an immigrant, and a woman. According to Adwoa Bagalini, intersectionality bias describes how different elements of a person's identity—again, race, sexuality, age, religion, or disability and so on— can be combined or "intersect" and discriminated against—with negative outcomes. Businesses that don't consider intersectionality bias in diversity and inclusion programs may ultimately lose out from high staff turnover (Bagalini, 2020).

Finally, *maternity bias* is founded on the false assumption that women are less committed to their careers and even less competent after motherhood. These are the most prevalent unconscious gender biases that most women in the workplace battle with daily. Every group of people regardless of their background are susceptible to having unconscious biases. But diversity, equity, and inclusion (DE&I) can work in every direction. Let's flip the script to not discriminate against any group—period.

As a leader, we have the opportunity and obligation to enable all our talent to reach their full potential, creating a culture where people feel valued because of their differences, unique needs, and perspectives. Please pay attention to your own biases, open your eyes to notice these and other tendencies in your leaders, and take corrective action once you see them. If you find yourself in a position where the people around you think, speak, and look like you, and only a few groups are represented and have opportunities to advance, that's a big clue to begin questioning how much your culture values diversity, equity, and inclusion. Connecting with your talent and understanding their perspectives and dynamics within the team and the company will provide a wealth of feedback.

I believe we're going to see a tremendous shift in education in the years to come. Society still places a lot of value on college degrees. However, I see a change in the mix. With the cost of education skyrocketing at a pace that parents and students cannot keep up with, self-education will grow. People will study to learn a specific skill rather than receive a four-year traditional college education. That means that as a leader, you may be interviewing a candidate who doesn't have a formal educational background for a position. Many who don't graduate from college have much value and experiences to contribute. As you interview and look for talent, keep this in mind—you may be speaking with the next Steve Jobs. Moving forward, consider people who don't have the same educational background as everyone else in the company. When looking at the talent pool, look for different avenues and at nontraditional sources. Get creative and focus on results instead of looking for people to fit a particular profile.

Leaders come in all colors, shapes, and forms, traditional and unconventional. Being open-minded, focused on the big picture, and on the results the organization needs will help you explore different options and embrace talent across a spectrum of experiences, education, genders, races, sexual identities, and backgrounds. We're all part of the talent pool. Question and bring rigor to your recruiting, training, and promotion practices. Measure your progress and when you identify gaps, generate solutions transparently and in supportive collaboration with other leaders and their teams.

LEADER SHOWCASE: PHIL ANDERSON

"Take a step. There is an opportunity for you to be part of the solution. Do something, it doesn't matter what, just do something."

Phillip Anderson, MBA, is an Executive Director at DTCC. Phil is a senior diversity leader with over thirty years of experience in management with degrees from the University of Pennsylvania and his MBA from Manhattanville College.

Please tell us a little bit about your background.

I work for the Depository Trust and Clearing Corporation. I've been here for about a year, but my career in diversity and inclusion (D&I) and leading diversity spans over twenty years. I've done diversity recruiting, diversity training, diversity development programs, and programming. And in addition to that, I have the responsibility for the strategy and the like. I take a look at it from the full employee life cycle. And it's been very inspirational for me in terms of trying to affect the lives of people and organizations with respect to diversity and inclusion.

What advice would you give leaders who are looking to develop a unique edge?

There are tons of studies that make a case for diversity and inclusion. Catalyst.org has shown, for example, that having women on the board typically helps the bottom line. Diversity and inclusion lead to innovation. And solving issues that come up are often tackled better by a diverse team. Being included automatically gives you a feeling of belonging. And because you belong, you want to give more and more. That inclusive skill set allows you to think differently and not have the same thought process that leaves you stagnant and vulnerable to disruptors.

To move the numbers, the first thing that has to change is behaviors. If you aren't changing behaviors, you're not making a change so that people can contribute, feel like they belong, and give their maximum effort. I believe we should set diversity goals, and notice, I didn't say "quotas." And that takes analysis. What kinds of skills do you need? What is the availability of talent in that space, both from a background and a skill set? Allowing us to be able to, with data, drive different outcomes.

Often, I hear about people saying, "Well, what about me? How does that affect me?" If I'm a white male I might think because we have diversity efforts going on, it might hurt me. I would tell that white male to sharpen his skills then and become more competitive. Because that's what we're talking about—making sure that there's a playing ground accessible to everyone so the best talent can be there.

Take a step. There is an opportunity for you to be part of the solution. Do something. It doesn't matter what, just do something. Here are some things you can do: mentor, educate yourself, demand a diverse slate when you're hiring, develop the team across the SWOT (Strengths, Weaknesses, Opportunities, and Threats). Be supportive and think about ways to engage your teams because that extra motivation comes from people feeling your empathy toward them. Not everyone is going to rise to the top, and that's okay. You want people to maximize their potential.

You can connect with Phil Anderson on LinkedIn.

Be Open-Minded

To genuinely value diversity, equity, and inclusion across the board requires that we embrace open-mindedness. Many of us want to believe that we are open-minded—who would like to describe themselves as otherwise? An inclusive leader brings an open mind to appreciate the differences and similarities among people, consider individualistic needs, and make people feel valued. This open-mindedness is a willingness to welcome new ideas, diversity of thought and perspectives, without instinctively shutting it down.

I've caught myself being close-minded. At the onset of my career, I recall sometimes being fixated on my solution to a problem and reluctant to entertain alternatives. Or when project members would bring up suggestions, it would take me a few beats to get unstuck and out of my single perspective to see the value in their new ideas. Although this is a simplistic example, it begs your thinking about how willing you are to listen and reflect on different ideas. Like me, you may notice a reluctance, albeit subconscious, to value a varying point of view. As a healing leader, expand the scope of how you look at your team members' strengths, contributions, and challenges, and seek to understand their perspectives. And take it one step further by incorporating components of your solution with features of theirs to arrive at a more inclusive and robust set of products, services, and culture.

Notice how open-minded your team members are. When you notice people stuck in their perspectives, help them expand by coaching them around it. Many of us are set in our ways; curiosity and empathy will allow us to fathom what else is possible. Know what you stand for, what you need, and your ideas. Similarly, consider what others stand for, what they need, and their ideas. Role model open-mindedness to influence better outcomes and results. When we don't open up, we miss opportunities to value other people's input. What can you do to promote a culture of open-mindedness that will support your people to feel valued and even loved as a team member?

LEADER SHOWCASE: LEANNE PUCHIR

"Don't underestimate your abilities."

Leanne Puchir is a Senior Analyst at PepsiCo and has over twenty-five years of experience at a Fortune 20 company where she had the privilege to lead small to large teams. She received her bachelor's degree in business from Fordham University, magna cum laude.

What leadership skills are more critical in this environment?

One of the most needed qualities is being open-minded. This pandemic has taught us that anything can happen, and we need to be prepared. As a leader, you also need to be resilient. Every day will be different, and it can be hard sometimes, and it's important not to give up the fight and keep going back. It would help if you also were flexible. And most importantly, for your team, you also need to have empathy. Even as a leader, you come to the table with what is on your plate at home and work. And that is the same for your team. You may not know everything that is happening to them before they walk in the door.

How should companies approach developing their leaders during this time?

On a proactive basis, companies could have a more formal leadership development program. They could have a rotation for their leaders to understand what it would be like to be in different roles and learn to relate better to their peers. And those programs shouldn't always be for the people who are picked to be in them. If an employee wants to be in a program like that, he or she should also have the chance to participate. It should be a two-prong approach. You might identify a potential leader, a manager, or a director. You might also look at your team and say, I think this person will be a superstar and I want to help him or her grow. Or it could be someone who does not have a mentor or sponsor looking out for him or her but who expresses interest in the program. They should also be allowed to participate.

What advice would you give to leaders who are looking to develop a unique edge?

First, learn to trust your instincts. You have a little voice inside you that is telling you personal and professional things that you should try, do, and follow. You need to pay attention to that and learn to trust it. And I believe the more you do, the stronger the voice gets. Lean on that, especially at work. Also, don't be afraid to try something new. Even if you're not sure, you don't have all the answers, jump in and give it a shot. Finally, don't be afraid to admit mistakes or admit when you don't know. As a leader, you are then an honest leader and can either resolve it or get the answers you need.

Don't underestimate your abilities. That's when you will try new things, trust your instincts, and go for it. You will learn so much from the opportunities that come from that.

You can connect with Leanne on LinkedIn.

Finding Strengths in Differences and Similarities

The interviews with the forty-one talented leaders who participated in our field study demonstrate the strength in celebrating diversity of thought, differences, and similarities of opinions and backgrounds. Their diverse experiences, ages, genders, areas of expertise, and industries create an interwoven backdrop from which to evaluate global critical leadership skills, ways to develop our talent, and ways to create new skills to create a unique edge during challenging times and periods of high demand. While many of them converge on related attributes, there's also vast differences in their responses, which are even more apparent when listening to the *Visionary Leaders Circle* podcasts and live interviews.

If we only pay attention to those who agree with us, we're missing the other half who do not—and therein lies the danger of "groupthink" and "silo thinking." Innovation and creativity are fueled by differences in viewpoints and approaches to solutions, creating stronger and better products and services. Remember this when you are hiring someone who comes from a different industry or has an atypical background compared to other employees in the organization. Differences can sometimes generate both conflicts and strengths. If you are developing a product and the engineering team members have different opinions, those differences will turn up questions. Addressing those questions and mitigating the objections are where you find the strength from the conflict. On the other hand, finding similarities, for example, the engineers agreeing on a feature or component, validates that the team is on the right track. There are strengths in differences and similarities, and our job as leaders is to bring those to the surface. We do that by asking empowering questions.

While reading *Man's Search for Meaning* by Viktor E. Frankl (Frankl, 2006, p. 86), a quintessential story of survival in German internment camps, I read a beautiful passage that's meaningful in this context: "Human kindness can be found in all groups, even those which as a whole it would be easy to condemn." Referring to the guards and prisoners at the concentration camp, he states, "From all this, we may learn that there are two races of men in this world, but only these two—the 'race' of the *decent man* and the 'race' of the *indecent man*. Both are found everywhere; they penetrate into all groups of society. No group consists entirely of decent or indecent people."

I believe in the race of *decent* people—those who live by a code that honors human freedom and dignity. We all have our challenges. Let's remember to bring our best Self forward as often as we can, do our best given our existing resources, and be kind to ourselves and others whenever possible. The more we take care of each other, the faster we'll populate the world with people in the "decent race."

Empowering Questions for Reflection

1. How is your organization creating work environments characterized by inclusive leadership, accountability among managers, equality and fairness of opportunity, and openness and freedom from bias and discrimination?

2. Individually, how are you being an inclusive leader, fostering accountability, equality and fairness of opportunity, and openness and freedom from bias and discrimination?

3. How can you relate to the seven types of unconscious bias outlined in this chapter?

4. How committed are you to paying attention to your own biases, opening your eyes to noticing these and other tendencies in your leaders, and taking corrective action once you see them?

5. What is your take on Frankl's statement? "From all this, we may learn that there are two races of men in this world, but only these two—the 'race' of the *decent man* and the 'race' of the *indecent man*. Both are found everywhere; they penetrate into all groups of society. No group consists entirely of decent or indecent people."

6. What can you do to promote a culture of open-mindedness that will support your people to feel valued and even loved as a team member?

15

Communicate Powerfully

Clearly Articulate Your Message

As a leader, engaging and influencing the talent, sharing the company's vision and mission, listening, inspiring, and enabling others to voice their opinions is all a part of communication. According to the leaders participating in our field study, communicating powerfully, clearly, and with transparency is the number-one leadership skill leaders need most especially during a time of crisis and uncertainty. At the core of your communication is the *message*, the *audience*, your *style*, and *listening*—we'll address all components. My communication skills were strengthened by understanding these four critical components after hosting a thirty-minute interview with Jane Hanson, a generous member of my professional network and nine-time Emmy award-winning television journalist, media coach, and former news anchor at NBC New York. Let's begin with *your message*.

Your message helps employees understand how their roles and responsibilities synchronize with the corporate vision and mission. Your message provides direction, connects employees to the purpose of the organization, and influences them to align their actions to move forward. What is your intention, and what do you want to accomplish through your message? You might want to encourage, comfort, and inform them about a significant change or transformation, M&A (mergers and acquisitions), layoffs, or an expansion to another country. Or maybe it's to rally the troops to prepare for the work ahead, elicit feedback, support, provide an update on the team's progress overall, or express appreciation. A leader shares respect, trust, loyalty, power, and authority. We do it through our messages. Again, the words that we use are significant; they transmit faith or fear.

Your messages can also inspire others to share their voices, be heard and understood by the team, share their knowledge, and collectively elevate the group's intelligence. When you *encourage* others to share their voices, you role model an open, free culture, and employees will go above and beyond what is required, not merely do the minimum. They feel their voices matter and that goes a long way. When we *motivate* people with physical rewards, they strive to meet the bar you set. However, when we *inspire* them with the bigger vision that you see for them, which they may not perceive for themselves, we enable them to soar. Your message has the power to do precisely that.

Your message also helps you increase your visibility. Be the leader who communicates across the organization, letting others know what you are up to, how you can support them, and how they can support you. Collaborate, join forces to move faster in generating solutions for the organization. As you build relationships across the spectrum and share a clear message, you will become more influential and thus able to promote the mission of the team more effectively.

Sharing your message authentically with your people is your right and privilege, and it's not one that should be taken lightly. You have a unique message to share, a perspective from which you see the world. Others who perhaps have been through similar situations will resonate with you, gravitate toward you, and your words will help them in their own healing. Own your story, your experiences, the lessons that you've learned over the years, and offer them up from a place of contribution, not ego, in hopes that your words are the medicine that your people need that day. With love, trust that your message will touch their hearts and minds.

and training, watching great orators, practicing at home, and delivering many keynotes and trainings while collaborating with ERGs (employee resource groups) at Fortune 500 companies and strategic partners in the industry. I appreciate being a motivational speaker and connecting with audiences through personal stories to share a compelling message that meets their needs. I aim to provide knowledge, give them tools they can use right away, and inspire them to see the possibilities in their careers and personal lives.

Connect with your message. Share what you already know. Inform and inspire your audience. Your voice matters, and no one has the same perspective you do. Your voice is your gift to us. We're waiting. Count on me to encourage you.

Listen on *all* Levels

As a certified professional coach, I trained to listen to my clients on all levels, that is, listening to their words, noticing their body language, gestures, speech rate, pitch, tone, breathing patterns, and so on. All those inputs are ways of listening. They are always critical components of communication but especially during times like this pandemic. As leaders, listening creates a container that allows people to feel safe and free to express themselves. To practice listening, ask an empowering question and then be quiet. The silence can be uncomfortable for you and the person. With practice, though, it becomes natural.

When I first began my coaching certification, I remember how uneasy I felt asking a question and sitting there quietly waiting for an answer. However, I noticed that by being silent and really listening, my practice partner relaxed and took the time to dig deep for the answer and then spoke. But simply being quiet doesn't necessarily mean you're *listening*. Maybe while you're waiting for the person to respond to your question, you're thinking of other things. Listening genuinely means being present and mindful at that moment, focusing on the other person and his or her words. Whether you're physically or virtually with the person or on the phone, you're creating a vast space for anything to emerge.

You'll know you're not *really* listening when you are already formulating what to say next while the person is answering your question, and as soon as the person pauses, you immediately plow through with your idea. To show the person that you're listening, follow the thread of the conversation by either asking a follow-up or clarifying question, for example, "What do you mean by that?" or commenting on something the person mentioned. Avoid making it all about you. And again, listen. Every leader, in my opinion, needs to master asking empowering questions. It would be a much more engaging culture if people asked each other empowering questions and listened to one another. But we can't do something we don't know how to do. Honing our listening skills applies to all areas of our life, not only our careers.

When you listen on all levels, you can use your intuition to guide the conversation and the follow-up questions. You may uncover so much that's not being stated by paying attention and naming what you see. For example, after somebody shares an update, you can say, "I get a sense that you feel uneasy about this, how accurate is that?" and then listen. Err on the side of listening. If somebody storms into your office and begins to unload, calmly ask the individual, "What's going on?" Ask the person to sit down and share with you, "Go ahead, I'm all ears," and hear what he or she has to say. If you are coaching this individual, resist the urge to go into problem-solving mode until the person is done, whether he or she is asking you specifically for the solution or you want to help him or her arrive at that solution on his or her own. As Cynthia Kersey shared during our engaging interview, use the expression "I hear you," and I often use, "What else?" until there's nothing left. Listening first will inform your answer or how to proceed.

When you are careful and thoughtful about crafting the message that will meet the needs of the audience, deliver that message authentically as the expert you are, adjust your style, and listen on all levels. Your communication skills will catapult to a whole new level.

Empowering Questions for Reflection

1. What is your message?
2. What is your intention, and what do you want to accomplish through your message?
3. What are your audience's objectives?
4. What is your audience most concerned about?
5. What will be valuable to your audience?
6. What are your audience's "pain points"—areas they struggle with and find challenging?
7. How do you engage your audience now? And do you plan to engage them in the same way in the future?
8. How do you adjust your style based on the audience? formal setting vs informal setting?
8. How are your listening skills? After reading this chapter, what will you do differently, if anything?

LEADER SHOWCASE: ALETA MAXWELL

"Get courageous or fearless, which is staring down your fear, knowing that it's there, getting comfortable with it, and proceeding anyway."

Aleta Maxwell, SHRM-CP, CPC, is a former Chief Human Resources Officer in the hospitality industry. She now serves as an Organizational Consultant, Leadership Coach, and founder of Uplifting Leadership, LLC. Aleta has more than twenty-five years of experience in the industry, receiving her degree from Kaplan University, and published her number-one bestselling book, Uplifting Leaders, in nine countries.

What leadership skills are the most critical? And can you give us a little bit of your background?

My experience is primarily in the hospitality industry in operations and then later in finance and HR. Over the last eight years, I've focused on HR.

The most critical leadership trait is effective communication— whether that is awareness to understand problems before they become huge issues or to collaborate with individuals to develop strategies to tackle both the company's issues and every unique individual's needs or transparency and communicating the whys. I hear most often that people feel frustrated by leadership not having transparency during this time or not communicating why certain decisions are being made.

And the last trait is vulnerability. The more leaders can be vulnerable allows their entire team to show up in that way as well, which to me leads to better connections down the road. When I say vulnerability, you don't want to cross that line into best-friend territory and give too much away. But the ability to say when we don't have all the answers—to say I was wrong on this; this is why I was wrong. It's the ability to ask for help, seek different answers, and be curious.

A couple of things get in the way of some people being effective communicators. First, the idea that they need to have all the answers means that they can't be vulnerable and say, "I don't know, this isn't my wheelhouse, help." The ego gets in the way for some leaders. And then, the fighting for position will come into play. If I show any vulnerability, any weakness, maybe they'll replace me with somebody who does have all the answers. Challenging narratives is important as leaders—to make sure we're dealing with facts and not some stories that we've created in our heads that might be holding us back.

What message would you like to leave our audience?

Get courageous or fearless, which is staring down your fear, knowing that it's there, getting comfortable with it, and proceeding anyway. Many people, including myself, have been able to do remarkable things that we never thought possible by taking that first step, even though we were fearful, and summoning up the courage to continue the journey. With my new book, *Uplifting Leaders: How to Have Difficult Conversations*, which is now available, and with our coaching services, I am super pumped to help and support HR leaders—as I believe HR is one of the loneliest positions in an organization.

You can connect with Aleta at www.upliftingleadership.com and LinkedIn.

16

Set the Vision

Develop a Strategic Perspective

As individual contributors, it's pretty straightforward what we need to do. However, as leaders, we have to account for our own responsibilities, including the overall well-being of the team and achieving the results that your group has been mandated to deliver. Strategic leaders look at options and different pathways to achieve desired outcomes. They plot the path forward toward a compelling vision. They imagine the possibilities, the advantages, and disadvantages of each path and develop a road map that helps the team achieve the objective and meet the stakeholders' needs along the way. Is this strategy feasible? How can you bring others along to implement it? How do you get all the inputs you need to finalize the strategy? Collaboration and inclusion is the key. Creating a compelling strategic vision is an exciting activity.

When I started my company, I wasn't 100 percent clear on what I would create. I knew the results that I wanted to have: I wanted to influence a healthier workplace culture and outcomes and directly impact leaders' lives, financially and emotionally, while supporting them to navigate the landscape and reach their full potential. How I was going to accomplish this was a bit of an enigma for me. As time went on, I began to deepen my understanding of my strengths and superpowers. I began to picture how I could meet my objectives by coaching individual leaders, creating leadership curricula, and training leadership dream teams at the corporate level. And I envisioned reaching large audiences with my motivational talks in companies, at conferences, summits, now virtual events, and through my books. The strategy that I used to pursue my objectives became clearer and evolved as time went by.

My resources are limited, like everybody else's. Knowing my strategic vision for my business helps me conserve resources. I only spend time, effort, and money on activities that will propel me closer to that compelling vision. Creating my strategy has been the result of collaborating with other subject matter experts in my field. I remember reaching out to Cynthia Lett on LinkedIn in 2018 at the outset of my motivational speaking career. Cynthia is a bestselling author, speaker, etiquette, and protocol expert and the creator of KeepMyStory.com, Cool2Color.com, and LettGroup.com. During our cyber-coffee, she taught me all there is to know about crafting a compelling speaking agreement, how to add the most value to partners, and how to structure the pricing model. Her generosity with her knowledge, expertise, and time were invaluable. Reaching out to a subject matter expert in my field and spending minutes on the phone with her saved me years of trial-and-error. I sat with her and asked her questions that helped me clarify how I could bring my strengths to the marketplace and accelerate the results that I wanted to see.

At this stage in my business, I have a virtual team supporting me across the spectrum of activities that I need to perform on a daily and weekly basis. I also have strategic partners that I rely on to run targeted marketing campaigns around product launches. I work with my book production team to publish my books, from my book consultant who knows the ins and outs of book publishing to my book editor, book cover designer, and layout professional. They are in the know. They know the latest trends and changes in regulations; they help save me time by giving me that information.

Ask questions, listen to experts, anticipate, and prepare. Begin to imagine what your mission could look like, get informed, take one step at a time, and be open to what develops. As you move forward, bring your team along. Create a support system that will help you realize your vision.

Get Clarity on the Future

One of the six human needs is *certainty*. People want to know what's happening when, how, and who is involved. As a leader, when you are clear on the vision for your team and the business, it helps everyone buy into that vision and understand how they can contribute to it. What is the higher vision for the team, your company, or mission you lead? Align your view with the people around you to ensure that everybody is committed to elevating the organization's higher purpose.

When so much is uncertain during a time like this pandemic and others, leadership adds value by being honest about what they know and what they don't know. Getting clarity on the future when there is so much ambiguity can be tricky. Whatever the changes, the company's values and devotion to do the best for its people are critical—even during times when we need to make tough choices to ensure the entity's survival such as having to close individual branches or shut down operations in entire countries.

There is no way to reach a destination unless you know what the destination is. Ensure that your team and everyone is clear on that vision and the endgame. Break it down into manageable chunks, either monthly, quarterly, yearly, or five-year plans. Be nimble and agile, knowing that things will definitely change, and be willing to revisit and adjust your approach.

Believe in Your Vision

Dear healing leader,

I know whatever you're doing right now or plan to do in the future will be filled with love, passion, and compassion. You inspire life and give all your soul to family, friends, clients, and all those you touch. Keep the faith, stay the course, and always remember that you are divine. And I'm here to provide for all your needs. All you need to do is ask, and I provide love, joy, health, happiness. All those things you crave and dream of are yours to have. Stay true to yourself and dream big. Keep asking, and I will guide you all the way. Laugh, have fun, otherwise, what's the point of all of this? You are magnificent magnetic light and love itself.

Love, the Universe

–Dr. Ginny A. Baro

Leaders inspire others to follow them. When you believe in your compelling vision and that of the company or mission, you exude certainty to those you daily interact with. If you don't believe in your vision, it's time to step aside and let someone else lead. Your enthusiasm is contagious and will rouse your team to take proactive steps to achieve the vision. How do you show that you believe in your vision? You speak words that exude that certainty. You take actions that demonstrate you believe in your message. When you articulate your vision, it will let people know how you feel about it.

One of the biggest problems with diversity, equity, and inclusion (DE&I) training is that we're not making significant progress. What is the vision around DE&I? On many occasions, leaders are good at giving this topic lip service and not genuinely believing that it matters. The leaders in our field study concur that without inclusion, there is no leadership. If you say you believe in diversity, equity, and inclusion, and your actions do not reflect your belief, it is evident that there is a misalignment.

Beliefs are proven by measuring. When you begin to track the elements of your vision, such as DE&I, that's when you genuinely stand behind it knowing there will be physical proof that shows how well your company is progressing or not. And when the senior leader stands behind a vision, the beliefs trickle down to the rest of the organization. Your direct reports will fall in line, and if they do not, have conversations with those individuals. It may seem ingenious to check a box and pretend that a topic such as DE&I is essential to you when it's not. It's not good for your reputation, character, or integrity when people see that you are not following in reality what you advocate in theory. In other words, practice what you preach!

If you don't honestly care about a topic, don't pretend that you do. It doesn't work. Don't waste your time or other people's time. Instead, respect them, step aside, and let someone else lead who believes in the vision you're selling but not buying. This type of honesty is vital to healing our leadership. What is going on, truthfully? The vision that you believe in is the right one for you—your truth. Lean on it with love, passion, and compassion. If it's different from your organization's vision and truth, maybe it's time to reconsider your next steps and seek that alignment with another organization.

Empowering Questions for Reflection

1. How can you bring others along to implement the strategy?
2. How do you get all the input you need to finalize the strategy?
3. How well do you practice collaboration and inclusion?
4. What is the higher vision for your mission or the team or your company that you lead?
5. How do you show that you believe in your vision?
6. What is the vision around diversity, equity, and inclusion (DE&I) in your organization and for you personally?

LEADER SHOWCASE: ANNA TOLMACH

"Career and life are very interesting adventures. They are the paths that you're walking in. It's better to enjoy them."

Anna Tolmach, CSM, CPC, is a former Scrum Master/Agile Project Manager at S&P Global with more than twenty years of leadership experience in financial services and technology. Anna earned a BS in computer science from Montclair State University. Today, she serves as a Certified Professional Coach and founder at Holistic Insighter, LLC, supporting talented professionals to thrive in their relationships while leveraging her gift for intuitive coaching.

Please tell us about your background.

I came to the United States at the end of 1994 from Russia. I graduated from college and landed my first job. It was so exciting because I ended up on Wall Street. I've worked for major financial companies over the last twenty years. At one point, I managed around seventy people in technology. I worked for UBS, S&P Global, U.S. Trust Company, and JPMorgan Chase.

What leadership skills are most critical in this environment?

There are many skills that leaders should have to drive people forward. Leaders should see what's coming up next and should prepare their teams for what's coming. Visionaries, as I would say, are most needed in today's world. The opportunity to see into the future and prepare your team for what's happening is a wonderful quality for leaders—and when things happen, people will be ready for them. And this includes training the mental capacity to deal with what's coming and also to develop trust. That's the reason people will follow you.

What components were present when you felt that you could trust your leaders?

They always had my back. I could rely on them. And in business, situations come up very often. I worked at one point in my career doing production support for a company. It was crucial that if something broke, your team would fix it right away. And I had great managers who helped me during those times when everything went crazy. It's very important that there is a person who supports you and you can rely on as your manager. Trust doesn't happen in one second; it develops over time, but it can be destroyed in one second.

I want to highlight another quality. I worked for many managers. There was one lady at S&P Global whom I admired the most. She was basically coaching me, and coaching was the most important part because we can always improve. She gave me insights into what was happening—I felt welcomed. She was developing me in ways that I could never have imagined.

Career and life are very interesting adventures. They are the paths that you're walking in. It's better to enjoy them. You helped me navigate through my last years in corporate and gave me the tools, insights, and practical advice to build my practice and work on my plan B. I dreamed about it for twenty years and never knew how to do it. Thank you for being there for all of us.

You may connect with Anna via Anna@holisticinsighter.com and LinkedIn.

17

Focus on Results with a Human Lens

Solve Problems

Without delivering results or on the company brand promise, there won't be anyone to lead—we would be out of work. Every organization has a series of problems daily. As leaders, we take the baton to advance the organization's causes and mission. Do you want to make yourself a valuable leader who leads, engages, and influences others? Look for the most significant problems to solve with an orientation toward the human element and the talent's well-being. The straightforward issues serve as a medium to uplift your confidence. The considerable challenges become the most rewarding, and potentially, simultaneously, the most frustrating. Solving problems with our team is one way to deliver results that matter.

When I look at my leadership development, I see how substandard and at times ineffective the training was for over thirty years in the industry. I recognize that we had a big problem with lack of customization to address specific individual challenges; lack of depth; inept integration into actionable takeaways; and nonexistent support structures that a leader could count on posttraining. Throw into the mix the elements of delivery, scalability, and cost. How can organizations develop their leaders effectively, efficiently, affordably, and see sustainable results long term? What can we do to enhance leaders' learning experiences?

These were the problems I set out to solve when I created the *Fearless Leadership Mastermind*™. The entire leadership training program is customizable for each leader through a series of personalized tools. Each training module can be adapted to a leader's situation and requirements and integrates daily practices and feedback to make it relevant. It provides a support structure for six months to a year where the leader can practice, with a soft landing, to ask and answer questions. It is scaled to handle many participants with a viable pricing model, and it's completely accessible virtually. From speaking with strategic corporate partners who were struggling to develop their leaders, it became apparent that the best leadership development solution needed to include flexibility, structure, and unique features, which we ended up implementing in our program. Listening to the different voices in the room will always turn up a more robust end product.

Collaborating and eliciting feedback from your team and others within the company accelerates identifying the best approach and course of action to solve the problems at hand and generate solutions. As the leader, set guidelines that prevent anyone from sabotaging the collaboration; discourage people who only want to hear themselves speak, shut down, or interrupt the quieter voices.

Look around you. What are the most significant problems you see, including challenges around improving your people's well-being, and how can you help solve them?

See the Human

Despite the latest technological innovations, AI (artificial intelligence), machine learning robotics, and so on, in my opinion people will never be replaced by technology 100 percent. It is true, however, that automation and digitization have forever changed our industry and jobs.

According to a McKinsey report (McKinsey&Company, 2018), the speed of skill displacement driven by technology changes is projected to double by 2030—50 percent of workforce activities could be automated with existing technologies, but only 15 percent of workforce activities have been automated as of the time of this report two years ago—the pandemic has most likely accelerated this rate. The report predicts that over 30 percent of US workers will need to change jobs or upgrade their skills significantly by 2030.

However, we will need humans to write programs, engineer the machines, service and maintain the operations, solve new problems, strategize, connect the dots, collaborate to generate ideas and innovate, and so on. There are human beings performing these functions and they have personal lives, families, concerns, dreams, and aspirations. They want to feel significant, that they matter, and they want to connect with their jobs and employers, grow, contribute, and have fun. By focusing on the human aspect of the operations and the business, you foster a culture where the *person* matters—creativity and innovation depend on it.

When machines ultimately perform many of our jobs that we do today, we will have more personal bandwidth to focus on higher-level activities and critical and strategic thinking. Our workforce and society will need to reskill to meet the new demand and adapt to technological advances. That preparation begins today by working on yourself first and then supporting your team to do the same.

Empowering Questions for Reflection

1. How do you want to make yourself a valuable leader who leads, engages, and influences others?
2. How can organizations develop their leaders effectively, efficiently, affordably, and see sustainable results long term?
3. What can we do to enhance leaders' learning experiences?
4. What are the most significant problems you see, including challenges around improving your people's well-being, and how can you help solve them?

LEADER SHOWCASE: PILAR AVILA

"I cannot see an effective leader achieving anything without empathy, communication, and focusing on people."

Maria del Pilar Avila (Pilar) is an Organization Change Management Consultant and founding leader of interDUCTUS. Pilar is also the founder and hostess of Renovad. She has over twenty-seven years of business experience. Pilar received her bachelor's degree in business administration, hospitality and convention management from the University of Central Florida.

Please tell us a little bit about you and your background.

I am currently the founder of InterDUCTUS. It means "among leaders." It's my consulting practice mostly focused on supporting the growth and success of clients in the private sector. And then, on the nonprofit side, I have been consulting with some foundations and nonprofits that are doing work across environmental projects. I'm also the founder and hostess of Renovad, a women's retreat initiative that brings together wonderful women to travel around the world. I have found a tremendous community of business owners like you, and things have been extremely rewarding and exciting over the last four years.

What leadership skills are the most critical in these times?

Right now, leaders need to focus on everything that relates to people, lifting people, lifting their teams, lifting their colleagues. And I would recommend leaders focus on empathy, compassion, and communication. Everything starts and ends with our people, human capital. And no matter what's happening, but particularly right now, I cannot see an effective leader achieving anything without empathy, communication, and a focus on people.

What advice would you give the leaders who want to develop a unique edge?

More than ever, leaders need to open their eyes and look at the future to anticipate and prepare our teams and our businesses for success. They need to be visionaries who move in a courageous manner and with a decisive approach. Because, sometimes, you can be bold but not take the necessary steps. You need to feel the strength but also take action. And sometimes, the decisions might not be the popular decisions. You have to be a leader who believes in your approach to moving forward.

Given all that you've experienced as a leader that has either helped you or challenged you, what would you say to leaders today?

You need to put yourself on the priority list, nurture yourself first. Ensure that you are healthy and have the energy and time to be reflective, and that requires discipline. This is part of the transformation of leaders and the rise of women in leadership. Even though I would say that sometimes we are the worst at putting ourselves on the list, but we're learning. I created Renovad Retreats as a space for women to take the time away from their daily grind, family, and business and reconnect with themselves and also open up and connect to other wonderful women who are part of this experience.

Maria del Pilar Avila is accessible at www.renovad.co, www. interductus.co, interductus@gmail.com, or LinkedIn.

18

Encourage Innovation and Bold Action

Look for the Lessons in Failures

We have taken painstaking steps to hire qualified individuals onto our teams. They are smart, hungry, and want to contribute. What can prevent them from being as innovative and creative as they can be? Watch your culture and how that culture may be stifling or encouraging new ideas and those taking bold actions. How does your culture encourage, champion, and celebrate innovation? Or is there retaliation when new ideas go sideways?

The culture you cultivate can either promote or squash innovation and calculated risk taking. Often, leaders prefer to play it safe, follow the status quo, and not make waves. How your culture handles failures sends a message to your talent that either inspires or discourages creativity. Suppose leaders fear retaliation when new ideas fail rather than looking for the lessons and growing from the experience with a growth mindset. In that case, they will shy away from trying, and your culture will stifle innovation.

In a *Forbes* article, Dan Pontefract (Pontefract, 2018) highlights that "fail fast, fail often" is often misused to imply that it's beneficial to embrace a culture where failure is celebrated. Originating in Silicon Valley, he indicates that the real aim of "fail fast, fail often" is not to fail but to be iterative.

To succeed, we must be open to failure, of course, but the intention is that we learn to be *iterative*, that is, learn from our mistakes as we tweak, reset, and then redo, if necessary. This scenario is where you reap the benefits of fostering a growth mindset culture.

Thomas Edison, by example, "failed" nine thousand times before succeeding at inventing the lightbulb. Pontefract recommends embracing experimentation combined with making judicious, thoughtful decisions and spending the time we need on creativity and critical thinking. Both Edison and Elon Musk, et al., at SpaceX, were iterative. Edison and Musk balanced their creative and critical thinking with the need to apply their learning iteratively.

Pay attention to the culture you're creating to support innovation. It's always important to communicate with your team and demonstrate your company's appetite and tolerance for trying out new ideas through actions. Ensure that your words and actions align with the vision you communicate.

Embrace New Ideas

Creating a safe space for new ideas to emerge is our responsibility as leaders. Setting our egos aside and letting everyone contribute to the best of their abilities will bring out the best ideas in the room. How we react to new ideas in front of everyone else is a significant indicator to the audience whether it is safe to share their thoughts.

Nothing stifles creativity during a brainstorming session more than hearing these phrases: "That's not how we do it here," "We tried that before, it didn't work," "That might have worked in your previous company, but it won't work here." That shows close-mindedness. If you have team members who are saying these things, they need to be mentored and coached on being more open to other perspectives.

The truth is that most people do not like to be embarrassed, especially in public or in a group. You can create some ground rules around the brainstorming session that indicate no idea is a bad idea. If you have something to share, share it, and we'll discuss it. You can also establish that when someone brings up an idea, provide background, pros, cons, potential problems, and critical benefits of it. Create a structure to help them produce more quality ideas.

While working on a project for my MBA program, my team and I came up with a novel marketing idea to generate income and enhance a company's brand. The idea was to establish partnerships where private companies would "sponsor" stadiums, and in the process, raise brand awareness in target markets. This project happened in the '94-'95 time frame. Not too long after we presented this idea and earned an A on the project, we began to see our idea occurring in the marketplace. In East Rutherford, New Jersey, the Meadowlands Arena was renamed the Continental Airlines Arena, subsequently Izod Center, and now MetLife Stadium.

How many Steve Jobs or Grace Hoppers are working for you right now? Jobs founded Apple Inc. in 1976 and transformed the company into a world leader in telecommunications. Grace Hopper designed the Harvard's Mark I computer in 1944, invented the compiler, which translated written language into computer code, and later coinvented COBOL, the first universal programming language used in business and government. As you connect with your people, learn about them and their capabilities and strengths; you can even challenge them to stretch and generate new ideas. Appreciate them for their contributions every step of the way and encourage them to go for it.

Be Courageous

"You cannot discover new oceans unless you have the courage to lose sight of the shore."

–André Gide

Leadership is not a popularity contest. Being a bold leader requires courage and fearlessness, acting despite fear. Most of us prefer to play it safe, be liked, and go with the flow. However, reflect on what has happened in your life when taking calculated risks and making bold moves. What has been the result?

In my personal life, filing for divorce was a painful and bold move, not one that I took lightly. The trajectory of my life would be vastly different today had I not accepted those conditions. I was not frivolous or flip about my decision. I spent over a year working on the issues. Life is too short, but it feels like an eternity when we don't feel aligned.

Being courageous carries a lot of weight because we have to live with the consequences of our decisions. Some of those decisions are irreversible. Being strategic and having a plan B is helpful. It also gives the team the certainty to pivot. My business would most likely not exist had I not taken those bold moves without knowing that I would be successful, but something I could do was count on my beliefs in my potential and abilities. That's what the team needs to lean on.

What have you done and accomplished before, as a team, and can you pull this off, too? There's inherent faith in being courageous and bold. We take steps without seeing the full picture. With confidence, the floor will show up under our feet when we take the next step. Leading in this type of environment and seeing in the dark requires a true leader.

Empowering Questions for Reflection

1. What can prevent team members from being innovative and creative?
2. How does your culture encourage, champion, and celebrate innovation?
3. How does your culture respond when new ideas go sideways?
4. How many Steve Jobs or Grace Hoppers are working for you right now?
5. What happened in your life when you took calculated risks and made bold moves?
6. What have you done and accomplished before, as a team, that can help you get through a current challenge?

LEADER SHOWCASE: JEROME PERIBERE

"I am asking you all one thing. I am asking you to be courageous."

Jerome Peribere retired in 2017 as President and Chief Executive Officer of Sealed Air Corp. Before joining Sealed Air, Jerome worked at the Dow Chemical Company for thirty-five years. With over forty years of experience, he is on the Board of Directors for Ashland and Xylem Inc. and received his bachelor's degree in economics and finance from Institut D'études Politiques de Paris.

Please share a little bit about your leadership background.

I was the CEO of Sealed Air for five years, between 2012 and 2017, and have retired since then. Before that, I spent my whole career at the Dow Chemical Company, starting as a salesman in Paris, France, and ended up as an executive VP in the executive committee in charge of one division. Sealed Air is a packaging company listed in the S&P 500 and the inventor of bubble wrap. It today is the global leader in protective packaging and protein packaging.

Managers are in oversupply. Leaders are in short supply. There is a world of difference between a manager and a leader. Being a leader has nothing to do with hierarchy. I have witnessed low-level employees who were extraordinary leaders. My definition of a leader is the one you go to because you trust him or her. You trust the judgment, the counsel, and the advice. A leader is somebody who has managed to instinctively create that trust.

What are key leadership skills that leaders need most during this time?

In very tough times, a leader has to be optimistic, yet realistic; a leader has to have faith and be able to communicate that faith. A leader is calm and he or she projects it. Leaders have to think that it's going to be okay. They need to be resilient and persistent, showing stamina.

The leader's number-one role is to communicate faith in the future; communicate with optimism while ensuring trust at the same time. A leader always tells things as they are and treats others as adults. You don't make it up because people remember what you told them, and it has to match.

Leadership is the art of creating "followship." People don't follow you because you are the supervisor but because they have decided that you walk the talk, that what you say and do make sense, that it is "worth the trip" to fight for what you try to build, and that you are taking them to the right place. You give them purpose.

If they had to develop this je ne sais quoi attitude around their leadership, what else would you tell them?

I'd say to them what I said to the Sealed Air employees when I made my farewell speech as I retired: "I am asking you all one thing. I am asking you to be courageous." Courage is a very unique skill. To be courageous means that you have to be passionate, accept that you're not necessarily right, but that you have the will to stand up and express yourself when you see an opportunity or there is something wrong. And above all, offer solutions to grab the opportunity or correct the issue. Being courageous will demand more work from you and will take you out of your comfort zone! But if you create "followship" as others believe in the idea, they will see you as a courageous leader. I also told them, "If you are courageous, everything's possible, and everything's going to be alright because that is the beginning of great things, and there is nothing to fear."

Connect with Jerome on LinkedIn.

19
Elevate and Inspire Others

Open Doors and Create Opportunities

How do you uplift and inspire others? One way is to open doors and create opportunities for others to thrive, fairly supporting them to reach their full potential. Leaders are looking for talent as much as talent is looking for opportunities to grow and contribute. As a leader, fairly opening doors is crucial. And to be fair requires familiarity with your team's skills, strengths, and challenges, in other words, connecting with your team and knowing them well.

When there is an opportunity, open the door for those qualified to go for it and give it their best. Do you remember what it was like wanting to ascend through the ranks? If you are in a position where you have the privilege to appoint talent to different roles, remember to "send the elevator back down" and reach out to people who aspire to one day reach your position. Help them by introducing them to other leaders across the organization, industry, and other connections that can support their ambitions and career goals.

This matter highlights the importance of DE&I (diversity, equity, and inclusion). Suppose we only feel comfortable with a particular set of people because they look, sound, and talk like us. In that case, you will be limited in the opportunities you're making available to all your talent. One of the factors holding back women specifically from ascending through the senior leadership ranks is not having access to mentors, sponsors, and the informal networks that their counterparts have. As a leader, you can be doing a great deal of good by introducing women in your circles to other senior leaders. Open doors to those introductions and allow them to expose their value. Being intentional and deliberate in making those introductions will generate opportunities for their growth and service in a higher capacity.

Safe leaders don't feel threatened by talent. They embrace it and encourage it. You know when someone working for you is potentially overqualified or capable of potentially surpassing you in terms of the organizational hierarchy. Contribute to your talent and let everybody's strengths elevate them. Be the sounding board and mirror for them to see what those strengths and potential are. Unfortunately, some people have a higher perception of themselves than their work shows. Those people require coaching from your end to highlight the areas that they need to improve. You can also create opportunities for your people by bringing up their accomplishments to your senior leaders and peers. Shining a light on your team's performance will help you promote what you do as a business and it also highlights the individuals responsible.

Appreciate Their Contributions

Like the *Five Love Languages* (Chapman, 2010), people express and receive appreciation based on their preferences. For some, appreciation is an acknowledgment for a job well done, more flexibility with the work schedule, or getting the break to pitch a new idea to senior management. To understand what form of appreciation speaks to your team members, pay attention to what they share about old projects, previous managers, or ask them directly.

Make it a habit to practice self-acknowledgment. Appreciating others' contributions will then become much easier for you. When people feel valued for their contributions, they are more likely to find meaning in their work and perform at their best. As a coach, one of the most prevalent gripes I hear from employees who aren't happy with their management is that they don't feel appreciated for their contributions or valued for their opinions. There are ample instances when leaders are delighted with their employees and yet don't make any effort to articulate this appreciation.

Appreciation is free. It only requires you to take a moment to highlight an attribute, a job well done, a problem handled well, or ideas well thought out. Acknowledgement and appreciation makes people smile and brings pep to their steps. It highlights that you're doing something well, and it encourages you to continue. As humans, we all need to feel *significant*. We want to be validated for our work—even though having an external locus of control is not the goal; it is to inspire. Leaders who know about this human need can use it as an opportunity to inspire and elevate others.

Recognize the Talent

Unlike appreciation, which is free, recognition typically involves a material display of appreciation. It can take many forms: getting paid time off, an award, a promotion, a salary increase, additional vacation days, or more resources at work. Stay closely connected to your people and your leaders to cultivate a culture of appreciation and recognition. Be honest if you are not able to reward them materially and share why.

In some cases, people don't know how to reach their next level. The standards are not clear, which creates a culture of confusion and favoritism. If you create and establish clear benchmarks for recognition, it removes the bias that some employees feel when someone else is recognized and they are not.

Empowering Questions for Reflection

1. How do you uplift and inspire others?
2. How do you open the door for those qualified to go for an opportunity and give it their best?
3. How are you introducing women in your circles to other senior leaders to create access to mentors, sponsors, and informal networks that allow them to expose their value and service in a higher capacity?
4. How do you contribute to your talent and let everybody's strengths elevate them?
5. How can you be the sounding board and mirror for your talent to see what those strengths and potential are?
6. How often do you create opportunities for your people by bringing up their accomplishments to your senior leaders and peers?
7. How do you practice self-acknowledgment?
8. How do you acknowledge, appreciate, and recognize your talent?
9. How do you establish clear benchmarks for recognition and remove the bias that some employees feel when someone else is recognized and they are not?

LEADER SHOWCASE: DORIS CASAP

"If every single person can feel part of the greater mission, that would be the best."

Doris Casap, MBA, is a former senior film and television executive, and now producer, investor, founder and CEO of Mother Films. Doris branched out after spending twenty-eight years working at HBO and leading a team as a Senior Vice President of Film Programming. She attended Vassar College and received her MBA from Harvard Business School.

Please tell us a little bit about you.

I live in New York and worked for HBO from the time I left business school until last fall [2019]. I was in charge of relationships with all the major studios, ran a team of ten people, and attended film festivals. It was interesting work. However, I was burnt out because I had also been incredibly active in political and social causes over the last five years. I needed to slow down and take a break. In the last year, I have sold two movies and am executive producing another movie right now.

I am an immigrant from Bolivia. My father worked for Bolivia in Foreign Service and then for the United Nations. We didn't have a lot of money at all. That idea of an immigrant where you have to produce, produce, and produce and achieve, achieve, and achieve is completely understandable. And yet, it can lead you down a path where you run roughshod over your own needs, your self-image, and your value as a producer versus your innate value as a person. Now, taking care of myself is a must.

How should companies approach developing their leaders?

It starts at the top. Honesty, clarity of mission, giving feedback should be at the top as well as supporting your leaders in being that way, too. Allowing different styles of leadership with those core values still in place is a big deal. And that gets you straight to diversity and inclusion. When you think about what it means to have your own edge in a leadership role, for me, it was my sense of humor. I find the absurd in everything. For instance, as top leaders, you need leaders who may be more serious, may be more soft-spoken, perhaps more outgoing, and cracking jokes. Empower them with training that speaks to the needs of today. Provide training about how you talk about differences, celebrating differences, and listening. How to listen is an important skill and an excellent tool for corporations to use to help their department heads and leaders.

Be clear in your strategy and your communication to your leaders so that they can do that in turn. Being on many diversity councils, I still found that a lot of the issues that would come up, even in these diverse settings, were about basic, good management skills: listening, following through, clarity, being available, making sure everybody is listened to and heard and has a role, and people understanding their roles and the way they play into the greater strategy so that they can feel appreciated. If every single person can feel a part of the greater mission, that would be the best.

You may connect with Doris through LinkedIn.

20

Developing Talent

"I love to mentor and advise the younger generations—especially women—on the realities of running their own businesses and how to set themselves apart from their competition."

–Cynthia Lett

Mentoring

Healing leadership can be a blast and personally rewarding when we put on our mentoring and coaching hats. We spoke at length about the role of mentors and sponsors in chapter 9. In this chapter, we delve into mentoring others.

Think about your favorite mentors. How do they show up for you? What kind of advice do they give you? What do you love about them as leaders? We all have a responsibility to mentor our people, and it begins with the spirit of contribution. Concurrently, while you're mentoring them, you'll also receive and learn in the process. Mentoring with curiosity leaves plenty of room to explore what you and your mentee are cocreating. What does your talent need to become the next version of who they are? The answer can be a two-way conversation, what they expect for themselves, and what you, as their leader, would like to see them become.

Mentors develop trust, safety, and honesty by listening mindfully, being impeccable with their word, not judging, but instead seeking to understand others' perspectives and challenging points of view curiously and respectfully. There is no age requirement for mentoring; mentors can be younger or older than their mentees. And typically, mentors have experience in the area of interest to their mentees. Mentoring your talent is an accessible and free vehicle for developing them.

How do you develop talent, especially under a virtual model and amid heightened concerns for people's safety and the likelihood of decreased engagement? Mentoring your team may be easier than you expect. Here's an example. As a leadership coach, I created the *Fearless Leadership Mastermind*™. As I mentioned, it is a six-month leadership development program where up to ten members meet weekly, virtually, in a group setting. The *Mastermind* setting provides every member an opportunity to bring up questions about the training curriculum and challenging situations where they need coaching and support. As their coach and mentor, I establish the guardrails for safety, confidentiality, privacy, mutual encouragement, and nonjudgment. Each member takes a turn to "check-in," and when one of the members asks a question about the training or a challenging situation at work, I make sure to answer the question and share insights that will benefit the whole group. If it helps, other group members also have the freedom to chime in and contribute to the person who asked the question. This framework is a very effective way to connect with your team, mentor them, and support them to contribute to each other. However, it requires that you possess foundational coaching skills and a structure that builds a framework for constructive discussion and dialogue. We'll discuss this topic momentarily.

When looking for your team's mentors, clarify what you both want them to get out of it. You may want them to expand their network across the organization or industry. They may need guidance and suggestions in a particular area, especially when innovating. Seeking the mentorship of others who are familiar with that area can save them headaches and wasted time. They may need support navigating the environment and can learn from other leaders in the organization about their respective groups.

Once the goals are clear, mentor them on creating an agenda. Perhaps they need to develop their emotional intelligence or business intelligence and you know other leaders who are highly emotionally intelligent or possess the business acumen these people need. Based on the team's individual needs, mentor them to be specific about why they are reaching out and narrow down the agenda.

Mentoring is a commitment to your team and your company. This level of care and connection is bound to enhance your team's engagement, and the business results will speak volumes about its effectiveness. Incorporate mentoring your team into your week, in the group setting, or as discussed earlier, individually. To guide your team about approaching others for mentoring, invite them to read chapter 9, "Develop Relationships." Happy mentoring!

Coaching 101

The leader who coaches builds and holds a safe environment and enables team members to work through situations that may be personally or professionally challenging, creatively solve tactical and strategic problems, generate ideas, and so on. The coach helps the team member feel empowered and confident in his or her abilities. These principles and coaching skills promote a growth-minded coaching culture and effective communication. These will support you to create a holistic foundation from which to help your team develop and address situations to deepen relationships professionally and personally. Use thoughtful occasions, such as regular check-ins, feedback sessions, and private or group meetings to coach team members and help them grow.

Learning these skills while earning a coaching certification has been pivotal in my career and transformational journey. I'm grateful for my dear teachers, Richard Michaels and Madhu Maron, Martha Lasley, Guthrie Sayen, and others for role modeling for us the power of coaching for transformation. The textbook, *Coaching for Transformation* (Lasley, Kellogg, Michaels, & Brown, 2011) is chock-full with the fundamental concepts every coach needs. I highly recommend it.

As a coach, your role is to keep your ego in check and bring awareness, intuition, curiosity, and natural flow to the conversation, listening on all levels. It requires you to be fully present, paying attention to the person while self-managing your state and emotions. To prepare for a coaching conversation with mindfulness, become aware of any *parts* of you that may not be present, the *parts* that may be judging, problem-solving, analyzing, and so on. This awareness will help you harness a critical mass of your highest Self and coach from this stance versus showing up frustrated, angry, resentful, and so on. Clear your head, take a few deep breaths, and set your plan aside before you begin a coaching conversation—that's how you show up fully present.

A coach calls out the team member's power and is not necessarily wearing the hat of the subject matter expert in the room to problem-solve on behalf of the team member. As a coach, you establish the guardrails for a healthy and productive conversation that honors the knowledge, freedom, and resourcefulness of all involved. Coaches value diversity and the fullness of a person's experience, for example, when a person feels both excited about a promotion and fearful of the challenge. We believe that everyone is positioned to be creative and to know themselves better than anyone else. These beliefs help you show up to a coaching conversation embracing all that is possible. In simple terms, the coaching conversation arc includes the topic or agenda, the transformational or coaching conversation using empowering questions, and the conclusion, which consists of a combination of a call to action and an acknowledgment of the person.

The most prominent tool in your coach toolkit is asking *empowering questions*. Use them while coaching, mentoring, and developing team members, and with colleagues, friends, and family members who rely on you for guidance. Once you create a private, safe space and time frame to host a compelling coaching conversation and bring your whole Self in, ask *empowering questions* to evoke reflection, insights, and actions. You've seen them throughout this entire book. And the first question to establish the agenda is, what's on your mind? Or perhaps you have a specific topic in mind related to work that is the main agenda for the conversation.

Empowering questions are open ended, carry no judgment, and also elicit exploration and clarity. Empowering questions start with words such as *how*, *what*, *who*, and *when*. Why questions are typically not empowering and project judgment. Whenever possible, replace why questions with what or how questions, for example, replace why did you do that? with what did you intend to do? Some of the few instances when why questions are powerful are when asking, why do you want to be successful? or why is that important?

When in a coaching conversation, in addition to asking empowering questions, rely on your intuition and social awareness to acknowledge what is present and call it out, for example, "I'm sensing this is very exciting for you," or "I'm noticing some apprehension," and wait for a reply. We call these "natural openings," a chance to explore more of what is alive in the moment for the other person. You can also bring up what is present for you as you listen to an insight from the person and use it to acknowledge him or her, for example, "Thanks for bringing that up. It is a nice reminder." Follow the conversation flow by using the answers to ask follow-up questions, which explains the significance of listening on all levels.

Ask quality questions to generate high-quality answers and solutions. A few helpful and classic empowering questions include: What's important about that? What can you improve based on what happened? How can you break that down into smaller steps? What's another way to look at this? If you only focused on one thing, what would it be? How can I support you going forward? What are your choices? What do you care about in this situation?

When asking yourself questions, ask empowering ones. Get curious and look to understand the root cause, how to fill the present needs, and how to move forward to honor your "endgame" by asking yourself open-ended, quality questions. Every situation will have its own line of inquiry, and when you form the habit of primarily asking empowering questions, they will roll off your tongue.

To close the coaching arc, conclude with a statement acknowledging the person's progress—avoid making it about you, and if appropriate, create a "call to action" to help the person move forward, for example, what will you do after this? And you can even invite your team member to take on a challenge related to the coaching session. For example, what about reaching out to one person each day for the next week? And be flexible about whether or not the person accepts it.

Trust your instincts. The solutions will emerge as you ask these types of questions. In the process, your team will also learn how to ask and use these questions. As you role model for them, the culture overall benefits as a by-product. These coaching tools will prove invaluable and transform how you interact, support, and develop the talent and people who rely on you for guidance and encouragement. Leverage their resources and help them see their own potential.

Invest in the Future

Every single employee facilitates the benefits to consumers by being part of the *machine* that creates the company's product and services. Yet, training our talent is sometimes relegated to checking off a box once a year or so, if at all. The fear may be, what if I train them and they leave? My retort is, what if you don't train them and they stay? I heard these questions and they have stuck with me over the years. Developing our talent is one of the areas where I feel deeply passionate. Even when my role did not directly involve talent development, I proactively got involved and my team took ownership for coordinating the resources for the people in the Technology Division of my company to have access to technical and soft skills training.

A team that is up to date on the technology, trends, compliance, regulations, processes, and in the know with the vision of the company are your biggest assets. As a leader, investing in the future of your talent and their development is not only the right thing to do, it's the smart thing to do. Developing talent and leadership development require going inward to go outward. You must have reliable, scalable, and sustainable methods to develop leadership teams for individual, team, and corporate success.

In the past, many of us learned leadership skills on the job and didn't receive a foundation that set us up for success. We were lucky if the role models around us were inclusive and fair leaders. Unfortunately, that's not always the case, and our role models may not have the self-awareness to lead, engage, and influence the talent in a way that engenders an inclusive culture that is productive and inspired. When you know your people, you can assess the type of development that they require.

If you're not developing your people, this is a compassionate wake-up call. And if you are, consider the effectiveness of the training. From the time I decided to go into business for myself, I'm methodical about identifying the next set of skills I need to advance and deliver more value to the leadership dream teams I develop. Over the past five years, I've invested over fifty thousand dollars in my self-development. Formal training, combined with mentoring and coaching, will ensure that your people are continuously growing and preparing to meet the demands of the future and fulfill the organization's vision. Some roles may require more training than others, but all leadership roles must ensure that each leader is self-led, which does not happen automatically.

Empowering Questions for Reflection

1. How do your favorite mentors show up for you? What kind of advice do they give you? What do you love about them as leaders?
2. What does your talent need to become the next version of who they are?
3. How do you develop talent, especially under a virtual model and amid heightened concerns for people's safety and the likelihood of decreased engagement?
4. How do you envision using "What's on your mind?" as an empowering question to establish a coaching conversation agenda?
5. How do you plan to use *what* and *how* high-quality questions to support your team?
6. How are you proactively investing in developing your talent to have access to technical, soft, and leadership skills training?
7. How well do you know your people to assess the type of development that they require?

LEADER SHOWCASE: JANNETTE SANTOS

"Companies that provide a people-centric culture will be the ones to attract the best talent under these circumstances."

Jannette Santos, MBA, CPP, is a Certified Payroll Professional with the American Payroll Association and has over twenty years of payroll experience in the financial services industry. Jannette received her BS in architecture from the NY Institute of Technology and her MBA in accounting from the University of Phoenix.

Jannette, please share your background with us.

I am currently the payroll manager for a major hedge fund in New York City and I've been in financial services for most of my career, specifically in human resources. I have about thirty years of experience, working in many different environments and cultures.

What are the most critical leadership skills that leaders need?

Under these circumstances, soft skills are going to be the most critical leadership skills to hone. We're always focused on our careers and how we can get to the next level, but this pandemic has put things in perspective as to what's really important. Showing empathy and gratitude for the people around us is more important now than ever.

How have you seen those soft skills used effectively, whether in your current work environment or the past?

The company that I work for currently is going above and beyond to make employees feel included now that they are isolated and may be feeling a little disconnected. We are using technology to schedule sessions with them to chat about things that are not work related and checking on them to see how they're doing personally with their families.

How do you recommend organizations develop their leaders during this time?

We have found that many companies have stepped up to face the new needs for virtual training. That's something that we're trying to take advantage of now more than before. I know I have a training budget for my team, and we would prefer to send them out to actual conferences to have sessions where they can ask questions and interact with the rest of the attendees. Taking advantage of technology and online training opportunities will be very valuable.

Coaching our leaders and sensitivity training are going to be the focus at least for the foreseeable future. I know my company is not intending for us to come back to the office at all in '21. That's a whole year to start planning for coaching and training sessions to help our leaders navigate through these difficult times.

What final message would you like to leave for our audience?

It's getting back to that human factor. We have to realize and understand that we're all humans going through our challenges during these times, and we need to put ourselves in other people's shoes. We may not fully understand what they may be going through. Not everyone shares their personal experiences, but think about them and keep them engaged to make it a better culture for everyone.

You may connect with Jannette on LinkedIn.

21

Be Persistent Not Perfect

"Take Imperfect Action"

Growing up as an immigrant in the United States and apart from my brothers, I was raised as an only child from the time I was five years old and my parents divorced. During my upbringing, I was often told to behave, not cause any problems, and be a good girl. Throughout my school years, I strived for perfect grades. In high school, I earned straight As. However, throughout college I struggled to adjust to the environment after being in the country for only four years. No matter how hard I tried to get the *perfect* college grades, I could never attain them. Once I became a young professional, I wanted to do my best and didn't always achieve that, either.

Adjusting to the truth and the reality that I couldn't be *perfect* became inevitable. I had been chasing a ghost. Today, I call myself a *recovering perfectionist*. As a leader in the industry, my perfectionism drove me to produce high-quality output, and it also pushed me to demand from my team the same level of quality I expected from myself. It wasn't always fun to work for me—even I will admit that.

Drawing from my self-awareness helps me realize how important it is to take "imperfect" action and be persistent in my business and personal life—that means doing *the best I can* at the moment without striving for the elusive state of *perfection*. I still catch myself wanting to make things perfect and quickly release it to keep adding value, *imperfectly*. As a leader, being a perfectionist prevents us from acting with urgency and decisiveness. And it can stifle our teams when we project it onto them. Doing the best that we can today is all we can do.

Take imperfect action and practice steps to move forward every day, including aligning your mindset to believing that what you want is possible. I won't pretend or mislead you into thinking that you can close your eyes, wish for what you want, click your heels, and it will magically appear. It requires you to show up and do the work. Bodheart's founder, mentor, and coach, Fabienne Fredrickson, taught me early on as I started the business venture to "take imperfect action." I thank her every day for making such an impact and helping me elevate my growth mindset and business.

Learn from your experiences, and if you don't see satisfactory results, tweak, pivot, iterate, and keep trying. You are a role model, remember? You've heard the saying, "Done is better than perfect." How is perfectionism impacting you today as a leader? What ideas are you holding back because they're not quite perfect yet?

Stumble Forward

When we fail, it is easy to stop trying. Sometimes, we negotiate our goals and settle. No matter the results, don't give up. Keep pivoting your way to the solutions, even when they don't turn out exactly how you anticipated. Sometimes the outcome is even better than you expected. I bring you the story of Colonel Harland Sanders (1890–1980), an honorary colonel (Klein, 2019), to inspire you and your team to stumble forward. It shows how perseverance, dedication, and ambition, along with hard work, can create success regardless of your age (Nafte, 2017). If you fall, dust yourself off, get up, and keep going.

At the age of sixty-five, after running a restaurant for several years, Harland Sanders found himself penniless. After retiring, he began collecting a monthly Social Security check of one hundred and five dollars. Harland loved his chicken recipe and got rave reviews from those who tasted it. So, he opted to sell the world on his chicken recipe. At first, Harland traveled door to door to houses and restaurants all over his neighborhood and later expanded his territory. He would cook his fried chicken on the spot for restaurant owners. If the owner liked the chicken, they would enter into a handshake agreement to sell it.

Colonel Harland Sanders heard 1009 nos before succeeding and building his Kentucky Fried Chicken (KFC) franchise, selling his trademark quick-frying chicken coated in his secret recipe of eleven herbs and spices. By 1964, he had six hundred franchises and eventually sold his company for two million dollars but remained its brand ambassador. In 1976, he was ranked as the world's second-most recognizable celebrity.

Every day is a new day and brings a new window of opportunity to create what we desire in our lives. Reset from what didn't work out yesterday. Revisit your goals (which implies that you have goals that you are working toward.) Without purpose, life can feel empty and humdrum. Follow your passions and dreams in business. It's easy to feel defeated and give up—it seems impossible or daunting at times, except when you are passionately working on a project that is meaningful to you—even when others don't get behind it, it breathes life into you and your team. My mentor, Steve Harrison from the Quantum Leap program, also used the phrase, "stumble forward," to close our online training. All the lessons begin to "click" and propel you forward. Take these lessons, too and apply what serves you.

What is my most significant takeaway from Colonel Sanders's story? He inspires me to be steadfast in pursuing my compelling vision of helping companies develop their leadership dream teams. And I also think of him every time I hear the word *no*. I know it's never too late to pursue my dreams.

How does his story land for you?

Stumble forward.

LEADER SHOWCASE: TELLE WHITNEY

"Each of you has something important and revolutionary to contribute. I encourage you to take risks and go for it."

Telle Whitney, PhD, is the CEO and Women in Technology expert at Telle Whitney, LLC. Telle is also the cofounder of The Grace Hopper Celebration. She has over thirty-three years of experience and led the Anita Borg Institute for Women and Technology for fifteen years as the CEO. Telle has a BS from the University of Utah in computer science and a PhD in computer science from Caltech.

Telle, let's start by telling us a little bit about yourself.

I passionately believe that women belong at the table creating the technology that changes all of our lives. That's my driving force. I came to Silicon Valley a long time ago, and at the time, I was passionate about participating in creating technology. I worked in semiconductors for many years. I'm a startup person and love the idea of creating ideas and products from scratch. And it's still true for me today.

Can you tell us a little bit about the Grace Hopper Celebration?

The Grace Hopper Celebration, founded in 1994 by Anita Borg and me, is a conference that celebrates the achievements of women in technology. At the 2019 Grace Hopper Conference, there were twenty-six thousand attendees. There's a large recruiting fair; it's a chance to get internships and jobs. There are well over three hundred companies that attend. Most bring their technical women, so Grace Hopper becomes an integral part of their retention strategy.

What are the most critical leadership skills leaders need?

The essential skills are resiliency and empathy. You need to approach today with the belief that you're going to get through it and not only survive but also find a way to thrive. Many team members are struggling with what to do, and to approach what you're doing with empathy is very important.

It is also important to be able to pivot. Many of the plans that we made were done with a different vision for the future. And understanding that you still have great ideas—but that you need to be able to pivot and approach the problems that you want to solve differently and more effectively—is important. If I reflect on my career, resiliency and determination are what have led me to my success.

What has led me to be an effective leader is the ability to overcome obstacles. I joined one startup, but we only had funding for six months. We had a vision of creating a voice-over processor, and we didn't even know if the company would exist. But you show up, create a product, and we were sold to a chip company and were quite successful. And I took over the Anita Borg Institute because my close friend and the founder, Anita Borg, had brain cancer. The organization didn't have any legs. We didn't know where our next paychecks were going to come from. And yet, we had people in the community who believed in what we were doing and were able to provide initial financial support. And we kept focused on the importance of women being at the table and continuing one day at a time to move forward. It became one of the most influential organizations worldwide in this space.

Please connect with Telle at www.tellewhitney.com or LinkedIn.

Learn as You Go

Taking *imperfect action*, *stumbling forward*, and *learning as you go* are a powerful trio fortified by a growth mindset. Take imperfect action and practice steps to move forward every day, including aligning your mindset to believe that what you want is possible.

Take appropriate steps to communicate goals and expectations, use what you currently know and what you do to enlist the stakeholders to be curious, evolve with the solution as the different components become known. Showing your team what perseverance looks like will support them in believing in themselves, their goals, and encourage them not to give up when things don't look perfect or the outcomes are not as planned. Adapting a *learning as you go mentality* that's in step with an agile, iterative approach makes you, as an organization, a nimbler and more responsive partner. If you are a leader with big ideas, who talks the big talk but doesn't implement, that also becomes part of your personal brand and reputation. Become a leader who puts into practice what you preach, someone with high integrity and character. The world needs you.

Empowering Questions for Reflection

1. How do you take imperfect action and practice steps to move forward every day?
2. What experiences can you learn from, tweak, pivot, iterate, and keep trying?
3. How is perfectionism impacting you today as a leader?
4. What ideas are you holding back because they're not quite perfect yet?
5. What is your most significant takeaway from Colonel Sanders's story? How does his story land for you?

LEADER SHOWCASE: KATRINA FUHRMAN

"Everyone is responsible for finding their own way to be innovative and manage their own presence on a virtual platform."

Katrina Fuhrman is a Project Manager and has worked for Verizon for over seven years. Through Forbes School of Business and Technology at the University of Arizona Global Campus, she is an MBA candidate expected to graduate in June 2021. Katrina is a Golden Key International Honor Society member, cofounder of the UAGC MBA Club, and holds undergraduate degrees in psychology, sociology, and business administration.

Please tell us what you do and what your background is.

I moved into sales and business after studying psychology as an undergrad. As I started moving up within management, I had the opportunity to join Verizon Corporate. I've been working my way away from a sales role and now into a supporting role. It's been an incredible journey in gathering a lot of different information, different experiences, and seeing things from all sides: from a consumer perspective, a sales perspective, and now from a supporting role.

How do you suggest companies approach developing their leaders?

The way I see it, it's a top-down approach. Upper management needs to implement and practice self-care, so when they're speaking with their people, they can be patient and not fly off the handle because of the stress and pressure that's coming in from the world around them, which all of us are feeling right now. It's a very saturated, stressful market. But if you take care of yourself first, your people will see that, and that's what they will replicate and pass down as a practice to their teams as well. It's a very passive approach, and it happens just by setting your own example. And then, a more proactive approach is scheduling weekly one-on-ones and turning your camera on to let people see what you're going through and make it a more human connection. Find ways to pivot. That's all you can do. You have to adjust for your current state of business and what's suitable for your action plan in the long run.

What are your last words for our audience?

Technology has developed over the years, and every generation has become more engrossed in it. Due to being forced to stay home during the last year, all humans worldwide are now fully immersed in the digital platform. Now, everyone is responsible for finding their own way to be innovative and manage their own presence on a virtual platform. That's really where your personal brand comes into play. And it's the only thing that you have control over. Companies shouldn't own it for you. It should be something that comes from within. And that's how you can connect, grow, and continue to develop as a human being. Even if you're stuck within your four walls like I am, make sure you make time for that.

Katrina is available to connect on LinkedIn.

22

Show Vulnerability

"Vulnerability is being willing to express the truth no matter what—the truth of who you are, the essence at your core, what you are feeling at any given moment."

—Oprah Winfrey

Overcome Fear

There are things you know and things you don't know. While you may feel very comfortable getting in front of a group and showing how much you know about a topic, providing guidance, and demonstrating your expertise, there is as much value, if not more, in letting people know what you don't yet know. An aspect of healing leadership is making room for people to be vulnerable and authentically express their concerns, dreams, fears, and ambitions. A safe leader shows vulnerability.

What are your biggest fears? Most likely, your team and others in your organization have similar ones. This vulnerability creates a bond from which collaboration and teamwork can lead to a clear path forward. We all have fears. Fear of failure transcends all levels of leadership. When your leaders show up vulnerable, let them know they have your support. This behavior will trickle down to the entire organization. Take a pause, acknowledge, and let them know you heard them and are willing to work with them. As you get to know your people and notice when they exhibit fear, vulnerably coach them. Ask them, what is your biggest concern or fear? What can we do to support you?

The best way to overcome any fear is to call it out and then dissect it. For example, you may be afraid of not finishing the project on time, that the client will not be happy with the results, or that the team disagrees with the direction that you're going. Once you pinpoint the fear, begin to ask empowering questions about it. What would happen if we don't finish the project on time? What can we do to mitigate the risks of not delivering the results the client wants? How can we prevent disagreements regarding our direction? In my view, fear is nothing other than a signal that you should pay attention to what you fear. It is a built-in warning mechanism. If we listen to it with wisdom, we can prevent messy situations. However, if we give in to it, we feel paralyzed and overwhelmed.

As a leadership team coach, we often deal with fears. I view them as messengers to help us get more clarity, question whether we are on the right track, and pinpoint what could derail us along the way. Typically, fear helps us prepare in a way that we usually wouldn't. Combined with our intuition, fear can be a tremendous resource. Questioning your fears helps you befriend them with curiosity and compassion, understanding that they are sources of insights and knowledge. What are your biggest fears today? And what is the message they're sending you? Listen to them carefully and heed their warnings.

Seek Support

"A fall is never final unless you stay on the ground."

—Marie Forleo

As a leader, showing vulnerability is also about relying on expert advice, seeking diverse opinions, and asking for help when you need it. Some of us grew up with the belief that asking for help was a sign of weakness. As a conscious leader who is self-aware about what he or she knows and does not know, seeking support is a sign of wisdom and self-care. Asking for help is another avenue that allows others to contribute to you not only as individuals but also as a group. You bring teams together when you collaborate and contribute from each other's subject of expertise. The by-product is an outcome that represents the efforts of the collective groups. If the focus is to create value in the end, asking for support can accelerate the results you're seeking on behalf of your business.

On a personal level, knowing when to ask for help can be enriching. As mothers, fathers, and partners, we take on a lot of responsibility for various reasons. We've used our mothers, fathers, and caregivers as role models or have a script about what a wife, mother, husband, partner, or father should do. We unintentionally bite off more than we can chew at times, overcommit, and don't say no as often as we should. Setting healthy boundaries, knowing when it's time to say no, and asking for help would tremendously benefit us. Sometimes, even our partners get used to us not relying on them, and after a while they stop offering to help us, too.

If you happen to be like this—I was—this message is for you. With love, stop the madness. It's human to ask for support, express your needs, and leave it open for the person to help you as he or she is able. Express your needs and then ask, how do you think you can help? and wait for the answer. However, we must ask since people cannot read our minds—yet! Telling people what to do can be off-putting and infringe on their "freedom"—I'm speaking as someone who values choice and freedom. Asking them what they're willing to do to support you is empowering for them and creates realistic expectations on your end. It's not fair to complain about having to do it all yourself if you have not taken the responsibility to express that you need help.

As you appreciate contributing to others, in a similar fashion others enjoy contributing to you. Give them the chance to do so by asking for support. What can support you right now? Who can provide that support? Let's get asking! And enjoy the help.

Be Humble

Another expression of vulnerability is displaying humility. When you admit what you don't know and get curious, you open up many possibilities to learn, grow, and let others exert and showcase their strengths. As leaders, we don't need to have all the answers all the time. In fact, it's not an answer that's most valuable. What's priceless is our level of resourcefulness to figure out how to find the solution. And then role-modeling for our teams and loved ones how we "fish"—as there will always be something we don't understand. When curiosity is substituted for the shame or embarrassment of not knowing the answer, everybody learns.

I am often humbled when I have conversations with my son who is thirteen years old. I didn't go through elementary school in the United States. When I ask him about school and what's going on with some of his classes, he tells me. There are times when he's learning material that I did not learn at his age when I lived in the Dominican Republic. I let him know when I don't know something, and I beam with pride when he proceeds to explain it to me in detail. Being humble about my knowledge, or lack thereof, inspires him to pour into me. And it helps him validate his knowledge base, which inspires confidence in his abilities.

Vulnerability is inspiring to our teams, too. Let them show you their unique value. You open the door and help them walk through it when you admit what you don't know. Your contribution to them is to mentor them and also share your strengths with them. As a humble leader, you can easily step aside to showcase and highlight your team's accomplishments—at any organizational level. When you share the spotlight, and their success does not intimidate you or make you feel inadequate, you'll benefit from a sense of joy and admiration for their talents and accomplishments.

As a humble leader, you see your team's growth and successes as if they were your own and celebrate them equally. Lead with humility, vulnerability, and confidence in what you know and who you are. It's a privilege to serve your team and your talent. It is a remarkable blessing and an honor not to be taken lightly. How can this perspective bring you closer and more connected to your team?

Empowering Questions for Reflection

1. What are your biggest fears?
2. What is the message your fears are sending you?
3. What will support you right now?
4. Who can provide that support?
5. How can the perspective that "it's a privilege to serve your team" bring you closer and more connected to your team?

When supporting your teams to address their fears, ask:
6. What can we do to support you?
7. What would happen if we don't finish the project on time?
8. What can we do to mitigate the risks of not delivering the results the client wants?
9. How can we prevent disagreements regarding our direction?
10. How can I help?

LEADER SHOWCASE: CAROL MANN

"Feel the fear and do it anyway. Because if you're not feeling fear, you're not growing and making change."

Carol S. Mann is the CEO at Mann Solutions Group, LLC. Leveraging over thirty years of expertise, her company specializes in high-growth change management, turnaround consulting, and interim management. Carol is a board member of the Abramson Center for Jewish Life, attended Lycoming College and Philadelphia University, and taught courses at Wharton Business School.

Carol, please share a little bit about your background.

I turn around troubled companies and help companies uncover hidden cash and profit in their businesses. I started turning around companies when I was nineteen. I've been a partner at two big-four consulting firms. And now I have my own firm specializing in the middle market because the middle market is underserved. It would have a big impact on the number of business failures in the United States if lower-end companies could get the help they need.

What is most critical for leaders to know and do today?

There are three qualities that I think are really important: One is humility. When people become afraid, they become protective and defensive. It's okay to admit to your company that you don't know or that you made a mistake. Whether it's with an employee or a customer, as leaders we should always be modeling the behavior we desire.

The third is to create a culture of humanity and kindness. If you're asking someone to be humble and then using humor, you can motivate people to do impossible things. And I'm the person that lays people off all the time. How can I do that and be respectful of what someone's going through if I don't have a kind way of approaching things? Focus on the good things to give them the room to be humble and exhibit those behaviors that you're looking for.

For the leaders looking to create a unique edge, what would you tell them?

I'm all about developing soft skills, how we engage with each other, how we relate to each other. Now, we have a workforce that is extremely educated, they spend their lives on their phones or computers, but they don't have a lot of soft skills.

And as a leader trying to develop an edge, I can say what I do for myself. I like to use humor, and I'm always learning, trying something I don't feel proficient at. It keeps me just a little bit off-balance, which on most days is very good. When you try something new that's physically unnatural to you, it brings out a different side of your personality. I challenge myself to try things that I know I'm not going to be good at.

I was paralyzed from the waist down; I'm not anymore, but I used to be a great dancer and a competitive cheerleader, but my feet don't work the same anymore. I take dance classes and I think, ugh, I used to be so good at this; that doesn't matter; what can I learn from this now? To challenge that edge for you to see things differently comes from challenging yourself and always pushing further in things that are not comfortable to you.

Connect with Carol at www.mannsolutiongroup.com or LinkedIn.

23

Deal with Conflicts Head-On

Solve Problems with Creativity

nhealthy conflict can be an insidious, invisible force, destroying team morale, relationships, and sabotaging outcomes. It is essential for a leader to have the courage to notice and address unhealthy conflict. *Healthy conflict* elevates the team to challenge ideas and raise the bar respectfully. However, when conflict strains relationships and interferes with teamwork and engagement, it becomes unhealthy. As we likewise deal with fear, looking at the disagreement and facing it head-on is the start of healing it. Call it out, look at the situation objectively with the stakeholders, focus on the behaviors and events, not feelings or personalities, and listen carefully. Notice if these behaviors signal that there are hidden agendas at work.

Notice where there are differences and where there's common ground. For disagreements, clarify what's most important and develop a plan to address each conflict area. Please don't ignore it, but rather create a plan and follow through, celebrate the successes, be realistic about expectations, and be willing and open to experience positive changes oriented more toward creative problem solving.

Fear sometimes obstructs our ability to resolve conflicts swiftly. Fears may emanate from the assumptions we make about the people involved and the situation and potential repercussions. As the leader, your team is watching you handle these situations—and they can be challenging at times. You'll be mentoring them to learn how to address these difficult situations. Admitting that

240

you don't have all the answers will help you disarm and deescalate the parties' emotions. Turf wars, egos, assumptions, taking things personally, dishonesty, filibustering are components that interfere with conflict resolution. Use your experience and knowledge with empathy and understanding of the different perspectives. Like dandelions that sprout on a beautiful patch of grass, if you don't get to the root of the conflict, it will take over the landscape and spread everywhere before you know it. Where is your team experiencing conflict? Get creative, enlist their support, and start weed whacking.

Look at the Big Picture

Team morale suffers when leaders don't deal with conflicts head-on. Look at the big picture to understand the different perspectives, identify the source of the conflict, and pinpoint what is most important. What is most important about this situation? What is the ultimate outcome that we want, what is the conflict about, and how would resolving it lead us to the solution? Looking at the big picture will help you view the problem objectively and strategically from different angles.

You may need to follow-up and have one-on-one conversations with the different parties involved and ultimately group discussions to ensure you are all moving forward with clarity and with the same vision. Ultimately, you want to solve the conflict intelligently and with integrity. This is the time to show your character, decisiveness, and fairness. Looking at the big picture and what's most meaningful for the organization will help you align the parties with that purpose, minimizing the risk of bias.

The alternative to focusing on the big picture is getting lost in the details, going down a rabbit hole, and entertaining unnecessary drama. If you recall, one of the six human needs is *uncertainty*. On some level, conflict is an unhealthy vehicle to meet our needs for uncertainty, mixing it up for variety's sake. Methodically exploring the root cause of the conflict will be time well spent and will serve you and the team in the short and long term. Where are you experiencing areas of conflict, and what's most important in the big scheme of things?

Negotiate for a Win

When the needs of both parties are met, you have a win. For illustration purposes, let's assume that you're one of the parties involved in the conflict. As a conscious leader, pretending to be the only one who deserves the win puts you at a disadvantage. You must negotiate on both ends of the conflict to successfully resolve the differences. What are your biggest fears? What are the other party's biggest fears? In other words, what do you fear would happen if you don't resolve the differences? What are your biggest desires and theirs? If you're able to answer those questions, you have done your due diligence and you understand the issue on a deeper level.

Teaching your leadership teams and role modeling how to resolve conflict not only among the unit but also across the organization will make you a better partner. Conflict resolution is a skill set you can apply across all areas of life—to both your professional and personal relationships, and all types of financial negotiations from buying a home or a car to a new job.

Let's start by getting clear on what it is that both parties want in resolving the conflict. What is their ideal and what is your ideal? What would the best outcome from resolving these issues look like? What about them? How do you find out what their ideal is? Ask them questions about what it is they're looking to achieve. If everything were to go well, what has to happen?

Similarly, ask them about their fears. Some of the questions you can ask are, what would happen if we don't resolve this situation? What is at stake? What are your biggest challenges right now? Those challenges can translate into fears. Ask empowering questions throughout the process to identify the other person's ideas, desires, goals, and fears.

The next step is to present your arguments. If you're going to negotiate this conflict, you know your ideal. You know their intent. What about your statements about why you want what you want? Let's get very clear on your must-haves, your wants, and your nice-to-haves in this scenario. And last, it's all about making it a win-win for everyone. By now, you have done your homework and have acknowledged their fears, goals, desires, and yours. You have a clear picture of your facts and your arguments and can express them in the context of the other parties' fears, goals, and desires. Express what you want, and knowing what they want, propose a solution or offer they can't refuse. And that's because you're going to consider all the information you've gathered from them to position yourself in a way that they see is a fair resolution.

I hope that this approach helps you powerfully frame your conflict resolution conversation. Resolving conflict using this technique is akin to negotiating for a deal. And there are times when negotiating and feeling confident about negotiating can make a big difference in our future because the negotiations' ramifications can have long-term effects. Similarly, if we don't resolve the conflict, it could derail your effectiveness in leading, engaging, and influencing your team and others.

Empowering Questions for Reflection

1. Where is your team experiencing conflict?
2. What is most important about this situation?
3. What is the ultimate outcome that you want, what is the conflict about, and how would resolving it lead you to the solution?
4. Where are you experiencing areas of conflict, and what's most important in the big scheme of things?

To negotiate, ask:

5. What are your biggest fears? What are the other party's biggest fears? What do you fear would happen if you don't resolve the differences? What are your biggest desires and theirs?
6. What is their ideal, and what is your ideal?
7. What would the best outcome from resolving these issues look like?
8. If everything were to go well, what has to happen?
9. What would happen if we don't resolve this situation?
10. What is at stake?

LEADER SHOWCASE: KATE CONROY

"Work hard, be nice, take no shit."

Kate Conroy, MA, IOM, is the Vice President of Strategic Partnerships at the New Jersey Business & Industry Association. Kate has over eighteen years of experience. She is the co-host of a fun and lighthearted podcast called Other People's Business and received a BA from Winona State University and her MA from Georgia Southern University.

Let's start by sharing your background with our leaders.

I'm the vice president of Strategic Partnerships with NJBIA. It's the largest statewide business association in the country, with about ten thousand members. I help members figure out how to best use their marketing dollars when they're ready to start sponsoring events and getting in front of audiences with speaking opportunities. I also help run the events department; the two go hand-in-hand.

What leadership skills are the most critical these days?

Because of COVID, we're going through all kinds of transitions. I know it's not always easy to act like a leader. Sometimes, I just want to flip over a table, stamp my foot, and go to bed for three days. We could do that, but we would still have the problem three days later when we got out of bed and had to figure out what the next step is. You have to be practical and say to your team, I get it. I'm feeling the same way. And the problem is still this: What are we going to do? It's not a very fun part of leadership, it's challenging, but I think it's the thing that sets people apart. Anybody can be a good team member. A leader is somebody who says, alright, we just ran into this problem, it's not our fault, it's now our issue, let's problem-solve and fix it.

It's being able to pivot successfully, getting your team on board with the pivot, getting them to buy in because it's the right thing for the organization. I love Brené Brown's quote, "A leader's job is to figure out what the next right thing is and then do it."

No man is an island. I'm an extrovert, but I'm also an empath, which makes me need the introversion space sometimes. And as much as I like sitting on my couch doing nothing and talking to no one, I also would be devastated if I never had interactions like this again. I think we all went through a little casual depression over the summer and spring when being with people was not allowed. Being with people is a necessity; needing people is a necessity. And even if you are not somebody who likes to ask for help like me, it's not an option. It's lovely to think that you can do it all on your own, but in practical terms, it's impossible.

Pivot and keep your team involved in the conversation through every pivot—you can't problem-solve every problem alone. It's something I wish I had known at the very outset of my career because I hated being vulnerable. For years, I never wanted anyone to think that I was not capable of the job. I couldn't express weakness of any kind. It took a lot for me to get from there to here. But allowing yourself to be vulnerable and allowing your team to know that you need their help is huge.

You can connect with Kate at KConroy@NJBIA.org or LinkedIn.

24

Embrace Constructive Feedback

Take the Pulse—Receive Feedback

As a leader, receiving and providing constructive feedback will help you and your team grow. It can help you improve your outcomes, processes, and behaviors. Knowing how to receive and provide constructive feedback is a valuable skill. If you want to increase your self-awareness, ask for feedback. It takes courage and vulnerability along with humility.

A type of question to ask your leader or board is, from your perspective, what should I be focusing on to improve? Yikes! You can ask for feedback ahead of time so the person you're asking has time to prepare his or her response. This exchange can be an opportunity to have an empowering conversation to deepen the relationship and demonstrate your character. If it's related to a specific work initiative, you can ask your partners and team for feedback especially if there have been conflicts. To get a deeper understanding of how you can improve, you can ask, what could I be doing better in this role? On behalf of your organization or your team, you can ask your partners across the organization, what can we improve upon, as a team, to support you? or, how can we be more supportive? Notice that this doesn't imply that you're not already supportive.

Your questions should evoke thoughtfulness from your partners. Sometimes, it may seem easier to lead the witness by asking yes/no questions, such as, are we doing everything you need? or, everything is okay, right? We can do better than that. Use empowering questions instead. Regularly take the pulse of others who work with you and your team to understand their experiences. Their perceptions become their reality, and with a growth mindset, you may discover how to enhance processes, teamwork, and services.

Give Feedback

Let your team know how they're doing, show them an appreciation for their contributions. Mean the feedback you're giving them, be honest and impeccable with your word. And let them know what you know and what you don't know. Giving feedback often to your staff will help them stay on track: Here's what you're doing well, and here's what you can improve upon. When you decide to provide feedback, make it about their behavior and not their personalities. Feedback could be part of the coaching and mentoring conversation, for example, "I would love to give you some feedback regarding this project" (or this meeting, or the interaction you just had with this person).

Create a culture where giving and receiving feedback is welcomed and expected. This activity will help you increase your emotional intelligence. You may find that you have a perception of yourself that is different from how others perceive you. It's essential to know how you come across to others. How they perceive you is their reality. Understanding that will be informative, and it will help you take any necessary corrective actions. When giving constructive feedback, provide useful comments and suggestions that would contribute to a positive outcome, a better process, or improved behaviors. Provide encouragement, support, and corrective measures and direction to the person who's receiving it.

The formal review should not be the first time that someone hears your feedback. Make feedback part of your regular check-ins and declare that you welcome and appreciate both getting and providing it. In giving feedback, be watchful of biases. Notice if you treat your group members differently. When you may notice or point out someone's performance, you should provide the same feedback to people whatever their gender. For example,

I know that one of my clients received feedback that she was too aggressive because she asked for a promotion. Yet, her male counterpart asked for one, too, and he did not get that feedback. Ironically, the manager who provided that feedback was a woman. So, notice that biases are not gender specific; we all have unconscious biases. Note how fair and consistent your feedback is.

Keep in mind the individual and his or her uniqueness; don't compare the person to you. Look at the overall picture, focus on the role, the ultimate goals of the position, the performance expectations, and the perspective of building up the relationship. An effective style, albeit different from yours, isn't a problem if the person performs the role well. Be proactive with your feedback and not reactive. Be swift and brave, instead of waiting for the problem to become so severe that the damage is nearly irreparable. Be clear on your expectations for corrective action in terms of the time frame or the next steps a person can take if he or she is doing fine in the current position or role.

Although it may seem like more work, pausing, getting clear on feedback, providing input, and having that courageous conversation will build a more cohesive team. I knew I was having issues with one of my virtual assistants. I was able to sit down with her and share both what was working well and the areas where she needed to improve. She appreciated the feedback. Unfortunately, I noticed that she continued to behave in similar ways by not communicating openly and proactively, impacting the work that we were doing together. I was grateful for her contributions but ended up parting ways when it was clear that we were no longer aligned. Most organizations have a formal mechanism for feedback. Whether you do or don't, giving feedback is what's most important. Make it clear, actionable, and do it often.

Empowering Questions for Reflection

Requesting Feedback:

1. What should I be focusing on to improve?
2. What could I be doing better in this role?
3. What can we improve upon, as a team, to support you?
4. How can we be more supportive?

Giving Feedback:

5. How often do you give your team members feedback to help them stay on track?
6. How would you benefit by pausing, getting clear on feedback, providing input, and having that courageous conversation to build a more cohesive team?
7. What is challenging about giving regular feedback that is clear and actionable?

LEADER SHOWCASE: CHRIS EKREM

"We need leaders today who listen and are willing to make the tough calls."

Christopher M. Ekrem, MBA, FACHE, is currently the Vice President of Business Development & Operations at Wiederhold & Associates. He has over twenty-three years of experience and attended Baylor University and the University of Redlands, where he received his MBA.

Chris, why don't we start by providing your background?

I'm with Wiederhold and Associates. I grew up in Southern California, nestled in the orange groves. My mom would literally turn on the lights at night and say, "We've got to keep working; we've got to keep planting flowers and trees." I ended up doing lots of things that I didn't necessarily enjoy doing, but I learned the value of hard work early on. I went to school at Baylor University in Waco, Texas. Then, I spent nine years after I graduated working in California and Florida for various hospital organizations. I was in finance, decision support, clinical performance improvement, and spent a decade in health-care administration as a CEO and COO. I'll never forget sitting in a joint commission survey meeting and I almost started falling asleep. I thought, if I'm this bored today, I'm probably not doing something that I'm passionate about. I decided that I'd like to do some recruiting and coaching. And that's what I've been doing the past three years. I'm an executive coach and help a lot of people find their dream jobs.

What are the most critical skills that leaders should be developing?

Number one is transparency. Tell your people what's really going on. Number two, you must be very candid with your people.

One thing I hear all the time right now is, "I don't really have any good feedback. Nobody ever tells me what's going on." People crave honest feedback. It doesn't mean we have to be a hammer, but it does mean giving some good feedback and being honest about it. There's a book that I like called Cowboy Ethics. In Cowboy Ethics, it talks about the top ten things that people need to utilize for Wall Street today, the Code of the West. I'm a big believer in that particular mindset of riding for your brand, being honest, and all these different things, be tough, but fair, and so on. All those things we really need today for good leaders.

How should leaders develop a competitive edge?

We all have blind spots; you need somebody to help you figure out what they are to be better in life, somebody who has your best interests at heart, not just anybody, is number one. Find a mentor, coach, or somebody who can help you along the way to figure out what those blind spots are. And then, figure out what you should be doing as a leader on a day-to-day basis that would make a difference.

We need leaders today who listen and are willing to make the tough calls, which goes back to the old cowboy way. Go shake someone's hand. That handshake is worth more than any contract you'll ever have. That is the type of leadership we need today more than anything else.

You may connect with Chris at Chris@wiederholdassoc.com or via LinkedIn.

"There is a thing stronger than all the armies in the world. And that is an idea whose time has come."

—Victor Hugo

SECTION 3
Strategies for Personal Development

25

Bet on Yourself

Get Clear on Your Inspired Goals

We are in the homestretch. This is probably one of my favorite areas, personal development. After spending over twenty-five years in my corporate role, I decided to start my own business. Four years ago, I put all bets on myself. It was a scary proposition at first. I was new to entrepreneurship and had so much to learn. I had confidence in my knowledge, my abilities to learn and figure things out. But I knew I would have to learn how to run a business from scratch, how to market and sell, manage remote teams, and scale my new business.

One of my mentors, Tony Robbins, says, "Take the island and burn the boats." What does that mean to you? To me, it means to go for it—be all-in on yourself, believe in your resourcefulness, and don't hold back. Harness the belief that you have what it takes to become the leader that you want to become. Believe in your compelling future and vision and in your capacity for growth and contribution.

As I launched into entrepreneurship and founded my business and the months passed, I identified a clear set of goals as a business owner and in this new era of my life. Professionally, I wanted to devote myself to coaching, speaking, and training leadership dream teams. I wanted to write my first book and learn how to get free publicity. I desired to learn marketing and sales and about business development to grow and scale the business. I also knew I needed an engaging website and a consistent social media presence. On a personal level, I craved for more peace of mind and wanted to deepen my Yoga and meditation practice. As a divorced, single woman, I also wanted to meet and date a nice man and future partner, vacation domestically and internationally with my family and continue to create memorable experiences, and enjoy activities in the company of dear friends and loved ones.

During one of my coaching sessions with a Tony Robbins coach, I learned the importance of connecting a meaningful purpose behind each of these goals. These goals were indeed critical and worth pursuing—propelling me closer toward the compelling vision I held for the business and myself personally. Engaging in these goals meant that I could create a purposeful livelihood that would sustain my son and me financially and bring us more joy and an abundance of experiences.

As the founder of Fearless Women @Work° and ExecutiveBound°, I would have the flexibility to work from home and be more accessible to enjoy and support my son. I could leverage my strengths, skill sets, experience as a leader, help others, and contribute my knowledge, leaving a legacy through my partnerships, work, and books. Extending myself beyond my comfort zone while taking this journey meant rising to my full potential—becoming the leader I knew I could be, having a positive impact on the well-being of other leaders, leaving this world a bit better, and delighting myself along the way. And so, I did. I put all the chips on me and invested in my future.

At this stage in your leadership career, and Self-leadership, what would it look like to bet on yourself? What dreams are still worth pursuing? What goals have you perhaps given up on that could potentially bring you tremendous joy?

Make Continuous Learning Your Norm

People who aren't learning on a regular basis are sitting on their laurels and may be feeling stagnant or "flat" in their careers. This is my assessment from my interactions with thousands of people a year. For the most part, almost every leader I speak with regularly makes continuous learning the norm, whether it's listening to podcasts, reading textbooks or paperbacks, consuming digital media, or engaging with colleagues in person or virtually. Most value and prioritize learning. It's easy to get complacent, and there is some comfort in that, except when the fear of becoming obsolete kicks in. My recommendation is that you learn from a place of abundance, with peace, without a lacking or scarcity mentality. This is not about living in fear but rather rejoicing in the knowledge that's readily accessible 24/7. If you are already an unrelentingly curious person who enjoys learning, you're in good shape, keep doing it. And if you're not, take one microstep by committing to developing yourself in a small way such as reading a book a year or listening to a podcast once a week. Make it whatever you want. What matters most is what works for you and how it makes you feel.

To develop the capabilities to accomplish my inspired goals, I sprang into action and chose to make a substantial investment in my development through time, effort, and finances. I had already completed a twelve-month program at the Client Attraction Business School (now Boldheart) with Fabienne Fredrickson and graduated from a nine-month coaching certification program with Leadership that Works in New York City. In 2017, I joined Steve Harrison's Quantum Leap, a twelve-month program, and his National Publicity Summit to learn how to get free publicity and to write my first book. That's when I also enrolled in Ann McIndoo's book-writing program to learn her methodology on "speaking" my books. In 2017, I also attended my first Tony Robbins programs, "Unleash the Power Within" and his "Business Mastery" class in January 2018—both were transformational, rich experiences that propelled me into new realms of possibilities and exposed me to a network of growth-minded leaders and entrepreneurs. I hired a Wix.com expert to design my new website, copywriters, and brand experts to help me launch it successfully. I purchased software packages —*MeetEdgar, QuickBooks, Zoom, YouCanBook.me*, and others—to support my business operations.

In the last couple of years, I've had the privilege to expand my virtual team to enable the smooth operations of my leadership training Masterminds—coaching, consulting, and speaking services—and hired a virtual marketing team to launch campaigns. I'm also committed to integrating my business with an ongoing self-care practice through the Visionary Shaman Circle with my friend Sensei Victoria Whitfield's twelve-month program. Early in 2020, I earned a Mastermind professional certification through the *Knowledge Broker Blueprint* program with mentors Tony Robbins and Dean Graziosi. Because of all this, my business continues to grow, and my clients receive the support they are craving to develop as leaders and make a significant impact on their lives and businesses.

On the personal front, I signed up for Yoga classes, became a member at my local cross-fit gym, and joined dating apps before meeting my partner, Dave. Since branching out on my own, I've enjoyed trips to Italy, Punta Cana, the Dominican Republic, Washington, DC, and other destinations with my son, Kyle, and my mom. Ever since my father, Joe, passed away in 2002, I take my mom on vacations with us—and it brings me so much joy when she and my son have fun and spend quality time together. I also made it a top priority to self-care and connect with dear friends as often as possible.

On my ride to the gym or the grocery store, I play one of my favorite podcasts. I take a few minutes a day to read an online article or watch a You-Tube video. My son and I research topics on social studies, history, elections, and others on YouTube. At any point, I typically have a stack of books by my night table that I read and enjoy at my own pace. Whatever area interests you and whatever you wish to learn, you'll find it readily available and most likely for free somewhere in the cyber world. Get hungry for knowledge and become insistently curious about the possibilities you can create. When it relates to your self-development, what lights you up? And what will you commit to doing once you finish this book?

Empowering Questions for Reflection

1. "Take the island and burn the boats." What does that mean to you?
2. What would it look like to bet on yourself?
3. What dreams are still worth pursuing?
4. What goals have you perhaps given up on that could potentially bring you tremendous joy?
5. When it relates to your self-development, what lights you up?
6. What will you commit to doing once you finish this book?

LEADER SHOWCASE: NICOLE WILKINSON

"One of the greatest things you can do is never stop learning."

Nicole Wilkinson, MBA, has been a Human Resources Generalist at Ocean State Job Lot over the last four years. She received her MBA degree from Salve Regina University and BA from the University of Rhode Island.

Can you share a little bit about your background ?

I started my journey at Ocean State Job Lot as an intern in the Leadership and Organizational Development Team. And one of my greatest projects that I still carry with me every day is our diversity and inclusion training. I see so much value in that today. It impacted who I am in my role and how I continue to learn, grow, and work with other people.

What would you suggest companies do to develop their leaders?

Companies need to encourage learning and inclusiveness. For me, the greatest thing about Ocean State Job Lot is that no matter what level you are, any idea is heard. Whether it's a silly idea or a great idea, it brings so much value and encourages creative thinking. For me, contribution is something that I strive for. I love to contribute, help others, and think about how we can improve different processes.

You work with Bob Selle, who we also interviewed. What's it like to operate, develop, and grow as a leader under these conditions?

From the start, Bob has always pushed understanding individual needs. What's going to motivate Ginny? What's going to encourage

Nicole? They may be different things, but how can we tie that back to the business? Speaking from a personal standpoint, each year I volunteer in Haiti. And right away, Bob was so encouraging.

Operating in the space of feeling cared for and supported by your management, how do you show up to work?

It all comes back to motivation. If we understand that Nicole likes to volunteer in Haiti, what can we do to help her and contribute to a cause that means so much to her? It's going to make me want to help this business grow and move forward. It's like an equal playing field; they help me in one way and I'll help them in another.

What advice would you give to leaders about how to create a unique edge?

One of the greatest things you can do is never stop learning—asking different questions, understanding why processes might exist today, suggesting ways that you could improve operations. Understand the business, encourage different learning, and welcome ideas about how we can further grow the business.

For people who may be intimidated from expressing their ideas, get out of your comfort zone. With businesses, it's so important to understand that you can't stay comfortable. I've learned the most from the things I was the most uncomfortable doing.

You can connect with Nicole on LinkedIn.

26

Create Opportunities

Be Resourceful

When you are into self-development, you embody an identity of resourcefulness, creating opportunities everywhere you turn from networking with interesting personalities and making connections in special groups you join. With a new level of self-awareness, you gravitate toward situations that generate the opportunities you are seeking. Creating a concise elevator pitch that outlines *what you do*, *who you do it for*, and *how you do it* provides a wealth of knowledge to the people you are meeting. In conjunction with what brings you joy and inspiration, you can quickly share how you add value, what drives you, and how they could relate to you and you to them. Here's one version of my elevator pitch:

"Hi, my name is Dr. Ginny Baro. I'm an international motivational speaker and leadership coach, career strategist, and number-one bestselling author. I partner with organizations to develop leadership dream teams and collaborate with individuals looking to get promoted or transitioning into a new phase of their careers. I have delivered leadership training, coaching, and keynotes for Fortune 500 clients and impacted global audiences larger than seven thousand. When I'm not working, I enjoy everything the outdoors has to offer, dancing Latin music, and spending time with friends and loved ones, including my thirteen-year-old son, Kyle."

The wider you expand your circle of influence, the more you'll be able to tap into all the resources available to you, from finding the services and support you need to connecting with them. Your resourcefulness supports your faith in yourself when you take on a new initiative, even when you don't know all the steps. Your belief in your resourcefulness is a source of confidence that lets you leap and take the opportunity, knowing that you will be able to figure it out as you go. Lean on your support network and approach your interactions as relationships, not transactions. You will generate a pool of knowledgeable and caring people who will become part of your tribe and super friends.

What is your elevator pitch? Spend some time answering these questions: Who are you? What do you do? Who do you do it for? How do you do it? Play around; make it sound like you. Practice it, and you will feel more confident as you share it when meeting people one-on-one or in small groups. It should convey the gist of who you are, what's important to you, the problems you solve, and show part of your personality. The rest will be history.

LEADER SHOWCASE: CYNTHIA KERSEY

"In any challenging circumstance, we must believe that there is ALWAYS a way."

Cynthia Kersey, MA, has been the CEO and founder of the Unstoppable Foundation since 2009. She is a transformational industry leader and a two-time bestselling author of Unstoppable and Unstoppable Women. She has over thirty-four years of business experience and received her MA from the University of Santa Monica.

Let's start by sharing who you are and the magic you bring to the world.

I am the founder and CEO of the Unstoppable Foundation, and our mission is to ensure that every child receives access to education. We move entire communities from barely surviving to thriving so that they can fulfill their highest potential in life. My background is in personal development and I ran a speaking and coaching company prior to running the foundation.

What are the critical leadership skills that leaders need these days?

Being resourceful and creative are two of those qualities. When the pandemic hit, everything changed not only for North America but also around the world. And it was most challenging for people living in vulnerable populations. When schools, local markets, and everything shut down in our communities in Kenya, the unintended consequences were that children no longer had access to their daily school lunches. Parents couldn't go to the local markets to buy or sell food. And within a short period of time, 95 percent of those employed lost their jobs. Suddenly, we went from communities moving up on the sustainability scale to not having access to food, which was becoming life-threatening.

To address this immediate need, we had to get creative. My team rounded up volunteers, and from morning until night, walked mile after mile bringing info and emergency supplies to remote community members. We ordered 1.5M meals that were distributed to those who didn't have access to food. Being resourceful and looking for creative solutions is critical, even if you don't know how to do it. In any challenging circumstance, we must believe that there is ALWAYS a way. It's a mindset that says I'm not going to be overcome by what's happening and will find a way through.

What would you say to leaders and companies looking to develop a unique edge?

Spiritual teachers and philosophers have been speaking about the power of giving for centuries. Now we have scientific research to prove its benefits. Dr. Stephen Post, author of Why Good Things Happen to Good People, runs an institute dedicated to exploring the extraordinary power of giving. Giving is the most potent force on the planet and generosity is in OUR best interest.

Sir John Templeton has been called one of the greatest stock advisors of the twentieth century. When he was asked what his best financial advice was, he had one word, tithing. Here is one of the top financial experts in the world saying that tithing is a key to prosperity. He went on to say that the only way we can really experience prosperity is through giving. People don't really experience their own wealth, whether it is a dollar or a billion dollars, until they are asked to share it. And by sharing their wealth, even if it is meager by other people's standards, it gives them access to their prosperity, access to their generosity, and access to their heart.

Connect with Cynthia at www.unstoppablefoundation.org or on LinkedIn.

Connect the Dots

We create opportunities when we begin to connect the dots. Over the years, I have attended dozens of training programs geared toward different modalities and observed a pattern. Everyone was rehashing similar concepts and presenting them with a new spin based on the instructor's preferences. Interestingly, all of us are "knowledge brokers." Anyone who reads a book and reviews what they read with a friend or colleague is brokering the knowledge they absorbed from the book.

When I developed the framework for the *C.A.R.E.S. Leadership Success System*, the primary focus of *Fearless Women at Work*, I integrated what I had learned throughout decades of attending formal educational and professional and personal training programs. Everything is connected. And when you think along these lines and begin to weave a thread through seemingly disparate concepts, you derive new interpretations and meaning from everyday encounters, situations, and information inputs. You develop an ability to be connected.

As a leader, looking for similarities, differences, and intersections among ideas, translating and adapting concepts in one field to another is the source of novelty and opportunities. You are an expert in your business, field, and industry, an exceptional individual with a unique combination of purpose, skills, and qualities.

What have you noticed in the intersections of knowledge across different areas? What patterns stand out when you look across your organization? Your insights will inspire you to identify a problem and the solution from a perspective no one else has. What's not working well? What do you know that could improve it even if it's not innate to that environment today?

Empowering Questions for Reflection

1. What is your elevator pitch? What do you do? Who do you do it for? How do you do it?
2. What's important to you?
3. What have you noticed in the intersections of knowledge across different areas?
4. What patterns stand out when you look across your organization?
5.. What's not working well?
6. What do you know that could improve the situation even if it's not innate to that environment today?

LEADER SHOWCASE: ALYSSA CHEN

"The most challenging times often prove to be our greatest moments of learning and growth."

Alyssa Chen is the Director of Partnership Development at Visa with over ten years of business experience. Alyssa attended Cass Business School, Harvard Business School, and received her BSBA at the University of Denver-Daniels College of Business with multiple awards.

Please share a little bit about your background.

I am responsible for managing large enterprise US travel partnerships at Visa, and managing strategic initiatives, business planning, and operations for our travel vertical. I've been in the payments industry now for about seven years. Before that, I was part of Target Corporation's Executive Leadership Management Program. I was thrown into the business world at age five, watching my parents run their own small business in Colorado Springs. I started working various roles at age five and got to the point of managing the business for them by the time I was nineteen or twenty years old.

What leadership qualities are critical for leaders right now?

For any leader in any industry right now, it's the ability to foster human connection and doing that digitally. We're in this unique time where everything is digital-first. Yet, leaders need to find a way to maintain the soul of their connection and demonstrate empathy and compassion as so many people are facing such unique circumstances and challenges. And as a leader, when you have that ability to stay connected with your team, clients, customers, and community, taking the time to understand what they're going through and how you can help is very challenging. But it also presents many opportunities to connect in a way that you probably wouldn't have otherwise done if it were the status quo. Leaders need to demonstrate and foster that human connection, showing honesty and transparency especially in a time of uncertainty.

How should leaders develop and create a unique edge?

The first point is remembering that leaders are defined and accentuated by their challenges and how they react toward those challenges. The skills, traits, tools, and access that they have is important. But there are defining moments when they became leaders, characterized by pivotal moments such as what we're seeing right now. When leaders reverse or identify that this is an opportune time, you move from challenge to opportunity. And a big part of that is embracing the fact that it is a horrible time right now. But after some time, when everyone reflects on this, they're going to see that it's been an incredible time of major technological transformation and significant evolutions in various industries, bringing things forward that would have otherwise taken years to do.

When leaders embrace that and think, what are the wild ideas that I wanted to test but didn't previously think were appropriate, given other priorities? Now is the time where they can introduce them. While we have this time where businesses or operations are closed, let's accelerate these technological advancements.

Alyssa is available to connect on LinkedIn.

27
Become an Expert

"Do the best you can until you know better.
Then when you know better, do better."

—Maya Angelou

Double Down

When you make learning your norm, you are motivated to learn all there is to know in your field. And there is a lot to learn, so make sure you're having fun while you're learning. You will most likely gravitate to an area that interests you. In my case, leadership is one of those. While I haven't read every leadership book under the sun, I am intrigued and excited to hear the real stories of leaders in their areas of expertise. That's what I have done in this book—exposed you to the insights and years of wisdom that each talented leader reveals.

Double down on your field of expertise whether you are a nurse, pharmacist, salesperson, project manager, supply-chain expert, lawyer, data manager, teacher, voice coach, and so on. Get curious about what interests you, go deep, and become very good at it. The more you do, the more "dots" you'll begin to connect. And with your unique background, you will be positioned to create and innovate in a way that solves real problems and delights your soul.

LEADER SHOWCASE: TARA GILVAR

"Take really big risks to invest in yourself."

Tara Gilvar is the founder and CEO of B.I.G., Believe Inspire Grow. Tara founded B.I.G. in 2009 to help women unlock their true potential and create a true work-life balance. Tara is also a partner at The VIP Exchange Consultants, which helps generate customized networking connections. With over thirty-four years of experience, she received her degree from Boston College and is an advisory board member of Seton Hall University's Transformational Leadership in Disruptive Times.

Please introduce yourself to our audience.

I opted out of the workforce after having children. After taking some time off, I knew I was meant for something more than motherhood. And I didn't know how to go about it. I felt a little paralyzed. One day I saw a bumper sticker on a teacher's car that said, "Remember who you wanted to be." And that was like a bolt of lightning from the divine saying, you are meant to do something here. Fast forward to today. B.I.G. is almost in its thirteenth year. We've had over six thousand members across multiple states. We were a little bit handcuffed about how many communities we could go to until COVID, when the world went on Zoom. In eight weeks, we have expanded to nine states, including internationally in Spain and Canada.

How should companies approach developing their leaders and talent?

Don't start with money. Money is one tool in the toolbox for validating work or effort. And I think they should have money if they meet specific criteria, but really, it's appreciation, it's value, especially for women. Women want to know that the effort they put in matters because they took their time from something else to give to this effort. They took the time from their family, their self-care, so it should matter. And number two, they want to feel valued for it. They want to feel smart for it, that it had an impact in some positive way.

People want to be happy. If you're going to spend eight hours at work in misery, what does that do for your life? I met this woman. She and her siblings inherited their parents' company—a very profitable, good company. When they asked her what position she wanted to be in, she said, "I know what I can do for this company to make this company more profitable, successful, and keep our employees happy." She's the chairperson of happiness. And it's a serious title. It's not human resources; she's creating a culture. And that's what companies have to do.

What message would you like to leave our audience with?

As we're in this new part of life, take really big risks to invest in yourself. Do that self-discovery work. Once you think you know who you are, take that risk to show the world and you will draw the right people to you like a magnet. And it might be a whole new opportunity. If you're not living a fulfilled, happy life, then you have to listen to your soul. It will tell you. Your Self will tell you the answer. The billboards are right in front of you. You have to open your mind to see it.

You can reach Tara at www.believeinspiregrow.com or LinkedIn.

Tap Your Full Potential

"We don't do what we can. We do what we think we are."

—Tony Robbins

What would underestimating your potential look like? You would stay fixed right where you are now. Suppose you don't learn anything new or apply what you know from this day forward. You know at this point that there is no further information coming into your periphery, no more insights or epiphanies. Everything stays status quo. Today, I don't think that's even possible. By only moving around in the world, you absorb input and information from the environment that would inevitably lead to new insights.

Tapping your full potential as an expert is to develop your intellectual, emotional, and spiritual capital, ideas, and resources to do whatever you'd like and become whoever you'd like to become. And it requires deepening and accessing all your resources, intuition, and divine guidance.

Get clear on what you want. It starts with owning your story—the good, the bad, and the ugly—and understanding how it impacts your purpose today. Is it helping you or holding you back from taking action? Take a chance. Trust and anchor in your source of strength, your faith, whatever you believe in, and if you don't believe in God, Source, Creator, or the Universe, believe in yourself and your abilities. And lastly, go for it. Do something. The more action you take toward your compelling vision and goals, the more results you'll see. As you see the results, you'll validate your beliefs that what you want is possible, and you'll continue to tap into more and more of your potential and continue to take more action. That's the momentum loop I learned from my mentor, Tony Robbins, and I'm passing it forward. However, the one thing that will hold you back from achieving your full potential in life is the *story* you choose to believe about yourself.

The stories you tell yourself, how you view yourself—your *identity frames*—and what you choose to believe is true about yourself are all linked to your sense of self-worth, your level of confidence, and your ability to pursue your dreams—to go after what you want most in life and what you think you can achieve. If you want to tap into your full leadership potential, tell yourself a great story, get behind it, and go for it! Yet, here's the problem. Your story is not factual. It's full of interpretations and assumptions and relies on your faulty memory. Your story today is what you perceived happened and the meaning you give today to those perceptions. How do I know that? You and your siblings, if you have any, or anyone else who has been in your life will have a different version and interpretation of the same series of events you experienced.

We build sturdy, invisible walls around us to *protect* ourselves and simultaneously, unintentionally, remain tethered and confined to the current situation. It's valuable to peek beyond those fictitious limits and expand your perception of what is possible, allowing yourself to dream big, grounded in your preferences and choices.

Here's a sample list of empowering questions to explore to expand beyond your current constraints. As you entertain them, have fun with it! Use these questions to bring to the surface ideas to support your self-care, to lead, love, thrive, and grow grounded in your compelling vision for a life and career you love. You may consider the different areas in the wheel of life to guide you: career, family, and friends, romantic relationships, finances, health, personal development, physical environment, recreation, community, creativity, and any other area that's relevant to you. Your challenge is to select and answer at least one question in each area—the questions that will make the biggest difference for you.

Empowering Questions for Reflection

Self-Care:
1. How are you spending your time? What should you stop doing or say no to?
2. What causes you the most stress/agita/fear, and what can you do about it?
3. How are you coping with stress now and what new practices will support you?

4. What are you doing to be healthy and energetic and what's important about that?

5. Which relationships nurture you, and which do not?

6. What are you committing to release (resentments, assumptions, expectations, anger, grief, people), why is it important, and how will your life be different as a result?

7. What thoughts bring you happy memories? Think more about them.

8. What thoughts upset you? Think less about them.

9. Where do you need to be more patient?

10. In what areas should you be more compassionate with yourself and others?

11. Where can you cut yourself some slack?

Identify a Compelling Future:
1. What do you love that you've been ignoring?
2. What strengths do you want to leverage more this year?
3. How can you advocate for yourself?
4. Twelve months from now, what do you want to see?
5. In the next twelve months, what would it look like if you stretched out your comfort zone?
6. Who can support you to achieve your goals?

Reflect:
1. On a scale of 1 to 5, 1 being low, how's your self-awareness and social awareness?
2. What is your unique value; how well do you articulate it?
3. What worked well this year, what didn't, and what did you learn from it?
4. What standard do you want to raise to enjoy a better quality of life?
5. Where could you lower your expectations and appreciate what is?
6. How are you empowering yourself to live the life you want?
7. What area of focus would benefit you and those you care for now?

LEADER SHOWCASE: ALYCIA BANKS

"Standing among the ruins of what was, you also have this unique opportunity to create what will be."

Alycia Banks, MA, is currently the Senior Vice President of Learning and Diversity for Columbia Bank New Jersey. Alycia has over twenty-two years of corporate experience. She received her BA at Bentley University and her MA in strategic communications and leadership from Seton Hall University.

Please share with our audience a little bit about your background.

I have been in learning and development for over twenty years. After graduating from Bentley University, I entered corporate America in marketing and sales. I was the first of my siblings to enter corporate America. I was at an organization that was launching a big initiative, and I started selling phenomenally. And then they asked me to teach the new hires how to do it. I went from being a ground-up foundation traveling trainer to then developing the stories. As my expertise grew in learning and development, I realized the value of having the manager involved in the employee's development. I began helping managers coach and lead their teams. This work led me to expand my skills in the area of talent development. I find that my ability to help leaders drive development and change with empathy has been most effective in creating inclusive cultures.

How should organizations approach developing their leaders?

Development is going to be multipronged, such as in-person, mobile learning, and self-directed learning. We will see an increase in leaders curating knowledge on social media platforms. Many legacy leaders are now learning more about technology and how to communicate on these social media platforms. Development for leaders will begin to include topics such as how to write a blog, creating podcasts, and posting on LinkedIn.

In addition to new topics, development will need to happen in short clips of time, sixty minutes or less. During this time, we will need to train on one topic or skill and have attendees practice or apply the skill upon leaving the course. Last, we need to get thought leaders in front of our leaders. This will help leaders learn the most relevant skills and increase credibility.

What would you say to the leaders who want to create a unique edge?

The individual holds the power right now. Whether you're newly entering the workforce or you have some expertise or find yourself more seasoned in your career, now's the time to look at your brand—who you are, your constant strengths, understanding where you have proven yourself to be valuable, what your contribution has been, and what you do naturally well. And begin to look at how you bring that on a greater level and a grander scale to your current teams, jobs, and organizations beyond your title.

Don't allow the ground to shake you into your fear. Move forward being brave. Because when you're in a situation where you're standing among the ruins of what was, you also have this unique opportunity to create what will be. Take the resources that you have—you're still standing, you're still here—and begin to craft and build the world that you want to see for yourself.

Alycia is accessible to connect via LinkedIn.

28

Invest in Yourself

Do what It Takes

With your dreams and goals in sight, doing what it takes to acquire the knowledge and strategies to advance your compelling vision will bring you tremendous joy. As I mentioned, to develop the capabilities that I needed to pursue my dream for the life I wanted to create for my son and myself back in 2017, I invested over fifty thousand dollars. I spent hours devoted to getting myself prepared, acquiring the skills, knowledge, and know-how to fulfill my new mission. And I did it with a lot of love, passion, gratitude, and a renewed level of self-awareness and self-care.

At first, it was quite scary waking up and not having a "workplace" to go to. I had been so accustomed to commuting and being on the go, being on my hamster wheel. I began to create a structure for myself; I would wake up and get ready for my business day as if I were leaving the house to go to work. I organized and planned each day to productively tackle each milestone on each initiative to launch the business, from establishing my LLC to crafting my ideal client profile, designing my website, and writing my first book.

In the process, I integrated my regular schedule with my son's, continued to self-care, taking walks, attending my Yoga class, and meditating regularly. I believed "failure was not an option." I knew it would take time. Joining programs, such as Quantum Leap, Ann McIndoo's book-writing program,

Business Mastery, Unleash the Power Within, The Knowledge Broker Blueprint, and others also gave me the resources and knowledge I needed to succeed. By attending those programs I learned that I was not alone in my pursuit of living a purposeful life. I met beautiful, inspiring, knowledgeable people on a similar journey, defining who they are now and taking their strengths and experiences out into the world. We're not crazy.

What actions do you need to perform to take your idea and your dream and bring them to reality? What does that look like? How would it disrupt your life, and how would it make it even more fulfilling? It's never too late. You may be in the second half of your life, but you're not done yet. There's so much beauty, love, and gifts that you're still here to share with the rest of us.

To get past the fear, come from a place of extreme generosity, vulnerability, and love. Think of giving and contributing; share those gifts that you have within. When you provide value and give more than what people expect, not only do you feel that you are reaching your potential but that's also when it comes back to you by the law of reciprocity. This law basically states that when you do something nice for people, they will have a deep-rooted psychological urge to do something nice for you in return.

LEADER SHOWCASE: RICHARD O'KEEFE

"Rolling up your sleeves and doing the best job possible irrespective of your role is the first building block "

Rich O'Keefe is the President of Your Tech Team, LLC, for over twelve years. He has more than twenty-three years of senior management experience in corporate IT and wealth management, management consulting, and international banking. Rich has a bachelor's in finance from Thomas Edison State College.

What are the leadership qualities that leaders must possess?

Everybody has something to contribute at every level of the organization from the janitor to the CEO. Make sure you are always doing the best job possible. Someone starting as a janitor could become the head of maintenance; there are always opportunities to advance. Rolling up your sleeves and doing the best job possible irrespective of your role is the first building block from a leadership perspective.

Look for ways to add value and ask first and foremost, what is my value statement as an individual contributor? And then, showing up and doing what you must do every day. It's not about punching in and punching out. Know when you must be there to provide services, whatever those might be, versus times when you don't need to be physically present. Or maybe you do things off-hours. It's about being flexible, too, showing value and making sure that you are delivering for the organization. That's going to come back and benefit you as well.

In too many cases, people may be apprehensive or want to get along with everybody so they don't give that constructive criticism or feedback. In fact, they do the opposite; they provide glowing feedback even though the person that they are reviewing is average in the role. But you are doing this person a disservice. You want to both pat a person on the back for doing a good job and displaying the aptitude to do more, because you want this person to be well-rounded and also help him or her grow by pointing out where those growth opportunities are and what things the individual could do to take corrective action and improve in areas that need improvement.

How should our audience approach personal and professional development?

You can become stagnant, so you need to look for opportunities. You should be learning something every day, whether it's about yourself or what you can contribute. Many people work in big corporations, but they have no idea what those companies even do from a business point of view and how they operate. Be inquisitive about that.

You have to go out of your way to build a strong team and understand that you're only as good as your weakest link. It's critical that you have folks who feel comfortable and confident working for you, irrespective of the role. Leading by example is the first and most critical step to building trust with anybody. We may have different roles and responsibilities, but nobody is above anybody else as it relates to being human beings.

You can connect with Rich by visiting www.YourTechTeam.com or through LinkedIn.

Capitalizing on Your Hard Work

Invest in things that bring you joy and get you closer to your compelling future. Back in 2016, I started taking lessons at the Jersey City ballroom dance studio. On the night of my class, I would bring my dancing shoes and practice dancing like a professional Latin music dancer. I had learned to dance at home at family gatherings. Of course, I didn't become a professional dancer—that wasn't the goal. I had a blast every Thursday, learning new steps and techniques and connecting with others who also loved dancing. It was exciting, it was super entertaining, and it put a smile on my face. When I moved out of Jersey City, New Jersey, I stopped the lessons, but those are some of my fondest memories from living there.

Everything I learned in all those programs I have integrated and metabolized into my overall framework for living an aligned lifestyle. I have integrated the different aspects of my life—my health and nutrition with my work, my fun, and recreation, my career, my family and friends, even my home and my physical space. I bring this perspective—my experiences, and all the principles, lessons, and information that I have collected over all these years—to my clients. I am capitalizing on all my hard work by adding the most value to the people that I serve and the leadership teams that I work, collaborate, and partner with. That is how I take advantage of my hard work. I put in the time, effort, and financial investment and I get to reap the fruits of my labor through a life that's more peaceful, harmonious, fruitful, and intentional.

How are you enjoying the fruits of your hard-earned work?

Empowering Questions for Reflection

1.. What actions do you need to perform to take your idea and your dream and bring them to reality? What does that look like?

2. How would taking these actions disrupt your life, and how would it make it even more fulfilling?

3. How are you enjoying the fruits of your hard-earned work?

LEADER SHOWCASE: NIKEVA BROWN

"You have to be eager to learn, open to feedback, and willing to invest in your own journey."

Nikeva Brown is a senior leader and expert in financial planning and analysis and data analytics in customer service, marketing, and database marketing. She has over twenty years of experience in senior-level roles at major financial institutions, including the Federal Reserve Bank, Citigroup, E-Trade, startups, and Sage Software. Nikeva earned a BA in mathematics from Bryn Mawr College and is an honored recipient of various fellowships with GE, Mellon, and NSF.

Please share your background with us.

My background is in financial planning and analysis (FP&A) and data analytics. For my first job out of college, I worked for the Federal Reserve Bank of Atlanta as a financial analyst. And then, I worked for Citigroup in the Credit Card Division and did database marketing. I spent the next fifteen years at E-Trade doing database marketing work and performing in various FP&A based roles—managing P&L, budgeting, strategic planning, and ad-hoc analytics, reporting and monitoring to enable critical business decisions by C-suite leaders. Most recently, I worked as a director of data for a steel start-up and as a regional finance manager. My work has been very rewarding.

How should companies approach developing their leadership teams?

People need to be encouraged to feel empowered and to have the autonomy to make decisions around whatever position they're in. And even outside of that, being a leader is more than just a title. It's an attitude, a mindset. Proactively seeking resources outside of the organization that could potentially help your organization, for example, bringing in coaches or finding programs that you think would benefit your team. Many times, there is expertise outside the company that will be more beneficial for employees.

What insights do you have for our leaders to develop a unique edge?

Always have an open mind, be curious, continue to learn, and want to learn every day. You must be eager to learn, open to feedback, and willing to invest in your own journey. It's nice if your employer is willing to sponsor you for leadership and different training and education opportunities, but be willing to spend some of your own resources to better yourself. Look for outside resources, but commit to yourself that you're worth it and spend the money on those types of things—It is critical.

I've always taken a few online courses here and there. When I started my current role, that's how you and I met. I happened to see you on LinkedIn and booked a complimentary consultation with you, and you had just started the Mastermind. I jumped in, and the material has been great. I've learned so much about myself. It's definitely been an investment well worth the money. It gave me a community of like-minded people to go to outside of the company. Even if it's asking questions about how to lead a project and motivate people, everyone in our group has different opinions on how to do that.

Be a life learner. Don't be afraid to speak your mind. It's our duty, as human beings, to ensure that we're adding value and our perspective.

You can reach Nikeva on LinkedIn.

29
Trust the Process

Account for the Time Factor

Patience will be your best friend as we heal leadership and develop Self-leadership, trusting the process, and then, knowing that things take time, prepare to stay the course. When I set out to reach my goals in 2017 after launching the business and starting a whole new life as an entrepreneur, there was an expectation about how long things would take. I always heard that the first five years of the business are critical. Many don't make it past five years.

As I write this book, I am four years into my business. So far, I have *positive expectations* that this venture will continue to scale despite both the foreseeable and unanticipated setbacks. In this case, it's the 2020 pandemic—I have a hunch this one may not be the last. I'm optimistic that whatever the obstacles, we'll overcome them, like our ancestors the cavemen did through the Ice Age. They role model for us that regardless of the circumstances, ingenious humans will figure it out. And between nature and us, we'll also regulate to protect our Mother Earth from imploding from the weight of our misuse.

From my experience, I realized that it might take more time than I anticipated. And I've noticed how the more aligned I become among my beliefs, thoughts, words, and actions, and connected to all resources, physical and metaphysical, the quicker I'm able to manifest my goals. I keep reminding myself to self-care and pursue my dreams from a place of abundance, not scarcity. Everything is fine as it is. I am safe, I'm fed, and my family is safe and fed. As a human, if we're not making progress, we don't feel fulfilled. I am walking the earth, I am here until I say good-bye, so while I am here I'm going to live with purpose. The time factor indicates when we have reached specific guideposts. Be patient, give yourself leeway, and as long as you are relishing the process, it's all going to be okay. That is my belief.

Stay the Course

As a leader on this growth and self-development journey, the road is long and winding and as picturesque as you want to make it. Stay the course with perseverance and consistency and with a structure that will support you. At every twist and turn, you decide what's best for you from a place of Self-leadership. In other words, you get to do whatever you'd like—not from fear, but love. If you're an emerging or established leader and aspire to continue to grow and contribute on a wider scale, or you're ready to transition into a new venture or role, great. If you are a business owner and you choose to stay in business or secure employment with a company and exit the business, that's a choice you get to make, too. No matter what you do, time will go by anyway; make it count. Celebrate yourself and others, forgive yourself, and forget those who have wronged you in your mind. They've done the best they can with the resources they have.

Healing leadership is not a project; it's a way of life. It's a more conscious way to walk the earth, to relate to others, and to share our love. It starts with you and radiates from you. It influences every person or thing that is in your presence. That is the magnificence of your presence and the influence that your energy exerts on the environment. It's undeniable and palpable.

Know that your value is not tied to your title, what you produce, create, say, or do. Your value is in your being here, now, with us. I thank those who brought you here, and I thank you for showing up.

Empowering Questions for Reflection

1. What is your response to this statement? "Patience will be your best friend as we heal leadership and develop Self-leadership, trusting the process, and then, knowing that things take time, prepare to stay the course."

2. What does it look like for you to stay the course with perseverance, consistency, and a structure that will support you?

3. How can you apply Self-leadership to make decisions at every twist and turn—not from fear, but from love?

LEADER SHOWCASE: SUSANA G. BAUMANN

"Stay on course. It's about finding new ways to get where you want to go. Be creative. This is a new road, not a new destination."

Susana G. Baumann, MAA, MALS, is the President and CEO at Latinas in Business, Inc. With over twenty-eight years of experience, Susana is an award-winning multicultural marketing communications professional, brand strategist, published author, and public speaker.

Please share with us, what is your background?

I am from Argentina, the country of passion for soccer and tango. I am currently the founder, president, CEO, and editor-in-chief of Latinas in Business Inc., a national nonprofit media organization that advocates for the economic empowerment of Latinas and other minority women entrepreneurs. I started this initiative out of my original business, LCSWorldwide, and became a nonprofit two years ago. We are growing organically; we now have over seventeen hundred members. And that has been tremendous growth because it shows there is a need for these promotional opportunities we provide.

What are some of those critical leadership skills our leaders need today?

You have to be prepared for the unexpected at any time. We call this moment in time an unprecedented time because we are experiencing a global public health pandemic, which we haven't had in our lifetime. But if you compare it to what other generations have gone through—such as wars, economic recessions, paradigm changes, or natural disasters—or what we have lived through in our country with hurricanes Katrina, Sandy, or Maria in Puerto Rico, leaders always had to face and prepare for the unexpected at any given time.

Companies face challenges all the time: Maybe it's time to scale up and become global. Maybe it's setting up a new vision because your organization needs a rebranding. Or maybe companies have to face a recent merger or acquisition. All of those are unprecedented times, too. If you don't prepare, then you're not developing your leadership skills. Stay on course, set the vision, develop creative, innovative strategies or ideas, and most important, engage your teams in your vision. If your team was not engaged before in normal times, they won't get engaged in a time of change or uncertainty—the same with your clients or customers. If you don't have enough engagement with your customers or clients, they're going to vanish because people were surprised and everybody was in disarray and in shock.

What advice would you give to the leaders looking to create a competitive advantage?

Having a unique edge comes from developing a very strong personal brand. But no matter how strong your personal brand is, you need to have a strong foundation for the company including setting a vision, creating innovative ideas and strategies, and having a pipeline, mentorship programs, and procedures in place. Otherwise, no matter how good you are at selling your personal brand, there's nothing behind it. There's no value, no continuation, no legacy to offer to your team.

Don't panic under the pressure of unprecedented times. If you panic, you lose sight of the vision. Stay on course. It's about finding new ways to get where you want to go. Be creative. This is a new road, not a new destination.

To connect with Susana, visit LinkedIn and www.latinasinbusiness.us.

30

Master Multiple Areas of Life

Create a Supportive Structure

When work and career are the primary areas of focus and are going well at the expense of other significant aspects of life, for example, relationships, we may feel that life isn't as fulfilling as we'd like it. And the same is true when we funnel most of our precious resources toward work-related activities and we're not enjoying the work. Over the past thirty years, I've learned from my own experiences and working closely with talented professionals that we feel the most "complete" when we integrate the various areas of our life that bring us the most joy, such as career, relationships, fun and recreation, health, community, self-development, spirituality, physical environment, and so on.

The integration of what you consider these essential areas creates a supportive structure that contributes to your holistic well-being. And how do we integrate them? The challenge is that even with the best of intentions, and in many instances by necessity, we devote most of our day to work-related activities. It's even trickier when on multiple levels work satiates our human needs for certainty, variety, significance, connection, growth, and contribution—yes, sometimes our work meets all our human needs. And so, our career activities may become addictive. The antidote that helps us create more integration—notice I avoid using the word *balance*—is setting healthy boundaries around work to leave room for other fulfilling activities. Especially when we're passionate about our work, this ideal, healthy life integration, eludes many—I'm the first to admit that. On certain days, I struggle to make myself stop working! There always seems to be a project or task lurking that *must get done!* And working from home exacerbates the situation; the lines between work and personal space blur. Getting accountability supports me. Let's do this together.

I'll start and provide a sample. In addition to work and career, I intend to use my creativity to make opportunities to have more fun and down time— silliness and entertainment. I'm committing to set official *business hours* and end my workday by 6:00 p.m. as often as possible—that's progress. When my son is home, I create a schedule that supports him and me. I'll incorporate a similar structure that prioritizes my silly and fun time more readily when I'm on my own. As I drill into other meaningful areas, I notice that I'm feeling satisfied with the level of attention I devote to these areas: enjoying family and friends, my partner, planning for financial stability, training at the gym, developing business and personal skills, connecting spiritually, nesting to make my home pleasant and harmonious, and writing and being creative. I also foresee expanding my reach and community as I continue to grow and share my message, the podcasts, and the books' contents. The intention of integrating these areas with more rest, fun, and entertainment is energizing and uplifting. There's plenty to "do," and I can *do* and *be* alert, replenished, grateful, and joyful with mindfulness and purpose.

Now, it's your turn. What structure will support you to integrate your life more holistically? Design the arrangement of these areas to help and serve your best experience now—what worked a year ago may not anymore. Give yourself time to sit peacefully. Ponder and gain more clarity about what you want in those areas of your life—pick up a new hobby, take a break, rest, kick back, and relax a bit. I'll be right there with you!

Mastery of various areas of your life isn't about ego and does not require you to work incessantly. It is about moving beyond dabbling and flowing between these areas deliberately, integrating more of what brings you joy from a bird's eye view. By intentionally bringing awareness to all the aspects that matter to you, assessing what you love and what you'd like to tweak, and then shifting your frame of mind around them, we will begin to transform them as we want to live them. Anything's possible beyond our imagination. We own the key and the combination to the lock of our potential and pleasure. Everything you want and need is within you. There's nothing to look for, there's nothing to gain or lose. Turn the key and you're inside.

LEADER SHOWCASE: MARIE WIECK

"How are you going to not waste the crisis for yourself? Pick one thing and try to do something about it every week; make that pledge to yourself."

Marie Wieck, MBA, MS, recently retired as General Manager after thirty-five years at IBM. Marie is currently Executive Partner at Ethos Capital, LLC, a Member of the Supervisory Board for Daimler AG, Member of the Board of Visitors for Columbia Engineering, and a Vice-Chair Member of the Executive Committee for Charity Navigator. She attended Cooper Union and earned an MBA from New York University and an MS from Columbia University.

Please share your background with us.

I joke that I'm still trying to figure out what I want to be when I grow up because I've had many different roles in technology. I started as a chemical engineer, switched to electrical, then computer science, but always have been in computer technology. I spent most of my career at IBM and have done hardware, software services, and most recently, I was managing Blockchain for IBM. But I recently retired and now am serving on some boards, so I'm involved in a different way.

What advice would you give individuals looking to create a competitive edge?

There's no substitute for learning. You have to learn something new every day. I had a mentor tell me, "You can never be perfectly at the place you want to be in your career or business. You're either going up or down because other forces are moving ahead, even if you think you finally got to your perfect job. You always have to be learning new skills, new technologies, new capabilities."

Right now, the biggest opportunity is how to maintain collaboration, contact, and insight that you get from people directly in a more digital world. How do you digitize and automate those processes that used to rely on face-to-face contact that we can't do right now? It's a great opportunity. Digitization, automation, and new ways of working and collaborating are going to be key.

How to accelerate the ability to develop and try new things is another crucial step. The more you can be a trailblazer for new things, whether those are technical or how you do the things you do in your company or your career, can be a real advantage because then you can help teach others. When everybody is digital, what's the unique opportunity? You constantly have to be thinking ahead about how to keep making it personal, how to get insight from what you're doing, how to connect dots that are no longer easy because you don't see people at the water cooler or the coffee bar. And ideas of finding answers to the things you are missing right now in your own life can be great ways to also enable differentiation in your business and your career.

Be brave. Pick one thing that you can do something about, whether it's in your job, your community or about diversity, equity, and inclusion. How are you going to not waste the crisis for yourself? Pick one thing and try to do something about it every week; make that pledge to yourself.

Marie is available to connect on LinkedIn.

Integrate Work and Life

The questions I often hear from our audiences are, "How do you do it all?" or, "What do I choose with all these options available?" Start by looking at all these topics we have covered in *Healing Leadership* and embrace them. Integrating them into our work and life may seem daunting. Begin by asking yourself, how do I want to feel? Get clear on the areas that you want to holistically master—to fill your cup. Accept where you are right now. And this is you being *whole* as of this moment. You are not broken or need fixing. You are a multidimensional being. Be kind and compassionate to all the aspects of who you are, all your parts. Integrate them all into your internal family. Recognize what's most important to you and what you can control, in a positive way, and focus on that intersection.

There is most likely nothing that I have mentioned in this book that you haven't already heard somewhere. What interests you the most? What areas intrigue you? Where are you strong? And where are you feeling curious? The prompts in each chapter are in no way intended to point out deficiencies. On the contrary, I want these themes help validate and contextualize what you may already be doing and then gracefully guide you using reminders and pointers about what you could implement in your compelling future and the vision that you hold for yourself, your team, your organization, your country, and your role on our planet.

I know I'm asking you to stretch often and step outside of your comfort zone. Let your inner voice guide you all the way. And wait with positive expectations for the many blessings for your family, friends, clients, and your audiences. May we heal and contribute to each other powerfully. I love, respect, and honor you. We are here as humble servants. Our people's wishes are our command. Don't forget that this is not about ego; it's about service and contribution.

To bring it all together and wrap it with a bow, I'd like to share a story that's near and dear to my heart, the story of three sisters. All three sisters were poor and lived in a small village near Haiti in the Dominican Republic. Their mom was only thirteen when she married their father. And by the age of seventeen, she had given birth to all three girls, Manuela, the oldest, Teresa, and Ana, the youngest. The story goes that their mom left to escape an abusive marriage. When their mother left, their dad and their grandmother did the best they could to raise them. All three sisters lived in the same home and shared the little resources they had available—food, clothing, toys, and education. All three sisters had to cook, clean, keep the house tidy, and go to school. Their father was very strict with all three, and he punished them when they did something that he disapproved of.

As the girls got older, Manuela, the oldest, left school before finishing the seventh grade. Teresa and Ana both completed eighth grade. Although they all had the same resources, very little money, and the same opportunities, when Teresa finished eighth grade at fourteen, she made a critical decision that transformed the trajectory of her life and her future family. Teresa begged her father to let her move in with her aunt who lived about three hours away so that she could continue studying and attend high school. You see, Teresa saw becoming a teacher as her "ticket out." She wanted to make something of her life above and beyond what she saw around her. Her father allowed her to go, and a few years later, Teresa became an eighth-grade teacher in her village.

All three girls became grown women. They all got married; they each had three children and created a life for themselves. All three sisters, unfortunately, married men who were physically abusive. Teresa divorced her husband and decided to try a new life in the city, outside of her comfort zone. To manage, Teresa left her two sons with her father in the village and took her daughter, five years old, with her to the city. She managed to get two teaching jobs to pay for rent, food, clothes, and support herself and her three kids, but Teresa struggled to make ends meet.

Teresa was out of ideas when an opportunity came up. Her mother had moved to the United States and could get Teresa a visa to live in the United States as well. And so, Teresa went for it. But immigrating to the United States was a big deal. Teresa didn't speak English; she didn't know what was going to happen once she moved to the United States. What she did know was that it was worth a try to create a better life for herself and her children.

She arranged to leave her youngest, her daughter, who was then twelve years old, with the landlord while she got settled in the United States and found a job and a place to live.

After spending over a year in the United States working in a factory making $3.10 per hour, she found a job working as a janitor at a local high school, earning $4.25 per hour. Speaking broken English, she asked one of the Spanish-speaking security guards who was Puerto Rican to ask some of the teachers whether they needed someone to clean their houses. He did, and slowly she began cleaning the house for one teacher, then two, and eventually, she left the janitor's job to start her own business cleaning houses to earn a decent and honest living.

While she was working during the day, Teresa was learning English at night and met Joe—they married about a year later. By the second year of her stay in the United States, Teresa had saved enough money to bring her daughter to the United States. Her daughter was now fourteen and was getting ready to start high school. A few years later, Teresa was also able to get visas to bring her eighteen- and nineteen-year-old sons to the United States. Joe became like a father to Teresa's three grown children. When Teresa and Joe were both fifty-seven, after twenty years of marriage, Joe was suddenly diagnosed with stage-four lung cancer and passed away within three months of the diagnosis. During their life together, they got to travel the world and enjoy many unforgettable moments.

At seventy-five years of age and for nearly forty years, Teresa has been running her small business and having a significant impact on the lives of the many families who hire her to clean their homes. She also enjoys supporting the families of the small crew of women who also earn a living as part of her team.

Choosing to get clear on what she wanted to do with her life, Teresa used her story to fuel her dreams and actions. Stepping out of her comfort zone with a compelling vision and courage, she went for it and sealed her legacy and uplifted the quality of life for her three children and future generations. Because of Teresa, her oldest son became a carpenter and worked in NYC's high-rises for over twenty-five years. He married and has two children.

Teresa's granddaughter will be graduating from college with a computer science degree in 2021. Because of Teresa's vision, her middle son became an electrician. He's happily married and lives with his wife and stepdaughter. Both sons raised their families here in the United States, giving them the best opportunities possible. And because of Teresa's persistence, work ethic, and resilience, her youngest daughter shares her story with you now in *Healing Leadership*.

I'm so delighted to share my story and use it to fuel my purpose and dreams, fulfill my potential, and help my son and my clients achieve theirs. I lean into my story, not to keep me down but to help me get clear on what I want and what's meaningful and essential in my life, to take chances and step out of my comfort zone, and to go for it.

What about you? What's your story, and how can you own it, fearlessly, to keep tapping into your leadership potential? May you and your loved ones be blessed. Your guides will support you to do what must be done. Answer the call and follow the lead with intention. You are loved more than you can imagine. You have been waiting to listen, and now you're ready—the portal is wide open and ready. Share your gifts. Be patient, don't lose faith. You will work as fast as required. Love is always our next deliverable. Be receptive, curious, and embrace that part of you that wants to be seen and heard, the vulnerable, fragile, connected, adventurous part of you. The challenges are a part of life. Cloaked with love and a growth mindset, we'll figure out how to move forward despite the fears.

Be loving, be kind, be you, and thrive, basking in your full potential and unique value.

Empowering Questions for Reflection

1. What essential areas bring you the most joy (career, relationships, recreation, health, community involvement, self-development, spirituality, physical environment, and so on)?

2. Realistically, how well do you integrate these areas today?

3. How would integrating these essential areas create a supportive structure that contributes to your holistic well-being?

4. What do you want in those areas of your life—to pick up a new hobby, take a break, rest, kick back, or relax a bit?

5. What structure will support you to integrate your life more holistically?

6. What healthy boundaries around work can you build to leave room for other fulfilling activities?

7. What would it look like to move beyond dabbling to flowing between these areas deliberately, integrating more of what brings you joy from a bird's eye view?

8. How do you want to feel?

9. What interests you the most? What areas intrigue you? Where are you strong? And where are you feeling curious?

10. What's your story and how can you own it, fearlessly, to keep tapping into your leadership potential?

Afterword
by Bob Selle, SPHR, SHRM, SCP

Dr. Ginny Baro has built on her success from her number-one best seller, *Fearless Women at Work: Five Powerful Strategies to Thrive on Your Career and Life* with *Healing Leadership: How to Lead, Love, and Thrive in Business and Life.*

From the moment I read the **The Five Reiki Principles**, I knew I was in for a valuable lesson. Ginny leveraged not only her life experiences but highlighted simple yet profound insights from a diverse group of leaders. The featured leaders are from all walks of life, including different points in their career journeys. Her ability to connect with readers and share what she's learned in her personal life really drew me in. Throughout the book, I felt like I was simply sitting with Ginny and friends, having a conversation about the responsibilities leaders have today.

As I read the words, a realization hit me: I recognized that we have one life, and we must admit to ourselves that the days of work being separated from home are in the rearview mirror.

Points that I walked away with and that readers will appreciate:

- **Use the "Empowering Questions for Reflections" at the end of each chapter.** By taking the time to look inward and be honest with yourself, it can prepare you for the next chapter.
- **Assess where you are.** If we can't assess where we are, we will not be able to impact the people we interact with daily.

- **Focus on your superpowers.** This is important: Do not try and emulate those around you. Be your authentic self and good things will happen.
- **Learn and evolve.** We are always learning and evolving, and we must embrace this to grow throughout our life.
- **Use your voice.** We all have a responsibility in this world and we need to use our voice to make a difference.

Thank you, Ginny, for reminding us that we are here for a higher purpose. We will shine brightest when we are continuous learners that embrace life and leadership authentically as ourselves.

Call to Action

Leaders are *healers*. We are here to heal ourselves and those we lead to see the vision of a unique, compelling future. In the process, we advance our business imperatives and our human evolution. *Healing leadership* is a responsibility and daily practice requiring mindfulness, resourcefulness, curiosity, and a great deal of care and empathy. As we continue our journey together, *healing leadership*, embrace a beginner's mindset and question everything, dig for the truth beyond the superficial. Let's open up to each other's perspectives grounded in our core values and mutual respect for what each of us uniquely offers to the experience. Getting our house in order will empower us to see the bigger picture and *work* collectively with our teams and talent toward an abundant, free, peaceful, and compelling future for *all* involved—not a few.

Please help me thank each of our leaders who were gracious and generous with their time and who eagerly answered the call to contribute to me and you. Connect with them on LinkedIn, listen to their full interviews on the *Visionary Leaders Circle* podcast, visit their websites, read their books, and bring them into your professional community.

Please visit my website, www.ExecutiveBound.com, to stay connected and access valuable resources supporting your leadership journey through our articles, books, podcast, speaking events, *Masterminds*, virtual leadership training, and more. All *Healing Leadership* related resources and bonuses await you at **www.HealingLeadership.com**.

Please connect with me on LinkedIn.com/in/GinnyBaro, Facebook. com/ExcutiveBound, Instagram.com/DrGinnyBaro, Twitter.com/Ginny-Baro or via e-mail info@executivebound.com.

Please write a brief review of this book on Amazon.com and share it with your team, colleagues, and friends to help other leaders find our resources.

There's no time like the present. You and your voice matter, and we are ready to support you to rise to your leadership potential. It would be my honor. Stay safe. I look forward to meeting you soon!

References

1. Bagalini, A. (2020, July 22). *Word Economic Forum*. Retrieved from World Economic Forum: https://www.weforum.org/agenda/2020/07/diversity-inclusion-equality-intersectionality/
2. Bradberry, T., & Greaves, J. (2009). *Emotional Intelligence 2.0.* New York: TalentSmart.
3. Brown, B. (2018). *Dare to Lead: Brave Work. Tough Conversations.* New York City: Random House.
4. Chapman, G. D. (2010). *The Five Love Languages: The Secret to Love that Lasts.* Chicago: Northfield Pub.
5. Covey, S. R. (2004). *The Seven Habits of Highlty Effective Pepole.* New York: FREE PRESS.
6. Deptula, B. (2018, March). *Ted.com*. Retrieved from Ted.com: https://www.ted.com/talks/bryan_deptula_leaders_are_born_to_be_made
7. Frankl, V. E. (2006, p. 86). *Man's Search for Meaning.* Boston, MA: Beacon Press.
8. Gallup. (2017). *State of the Global Workplace.* Retrieved from Gallup: https://www.gallup.com/workplace/238079/state-global-work-place-2017.aspx
9. Gallup. (2020). *Gallup.* Retrieved from Gallup: https://www.gallup.com/workplace/321032/employee-engagement-meta-analysis-brief.aspx
10. Harvard Business Review Press. (2017). *HBR Emotional Intelligence Series: Mindfulness.* Boston: Harvard Business Review Press.
11. Klein, C. (2019, August 7). *History.com*. Retrieved from History.com: https://www.history.com/news/8-facts-real-colonel-sanders-kfc#:~:-text=Sanders%20sold%20Kentucky%20Fried%20Chicken,so%20disliked%20Kentucky%20Fried%20Chicken's
12. Lasley, M., Kellogg, V., Michaels, R., & Brown, S. (2011). *Coaching for Transformation: Pathways to Ignite Personal & Social Change.* Discover Press.
13. LiteraryDevices. (2020, November). *William Shakespeare.* Retrieved from Literary Devices.net on November 15, 2020: https://literarydevices.net/william-shakespeare/
14. Malnight, T. W., Buche, Y., & Dhanaraj, C. (2019, September - October). *Put Purpose at the Core of Your Strategy.* Retrieved from HBR.org: https://hbr.org/2019/09/put-purpose-at-the-core-of-your-strategy
15. McKinsey&Company. (2018, July). *McKinsey.com.* Retrieved from McKinsey.com: https://www.mckinsey.

com/industries/public-and-social-sector/our-insights/
creating-an-effective-workforce-system-for-the-new-economy

16. McKinsey&Company. (2020, May 19). *Featured Insights*. Retrieved from Mckinsey: https://www.mckinsey.com/featured-insights/ diversity-and-inclusion/diversity-wins-how-inclusion-matters

17. Nafte, D. (2017, September 10). *Medium*. Retrieved from Medium: https://medium.com/@dennisnafte/ colonel-sanders-failed-1009-times-before-succeeding-ac5492a5c191

18. Nightingale, E. (2019, November 19). *YouTube*. Retrieved from YouTube: https://www.youtube.com/watch?v=NbBHR_CD56M

19. Orloff M.D., J. (2016, February 19). *Psychology Today*. Retrieved from 10 Traits Empathic People Share: https://www.psychologytoday.com/us/ blog

20. Pontefract, D. (2018, September 15). *The Foolishness Of Fail Fast, Fail Often*. Retrieved from Forbes.com: https://www.forbes.com/sites/danpontefract/2018/09/15/ the-foolishness-of-fail-fast-fail-often/?sh=472cf11959d9

21. Ruiz, D. (2018). *The Four Agreements*. Amber-Allen Publishing, Incorporated.

22. Sinek, S. (2019, December 17). *YouTube.com*. Retrieved from YouTube. com: https://www.youtube.com/watch?v=XGQo-Vge-WU

23. smarp. (2020, August 11). *smarp*. Retrieved from smarp: https://blog.smarp.com/employee-engagement-8-statis- tics-you-need-to-know#:~:text=1.,are%20engaged%20in%20the%20 workplace.

24. Spencer, J. (2019, July 8). *Zenefits*. Retrieved from Zenefits: https:// www.zenefits.com/workest/employee-turnover-infographic/

25. Weller, C. (2019, August 29). *NeuroLeadership Institute*. Retrieved from NeuroLeadership Institute: https://neuroleadership.com/ your-brain-at-work/what-is-growth-mindset

26. Whitfield, V. (2016). *Natural Intuition Now, Uplevel Your Life by Awak- ening Your Innate Spiritual Senses*. Westfield, NJ: Victoria Whitfield.

27. Wikipedia. (2020, October 21). *Wikipedia*. Retrieved from Wikipedia: https://en.wikipedia.org/wiki/Healing#:~:text=Healing%20is%20 the%20process%20of,diseased%2C%20damaged%20or%20unvital- ized%20organism.&text=With%20physical%20damage%20or%20 disease,resumption%20of%20(normal)%20functioning.

28. Zukav, G. (2014). *The Seat of The Soul*. New York, NY: Simon & Schuster.

About the Author

D r. Ginny A. Baro immigrated to New Jersey from the Dominican Republic at age fourteen and started with nothing more than a dream. Named one of the Top 100 Global Thought Leaders, she is an award-winning international motivational speaker and leadership coach, career strategist, and number-one bestselling author of *Fearless Women at Work* and *Healing Leadership*.

She leverages over twenty years' leadership experience in highly competitive environments in financial services and technology to support strategic corporate partners and to develop inclusive, impactful leaders and leadership dream teams. She is the CEO and founder of ExecutiveBound® and Fearless Women @Work® and creator of *The C.A.R.E.S Leadership Success System*™, the *Fearless Leadership Mastermind*™, the *Personal Branding Masterclass*™, and the *Visionary Leaders Circle*™ programs.

She has successfully facilitated leadership training and coaching programs for individuals and Fortune 500 companies with more than 140,000 employees and delivered keynotes impacting global audiences larger than 7,000. To learn more, please visit www.ExecutiveBound.com.

In 2009, Ginny earned a PhD in information systems, holds an MS in computer science, an MBA in management, and a BA in computer science (major) and economics (minor). She's a Mastermind professional and certified professional coach (CPC), accredited by the International Coach Federation (ICF).

Ginny is fluent in Spanish. With her programs, she and her clients help change the lives of those in need through the *Unstoppable Foundation, Feeding America,* and *other charitable organizations.*

She lives in rural Sussex County, New Jersey, with her son.